VISIONS OF PEACE

Justice, International Law and Global Security

Series Editor: Howard M. Hensel

As the global community enters the 21st century, it is confronted with a wide variety of both traditional and non-traditional challenges to its security and even survival, as well as unprecedented opportunities for global socio-economic development. International law will play a major role as the international community attempts to address these challenges and opportunities while, simultaneously attempting to create a just and secure global order capable of protecting and promoting the common good of the whole of mankind.

The Ashgate Series on *Justice, International Law and Global Security* is designed to encourage and highlight analytical, scholarly works that focus on the ways in which international law contributes to the management of a wide variety of contemporary challenges and opportunities, while, simultaneously, helping to promote global justice and security.

Also in the series

Ethics and the Use of Force
Just War in Historical Perspective
James Turner Johnson
ISBN: 978-1-4094-1857-3

The Prism of Just War
Asian and Western Perspectives on the Legitimate Use of Military Force
Edited by Howard M. Hensel
ISBN: 978-0-7546-7510-5

Peace Operations and Restorative Justice
Groundwork for Post-conflict Regeneration
Peter Reddy
ISBN: 978-1-4094-2989-0

The Law of War
Ingrid Detter
ISBN: 978-1-4094-6495-2

Visions of Peace

Asia and The West

Edited by

TAKASHI SHOGIMEN
University of Otago, New Zealand

and

VICKI A. SPENCER
University of Otago, New Zealand

LONDON AND NEW YORK

First published 2014 by Ashgate Publishing

2 Park Square, Milton Park, Abingdon, Oxon OX14 4RN
711 Third Avenue, New York, NY 10017, USA

Routledge is an imprint of the Taylor & Francis Group, an informa business

First issued in paperback 2016

British Library Cataloguing in Publication Data
A catalogue record for this book is available from the British Library

The Library of Congress has cataloged the printed edition as follows:
Shogimen, Takashi, 1967-
Visions of peace : Asia and the west / by Takashi Shogimen and Vicki A Spencer.
pages cm. – (Justice, international law and global security)
Includes bibliographical references and index.
ISBN 978-1-4094-2870-1 (hardback)
1. Peace–Social aspects–Asia. 2. Peace–Political aspects–Asia.
3. Peace–Religious aspects–Asia. I. Title.
JZ5584.A69S56 2014
303.6'6095–dc23

2013032329

ISBN 978-1-4094-2870-1 (hbk)
ISBN 978-1-138-26996-5 (pbk)

Contents

List of Contributors

Bruce Buchan is an Australian Research Council Future Fellow in the ARC Centre of Excellence in Policing and Security and the School of Humanities at Griffith University, Brisbane, Australia. His research focuses on the historical uses and transformations of political concepts. He is currently working on a project on the conceptual history of security and asymmetric warfare in the eighteenth century. His recent publications include *The Empire of Political Thought: Indigenous Australians and the Language of Colonial Government* (Pickering and Chatto, 2008) and *An Intellectual History of Corruption* (co-authored with Lisa Hill, Palgrave, 2013). He has also co-edited two editions of *Cultural Studies Review* exploring representations of mortality (2011) and another mapping interdisciplinary approaches to the study of noise (2012).

Shin Chiba is Professor of Political Thought at the International Christian University in Tokyo, Japan. His research interests encompass federalism, radical democracy, ecology and the relationship between religion and politics. His publications in English include *Christian Ethics in Ecumenical Context* (co-edited with George R. Hunsberger and Lester Edwin J. Ruiz, Eerdmans Publishing, 1995), *Toward a Peaceable Future* (co-edited with Yoichiro Murakami and Noriko Kawamura, The Foley Institute, 2005), *Peace Movements and Pacifism after September 11* (co-edited with Thomas J. Schoenbaum, Edward Elgar, 2008) and *Building New Pathways to Peace* (co-edited with Noriko Kawamura and Yoichiro Murakami, University of Washington Press, 2011).

Patricia A. Hannah is a Senior Lecturer in, and past Chair of, the Department of Classics at the University of Otago, Dunedin, New Zealand. Her research interests focus on the material and conceptual foundations for the artistic and social culture of Archaic and Classical Greece. Her recent publications have explored the links connecting ancient Greek imagery and popular thought, especially in the area of military theory and practice. She is currently working on a book on the visual representation of soldiers and their equipment in Athenian vase-painting.

Murray Rae is Professor of Theology at the University of Otago in New Zealand and Head of the Department of Theology and Religion where he teaches courses in Systematic Theology and Ethics. His research interests include the work of Søren Kierkegaard, theological hermeneutics, Maori engagements with Christianity and theology and the built environment. He is editor of the *Journal of Theological Interpretation* monograph series and his publications include *Mana Maori and*

Christianity (Huia, 2012), *Kierkegaard and Theology* (Continuum, 2010), *History and Hermeneutics* (T&T Clark, 2005) and *Kierkegaard's Vision of the Incarnation* (Clarendon Press, 1997).

Kaushik Roy is Associate Professor in the Department of History at Jadavpur University, Kolkata, India, and Senior Researcher at the Peace Research Institute in Oslo, Norway. He has written and edited 19 books from Oxford University Press, Cambridge University Press, Routledge, Bloomsbury, Ashgate and Brill among others and 45 articles in peer reviewed journals including the *Journal of Global History, Journal of Military Ethics, Journal of Military History, Modern Asian Studies* and *War in History*. His latest publication is *Hinduism and the Ethics of Warfare in South Asia: From Antiquity to the Present* (Cambridge University Press, 2012).

Takashi Shogimen is Associate Professor in History and Associate Dean (Research) for Humanities at the University of Otago, Dunedin, New Zealand. He has previously been Research Fellow, Clare Hall, Cambridge, and a Visiting Professor in History at the University of Helsinki. His research interests encompass medieval European political thought, comparative political theory and Japanese intellectual history. His publications include *Ockham and Political Discourse in the Late Middle Ages* (Cambridge University Press, 2007) and *Western Political Thought in Dialogue with Asia* (co-edited with Cary J. Nederman, Lexington Books, 2009).

Katherine Smits is a Senior Lecturer and Head of Politics and International Relations at the University of Auckland, New Zealand. She researches and teaches in political theory, specializing in contemporary and historical liberal thought, multiculturalism, feminist political theory and identity politics. She is the author of the books *Reconstructing Postnationalist Liberal Pluralism* (Palgrave Macmillan, 2005) and *Applying Political Theory* (Palgrave Macmillan, 2009), as well as several articles on liberal political theory, multiculturalism and national identity. She is currently working on a study of multiculturalist policies and modernity in Britain, Australia and New Zealand.

Vicki A. Spencer is a Senior Lecturer in political theory in the Department of Politics at the University of Otago, Dunedin, New Zealand. Her research interests encompass early modern European thought and contemporary political theory with a focus on issues relating to language, cultural identities, nationalism and multiculturalism. She is the co-editor (with Paul Corcoran) of *Disclosures* (Ashgate, 2000) and her most recent publication is *Herder's Political Thought: A Study of Language, Culture and Community* (University of Toronto Press, 2012). She is currently working on a project in contemporary theory on toleration, humility and recognition.

Kam-por Yu is currently Director of the General Education Centre at the Hong Kong Polytechnic University. He is also a Scientific Associate of the Philosophy Chapter of SIGENET-Health, Sino-Germany Research Network on Public Health and Bioethics, Berlin. His main area of interest is in ethics – including ethical theory and applied ethics, and especially Confucian ethics and bioethics. His latest publications include *Taking Confucian Ethics Seriously* (State University of New York Press, 2010) and *Social Ethics: An Introduction* (Oxford University Press, 2012), and a series of papers on the Confucian views on war, peace, harmony, civility and pluralistic values.

Acknowledgements

The genesis of this collection of essays was the international symposium 'Visions of Peace: The West and Asia', which was held at the Otago Museum in Dunedin, New Zealand, on 10–12 December 2009. Eighteen scholars from various parts of the world presented papers, and the editors would like to express their gratitude to the speakers, who could not contribute to this volume, for their intellectual contributions to the event. We are also grateful to the Japan Foundation and to the Division of Humanities and the Department of History and Art History at the University of Otago for their financial support, without which Takashi Shogimen could not have organized the symposium.

Unforeseeably we both experienced significant personal losses during the course of editing this book and we owe a heartfelt thanks to Ashgate and our contributors for their patience and understanding due to the inevitable delays that occurred in its production. Takashi's editorial work for this book could not have been completed without the support of his parents, Tadashi and Hiroko Shogimen. And Vicki would like to express her appreciation and gratitude to her family and friends in Adelaide and Dunedin for their loving support.

Finally, we would like to thank Margaret Younger for her speedy response to our many questions during the editing phase of the project, Brenda Sharp and Matt Irving for their smooth management of the publication process and Diane Lowther for compiling the index.

Takashi Shogimen Vicki A. Spencer

25 November 2013

Introduction

Takashi Shogimen and Vicki A. Spencer

This book is a collection of essays that explore diverse conceptions of peace in the Asian and Western historical worlds. The events of 11 September 2001 and the subsequent military conflicts have renewed interest in questions of war and peace in the new context of the 'war on terror'. Though the term 'war' was employed metaphorically in this context, the evident part that religion has played in recent terrorist attacks have challenged many to rethink the relationship between violence, religion and politics. The need to re-evaluate our cross-cultural encounters has likewise taken on an air of urgency. And since the United States readied for war first in Afghanistan and then in Iraq, scholars have engaged in a serious re-examination of the theory and practice of just war (Frowe 2011, Kelsay 2007, Lee 2007, Reed and Ryall 2007, Fotion 2007, Smit 2005, Elshtain 2003, Temes 2003).

Many, however, remained unconvinced that a just war was about to be waged in Iraq and, in February 2003, millions took to the streets in a co-ordinated global movement in favour of peace. Nonetheless, the United States and its allies disregarded the protests of their people; worse, the invasion of Iraq by the 'coalition of the willing'[1] on 19 March 2013 revealed the impotence of the United Nations as an institution that entailed the capacity to secure peace. Yet even as the original justification for the war that Saddam Hussein was harbouring weapons of mass destruction was exposed as a chimera and the numbers of innocent Iraqis killed in the invasion grew exponentially,[2] radically new visions of peace for our globalized world failed

1 On 27 March 2003, following the invasion, the official public list of the United States' allies in 'Operation Iraqi Freedom' contained the following 48 countries (up from 30 on March 18 2003): Afghanistan, Albania, Angola, Australia, Azerbaijan, Bulgaria, Colombia, Costa Rica, Czech Republic, Denmark, Dominican Republic, El Salvador, Eritrea, Estonia, Ethiopia, Georgia, Honduras, Hungary, Iceland, Italy, Japan, Kuwait, Latvia, Lithuania, Macedonia, Marshall Islands, Micronesia, Mongolia, Netherlands, Nicaragua, Palau, Panama, Philippines, Poland, Portugal, Romania, Rwanda, Singapore, Slovakia, Solomon Islands, South Korea, Spain, Tonga, Turkey, Uganda, Ukraine, United Kingdom and Uzbekistan. However, only the United Kingdom and Australia sent substantial military assistance to fight at the time of invasion compared to 34 countries in the previous war on Iraq in response to its invasion of Kuwait. See Bush 2003, Schiffers 2003.

2 Based on media reports, the Iraq Body Count organization (2013) estimates 115,294 to 126,494 violent civilian deaths since the invasion of Iraq. WikiLeaks (Goldman and Martinez 2010) revealed 109,032 deaths according to classified United States' government reports: '66,081 "civilians"; 23,984 "enemy" (those labeled as insurgents); 15,196

to emerge. The human imagination is invariably constrained by our historical and cultural contexts, and our imagination for a new vision of peace is no exception.

The historical and cultural limitations of our imagination are not, however, set in stone. The narratives of peace we have inherited have been subject to various forces, interpretations, encounters and chances so that some have come to dominate our imaginings while others lay hidden, neglected and underappreciated. The limitations on our conceptual framework are therefore contingent and fluid. They are subject to reinterpretation not only in light of changing circumstances in the present, but also through historical investigation aimed at revealing less well known visions of peace. The reverse side of these limitations is that human history constitutes an immense storage of past ideas that were generated in diverse historical and cultural worlds. These ideas may not provide a ready-made answer to our current problems; however, the excavation of historically and culturally diverse perspectives opens the possibility to inspire more creative thinking.

Little wonder, then, that one of the new trends in the rapidly expanding literature on war and peace is the examination of theory and practice from cross-cultural perspectives. This is particularly the case for studies on just war theories, where cultural diversity is increasingly receiving scholarly attention (Hashmi 2012, Fisher and Wicker 2010, Hensel 2010, Sorabji and Rodin 2006, Brekke 2006, Robinson 2003, Nardin 1998). The study of different cultural and religious traditions on warfare is thought to have the potential to create greater international consensus on ways to restrain war both with its initiation and in its conduct (Brekke 2006: xi, Johnson 1999: 227). Peace and war are interconnected subjects of investigation, but they also have their own separate characteristics (Gittings 2012: 3, Boulding 1978: 8). What is still lacking in the literature is a direct counterpart for peace: a cross-cultural exploration of different visions of peace. Existing surveys of the history of the idea of peace generally focus on the Western tradition (see Cortright 2008, Gittings 2012), as if peace plans were the monopoly of the West.

The scholarly constriction of *vision* is not merely cultural but also historical. Until recently the historical scope of existing studies on the idea of peace has generally been confined to modernity. Typically the tendency has been to focus on the conceptions of Leo Tolstoy, Mahatma Gandhi, Reinhold Niebuhr and Martin Luther King, as if the quest for peace is a distinctively modern phenomenon (Cortright 2008). When scholarly attention has turned to the historical world prior to 1800, attention has been focused – if not quite exclusively, certainly one-sidedly – on Immanuel Kant's essay *Toward Perpetual Peace: A Philosophical Sketch* (1795), as if he were unique among his contemporaries to turn his attention to peace. This narrative is perhaps most prevalent among scholars of international relations and, in particular, advocates of cosmopolitanism who see in Kant's essay the basis for the development of a cosmopolitan law necessary to ensure

"host nation" (Iraqi government forces) and 3,771 "friendly" (coalition forces)'. For a comprehensive discussion of various methodologies employed in determining estimates see Iraq: the Human Cost (2013).

justice, human dignity and peace at a global level. Although his cosmopolitan contemporaries are generally noted in passing, Kant's plan is depicted as superior in its scope, wider and more influential in its application and thus more worthy of our attention (Brown 2009: 7–8, Nussbaum 28, Wood 62).

That Kant's essay is the most famous and well known of peace plans in the European tradition is indisputable. This self-perpetuating narrative is nevertheless problematic at a number of levels. The commitment of European intellectuals to peace as a central issue of concern is evident from the thirteenth and fourteenth centuries and there was a veritable flourish of interest in peace plans during 'the Enlightenment'.[3] Nor was Kant alone in extending his vision to include non-European peoples; indeed, his plan was far more restrictive than the less known plans of some of his contemporaries examined here. The idea that the discourse on peace during the European Enlightenment 'reached its peak' (Gittings 2012: 127) in Kant's essay is thus open to serious challenge.

For those interested in global peace, however, broadening our historical perspective to represent better the diversity of the Enlightenment and the indebtedness of Enlightenment intellectuals to earlier European thinkers has to remain insufficient. It still leads far too easily to a celebratory narrative that traces the development of international peace plans and the current existence of multilateral organizations to the European Enlightenment (Gittings 2012, Adolf 2009). The part that those steeped in other intellectual traditions had in the development of current international institutions thereby becomes hidden and gradually fades from memory. It is important therefore to recall the key role that China played both in the formation of the United Nations and the subsequent drafting of the Declaration of Human Rights of 1948. Ethiopia, Egypt, the Philippines, Saudi Arabia, Iran and Syria, along with other non-Western states, were also among the United Nations' founding members. The desire for peace is a global phenomenon that is informed by on-going debates within a range of intellectual traditions.

Yet currently missing in the literature are studies that explore the idea of peace before the modern era from a global perspective. In the Western world at least, it remains the case that non-Western perspectives on peace are marginalized. The domination of the United Nations by the West with its holding of four out of the five permanent positions on the Security Council also contributes to the narrative that peace is the business of the West, while others are left to follow its lead. It is precisely, however, the adequacy of its lead and current institutions that are increasingly open to contestation in the current political climate. By pluralizing our conceptions of peace, the potential thus exists to expand our imaginations beyond the impotence of existing international arrangements.

---

3 The existence of 'the Enlightenment' as a unified intellectual movement has in recent years been highly contested. Here the term is employed simply to denote the long eighteenth century, that is, the late seventeenth to the early nineteenth century (see Israel 2006a; 2006b, Muthu 2003: 1–2).

The present book begins this task by exploring the diversity of past conceptualizations of peace across intellectual and religious cultures in Asia and the West before circa 1800.[4] The coverage of the book is not intended to be comprehensive. Rather, the emphasis is placed on hitherto underexplored conceptions of peace. The non-Western traditions our authors consider encompass Hindu, Japanese and Confucian visions of peace and war, while ancient Greek, early Christian and less known medieval and early modern conceptions of peace in the European tradition are also explored. Each chapter constitutes a study of a particular intellectual tradition or its representative example(s), in our attempt to rehabilitate 'forgotten' conceptions of peace and reclaim their contemporary relevance. This book is thus intended to provide contemporary readers with new perspectives on peace by shedding light on certain overlooked or underappreciated visions of peace in the global historical landscape.

The book opens with Patricia A. Hannah's exploration of the ancient Greek idea of peace. In ancient Greece, peace (*Eirēnē*) was both personified as a benevolent goddess and conceived as an abstract idea, the antithesis of war (*polemos*). As a female divinity, by the early fourth century BC she had an altar in Athens' civic centre, a prestigious sculptural image and significant cult observances. She was frequently invoked as a beautiful young woman, the bringer of wealth and the nurse of young men. In wartime, *Eirēnē* offered the hope of blessings associated with a return to a peaceful life, in which the seasonal cycle of the agricultural year could prevail. At the same time, as a concept *eirēnē* equates well with the English term for peace in a range of real-life contexts. Surprisingly, however, the Greek word comes only late into the diplomatic terminology of alliances and peace treaties negotiated between the often bellicose city-states. Friendship and association appear earlier as more achievable goals. Hannah thus discusses the extent to which the religious aspects of *eirēnē* were inherent in the sphere of interstate relations, thereby exploring the complexity of this dual construct from the point of view of some of the surviving archaeological and historical evidence.

In the following chapter, Murray Rae reveals that theologians of the first three centuries of the Christian tradition were unanimous in their opposition to war and to the participation of Christians in military service. They believed, on the basis of the life and teachings of Jesus, that there was a theological imperative to seek peace. However, that conviction was rapidly eroded following the conversion of Constantine and the adoption of Christianity as the official religion of the Roman Empire. Rae explores the origins of Christian pacifism and the reasons why it became a dissident tradition within Christianity. He thus considers the theological arguments of the sectarian groups of Christians that have tried to maintain the pacifist tradition, and examines the critiques of this tradition that have been offered by theologians in the mainstream churches.

---

4 Dates throughout this edition are given as BC, before Christ (= BCE, before Common Era) and AD, anno Domini (= CE, Common Era).

The following three chapters turn to three Asian conceptions of peace. In Chapter Three, Kaushik Roy offers a panoramic view of the Hindu idea of peace from ancient times to the present. Nowadays, largely due to the achievements of Mahatma Gandhi, Hinduism is commonly regarded as a religion of peace. Indeed, Gandhi's philosophy of non-violence was derived from the *Bhagvad Gita*. From a historical perspective, Roy argues, Hinduism is anything but a religion of peace. The classical Hindu texts make no watertight division between the two concepts of peace (*shanti*) and war (*yuddha/vigraha*). So, understanding Hinduism's view about peace requires insight into the Hindu attitude towards warfare. Roy shows that there are two schools of thought regarding peace in Hinduism: the spiritualist and the realist. The former position, which claims that penance and sacrifice lead to peace, constituted a spiritual foundation for Gandhi's pacifism. The realist school within Hinduism, by contrast, claims that while exercising force through authority is necessary for enforcing peace, enforcement of peace might also lead to warfare. Thus this branch of Hinduism developed a theory of just war. Roy demonstrates the influence of the realist position in contemporary India.

Chapter Four examines arguably the most influential intellectual tradition in East Asia: Confucianism. Kam-por Yu notes that Confucianism knew two visions of peace: peace as absence of war (peace in a weak sense) and peace as an ideal state (peace in a strong sense). Yu takes on board the task of investigating the Confucian idea of peace in a strong sense; thus he highlights the Confucian approach of handling value conflicts and the Confucian recipe for achieving harmony and peace. According to the Confucian view, Yu argues, conflicts occur not just between good and bad, but can also occur between different kinds of good, in addition to different understandings of the good. As a result, the ethical task consists not in doing the right thing and avoiding doing wrong, but also in balancing different kinds of good. The challenge of ethical thinking, therefore, is to see all the relevant values involved and strike the right balance among them. The Confucian vision of peace is constituted not by imposing an order or a state of stability on different parties, but by giving due recognition to all parties concerned.

Our eastward journey ends in Japan: in Chapter Five, Shin Chiba offers a survey of Japanese understandings of peace from the seventh century to the present. Acknowledging that East Asian countries share Confucian values that are historically disseminated in diverse traditions, Chiba examines ancient Confucian ideas of peace advocated by Confucius and Mencius including harmony, benevolence, courtesy and the rule of virtue in order to show the ways in which these ideas were inherited and developed in a unique manner by Prince Shotoku of Japan in the early seventh century. Chiba turns his attention, next, to Itoh Jinsai and Ando Shoeki in the seventeenth and eighteenth centuries respectively, both of whom criticized the conservatism of contemporary Japanese Confucianism and developed an alternative, equality-based peace theory within the broad framework of Confucian thought. In the nineteenth century, Yokoi Shonan developed a theory of international relations through a reinterpretation of Confucianism. The chapter thus concludes with a reflection on how Confucian ideas, a shared heritage in East Asia, can help to realize peace and reconciliation in East Asia today.

The following chapter looks at medieval contributions to peace in Western Europe. The popular image of medieval Europe, which is determined significantly by the Crusades, is belligerent and violent. In Chapter Six, Takashi Shogimen argues that European intellectuals wrote increasingly on peace in the late Middle Ages. Shogimen singles out two thinkers: the Italian poet Dante Alighieri and the English theologian John Wyclif. Criticizing the papal encroachment on the temporal sphere, Dante theorized about the universal rule of the Roman emperor, thereby imagining universal peace. However, unlike the classical Roman concept, Dante's idea of peace was not expansionist. John Wyclif's contribution to the idea of peace was through his critical engagement with just war theory; while Wyclif acknowledged the legitimacy of just war, he was deeply sceptical of its practical feasibility and magnified its spiritual danger. These two pioneering intellectuals exemplify the increasing interest in *temporal* peace, as opposed to perfect peace in the spiritual world, which had preoccupied the medieval mind.

The final three chapters shed light on some less familiar aspects of modern European conceptions of peace and peacemaking. The European Enlightenment is still regularly interpreted as an era in which civilized laws and limitations were imposed on war-making, and peace became a serious object of diplomacy. In Chapter Seven, Bruce Buchan argues that the European Enlightenment's apparent veneration for peace was underwritten by a complicated appraisal of the relationship between war, peace and civilization. Enlightenment intellectuals believed that European warfare was not only becoming more civilized, but a more technical practice, the scientific mastery of which promised European war-makers unparalleled power and reach. Uncovering the connection between claims about civilized and limited but scientific and overwhelming war-making, Buchan shows how closely war and peace were linked in the European self-imagining during the Enlightenment period. This self-imagining was heavily laced with fictional accounts of the civilized qualities of modern European war. Scottish Enlightenment intellectuals, however, attempted to provide a historiographical foundation for the presumed European accomplishment of peace by interpreting war as both an agent of peace and an index of historical progress. The corollary of such normative histories was that the emergence of increasingly civilized norms of conduct in Europe was tied to the development of sovereign states, effectively consigning peoples without such states to a parlous status awaiting supposedly superior European civilization and superior European military power.

In the following chapter Vicki A. Spencer excavates an alternative vision of peace proposed by Kant's contemporary, Johann Gottfried Herder. Although Herder rejects the notion of an eternal peace as unachievable until Judgement Day, he encourages every effort towards its realization. Only self-defence against a direct physical attack is to his mind legitimate. Spencer argues that Herder offers us in many respects an 'anti-plan' for peace by providing a democratic, grass-roots cosmopolitan alternative to the institutional state-based cosmopolitanism of his contemporaries. Responding directly to Kant's views on the war-like condition of stateless peoples, he recounts the story of the formation of the peace alliance between the Iroquois and Delaware nations in North America whereby the Delaware took on the role of peacemaker by donning female clothes and becoming the peace-woman. Ultimately Herder sees the Indian alliance as unsuccessful, like other similar attempts to stop war-thirsty nations in Europe and Asia. Nevertheless, it forms the inspiration for this own peace woman in whom he personifies his views on how most effectively to work gradually towards the elimination of war and the cultivation of peace. The key, for Herder, lies first and foremost in changing people's fundamental attitudes towards war and other peoples, something that we can all work to achieve. Spencer thus concludes that the empowering message in this grass-roots approach will resonant with activists today frustrated with the Security Council's domination of the United Nations and the veto right of its five permanent members that so often leads to inertia.

The book concludes with yet another alternative to Kant's peace plans: Katherine Smits examines Jeremy Bentham's defence of the viability of peace between liberal states from a utilitarian philosophical perspective that promotes the greatest happiness of the greatest number and is fundamentally different from Kant's philosophical approach. Bentham and Kant were both strong opponents of colonialism, which they saw as a leading cause of warfare. However, they differed on the degree to which a pacific international society could include the participation of non-Western and non-liberal societies. Smits compares the different liberal peace plans of Bentham and Kant, arguing that Bentham's pragmatic utilitarian philosophy recognizes that modes of government need not be grounded in specific cultural practices. Bentham's view is based upon the universal principle of maximizing the utility of all people and he recognizes the validity of cultural difference as a contributing factor to that utility. Since non-Western cultures are capable of accountable government, they have the capacity to form peaceful relations with other states. Smits thus shows that Bentham and Kant established competing liberal perspectives on the issue of universalism and cultural difference, which have continued to shape modern Western liberal thinking on international peace.

What emerges from this volume is that the idea of peace is historically and culturally contingent and diverse. At the same time, one is struck by the degree of continuity evident in the common search for peace that transcends time and place, and the development of just war theories by diverse cultures as a means to limit the advent of war or at the very least to minimize its destructive portent. As much as some wish to insist that war is endemic to and characteristic of the human species, the search for peaceful relations across cultures is equally evident. Even the most bellicose periods in our historical imaginings are revealed here to have been the birthplace for visions of peace. Proposals for peace are by no means confined to the purview of a handful of enlightened thinkers in the history of Western political thought. Throughout human history peace has been envisaged from a diverse range of religious, cultural and philosophical standpoints.

Though ancient Greek civilization and the goddess *Eirēnē* have not survived the ravages of time, the other conceptions of peace examined here form part of what are diverse and evolving traditions that are subject to continual debates. At the same time that the present is always shaped by the past, both are open to constant reinterpretation. The visions of peace reconstructed and rehabilitated in this volume will thus hopefully help to redefine and reshape debates on peace in our own time.

Bibliography

Adolf, A. 2009. *Peace: A World History*. Cambridge: Polity.

Boulding, K. 1978. *Stable Peace*. Austin, TX: University of Texas.

Brekke, T. (ed.) 2006. *The Ethics of War in Asian Civilizations*. London and New York: Routledge.

Brekke, T. 2006. Editor's preface in *The Ethics of War in Asian Civilizations*, edited by T. Brekke. London and New York: Routledge, ix–xv.

Brown, G.W. 2009. *Grounding Cosmopolitanism: From Kant to the Idea of a Cosmopolitan Constitution*. Edinburgh: Edinburgh University Press.

Bush, G.W. 2003. *Operation Iraqi Freedom* [Online, The White House] Available at: http://georgewbush-whitehouse.archives.gov/news/releases/2003/03/20030327-10.html [accessed: 14 February 2013].

Cortright, D. 2008. *Peace: A History of Movements and Ideas*. Cambridge: Cambridge University Press.

Elshtain, J.B. 2003. *Just War Against Terror: The Burden of American Power in a Violent War*. New York: Basic Books.

Fisher, D. and Wicker, B. (eds) 2010. *Just War on Terror?: A Christian and Muslim Response*. Farnham, Surrey, England and Burlington, VT: Ashgate.

Frowe, H. 2011. *The Ethics of War and Peace: An Introduction*. London and New York: Routledge.

Gittings, J. 2012. *The Glorious Art of Peace: From the Iliad to Iraq*. Oxford: Oxford University Press.

Goldman, R. and Martinez, L. 2010. WikiLeaks: at least 109,000 killed during Iraq war. ABC News [Online, 22 October]. Available at: http://abcnews.go.com/Politics/wikileaks-dumps-thousands-classified-military-documents/story?id=11949670 [accessed: 18 November 2013].

Hashmi, S.H. (ed.) 2012. *Just Wars, Holy Wars, and Jihads: Christian, Jewish, and Muslim Encounters and Exchanges*. Oxford: Oxford Scholarship Online.

Hensel, H.M. (eds) 2010. *The Prism of Just War: Asian and Western Perspectives on the Legitimate Use of Military Force*. Farnham, Surrey, England and Burlington VT: Ashgate.

Iraq Body Count 2013. [Online: Conflict Casualties Monitor]. Available at: http://www.iraqbodycount.org/ [accessed: 18 November 2013].

Israel, J. 2006a. *Enlightenment Contested: Philosophy, Modernity, and the Emancipation of Man, 1670–1752*. Oxford: Oxford University Press.

Israel, J. 2006b. 'Enlightenment! Which Enlightenment!?' *Journal of the History of Ideas* 67(3), 523–45.

Johnson, J.T. 1999. *Morality and Contemporary Warfare*. New Haven, CT: Yale University Press.

Kelsay, J. 2007. *Arguing the Just War in Islam*. Cambridge, MA: Harvard University Press.

Lee, S. 2007. *Intervention, Terrorism, and Torture: Contemporary Challenges to Just War Theory*. Dordrecht, the Netherlands: Springer.

MIT Center for International Studies 2013. Iraq: the Human Cost. 2013. [Online: the Human Cost of the War in Iraq]. Available at: web.mit.edu/humancostiraq/ [accessed: 18 November 2013].

Muthu, S. 2003. *Enlightenment against Empire*. Princeton, NJ: Princeton University Press.

Nardin, T. (ed.) 1998. *The Ethics of War and Peace: Religious and Secular Perspectives*. Princeton, NJ: Princeton University Press.

Nussbaum, M. 2010. Kant and cosmopolitanism, in *The Cosmopolitan Reader*, edited by G.W. Brown and D. Held. Cambridge: Polity, 27–44.

Reed, C. and Ryall, D. (eds) 2007. *The Price of Peace: Just War in the Twenty-First Century*. Cambridge: Cambridge University Press.

Robinson, P. (eds) *Just War in Comparative Perspective*. Aldershot, Hampshire, England and Burlington, VT: Ashgate.

Schiffers, S. 2003. US says 'coalition of the willing' grows: analysis. *BBC News* [Online, 21 March] Available at: http://news.bbc.co.uk/2/hi/americas/2870487.stm [accessed: 14 February 2013].

Smit, W. (ed.) 2005. *Just War and Terrorism: The End of the Just War Concept?* Leuven, Belgium and Dudley, MA: Peeters.

Sorabji, R. and Rodin, D. (eds) 2006. *The Ethics of War: Shared Problems in Different Traditions*. Aldershot, England and Burlington, VT: Ashgate.

Temes, P.S. 2003. *The Just War: An American Reflection on the Morality of War in Our Time*. Chicago: Ivan R. Dee.

Wood, A.W. 1998. Kant's project for perpetual peace, in *Cosmopolitics: Thinking and Feeling beyond the Nation*, edited by P. Cheah and B. Robbins. Minneapolis and London: University of Minnesota Press, 59–76.

Chapter 1
Eirēnē: Ancient Greek Goddess and Concept of Peace

Patricia A. Hannah

This chapter examines the vision of peace in ancient Greece by focussing in particular on the deification of the abstraction, *eirēnē*. The main discussion is divided into two sections, which will explore the topic from different angles on the basis of two forms of surviving evidence, one artistic, the other epigraphical. Then the conclusion will draw these separate approaches together and reflect on the subtle ways in which these complex layers of thought may have informed and enriched the vision of peace within the ancient Greek cultural context.

For the Greeks peace was a complicated and multifaceted concept, which changed and developed over time in a variety of sociopolitical, religious, literary, artistic and intellectual contexts. On the whole, though, to be able 'to live at peace' (*eirēnēn agein*), free from violence or the threat of it, was always seen as a desirable personal and civic ideal, as it is in the Western world today. That the achievement of that goal often eluded the Greek city-states in the Archaic and Classical periods (about 700–323 BC) says more about their fiercely competitive character and lifestyle than it affirms a belief in the inevitability of endemic warfare.

It is, of course, Greek warfare (its strategy and tactics, equipment, customs and memorials), not Greek peace, which has traditionally been studied in great depth by classicists and ancient historians, both political and military, for centuries. Indeed, some modern authors (see Sage 1996: 129) have claimed that war was a basic fact of life, the normal state of affairs, and any peace a short-lived aberration. To support this vision of a world constantly ravaged by acts of violence they invoke sayings like that of the Greek philosopher, Heraclitus, who stated about 500 BC, 'War is the father of all, and the king of all; some he has shown to be gods but others men, and some he has made slaves but others free' (Heraclitus 1979: 66–7 [fragment LXXXIII, D. 53]).[1]

War, it is argued, determined everything in life, while peace was so elusive that even the very idea barely registered in the Greek consciousness except as an impossible dream. Thus, the Cretan, Cleinias, in Plato's *Laws* (1926: 6–7 [1.626a]) asserts: 'What most people call "peace" is only a word, and in fact each city-state

1 The translations of all quotations are my own, based on the original Greek. I have included translations in the bibliography that are easily accessible, especially in the *Loeb Classical Library*, where the Greek text and an English translation appear on facing pages.

is always naturally in a state of undeclared war with all the others'; and 'it seems to me that he [the lawgiver Minos] observed the folly of the many since they do not notice that everyone is always at war continuously throughout his life against all the cities' (Plato 1926: 6–7 [1.625e]). For this speaker peace is an intangible idea, while uncontrolled aggression between communities is unavoidable and inherent in the natural scheme of things. His promotion of communities organized as if in a permanent state of war, however, is part of a philosophical dialogue on various governments and laws between an Athenian, a Cretan and a Lacedaemonian (Spartan), and it is ultimately rejected as not in the citizens' best interests long term. As the Athenian states, 'The best thing is neither war nor civil strife – and we must pray not to experience these – but peace with one another and at the same time friendliness' (Plato 1926: 14–15 [1.628c]). Even from Cleinias' point of view 'most people' do call something peace and mistakenly believe in its existence, but war was ingrained in the Greek male psyche.

Our surviving written sources tend to reflect the prevailing view of the elite in Greek society; they saw war as a brutal, but necessary, means to a positive end, whether that was the reaffirmation of a city's or individual's status and honour, the acquisition of more power or property, or simply a life of ease facilitated by the enslavement or elimination of one's enemies. With the constant reinforcement of the frequently recited Homeric poems from about 700 BC, revenge and the quest for glory, won through manly heroism, were also strong and acceptable motivators to military action. Accordingly, Bruno Keil's influential study of *eirēnē*, published in 1916, promoted 'a negative conception of *eirene* as "not-war"' (Alonso 2007: 209), and more recent studies of warfare still perpetuate a history of unremitting Greek bellicosity.

But the Greeks themselves certainly contrasted the two opposite states, war and peace. For example, in his *Histories* Herodotus (1924: 4–5 [8.3.1]) approves of the Athenian decision not to contest the leadership of the combined Greek forces against the Persians on the grounds that 'internal tribal strife is so much worse than a unanimous war as war is worse than peace'. And, according to Thucydides (1930: 244–5 [4.20.2]), the Lacedaemonian (Spartan) envoys say to the Athenians in 425 BC: 'let us be reconciled, and let us both ourselves choose peace instead of war and for the other Hellenes let us make a rest from their troubles'. So, what did they have in mind when offering this choice?

If we look for their vision of peace instead of war, there is first the question of terminology. In Greek, '*eirēnē*' seems to convey best what we mean by 'peace' in English in both private and public terms: that is, to define it broadly, feeling safe, having enough to live on comfortably and being in harmony with one's family, friends and fellow citizens. Other terms are also relevant and worthy of future study. Quiet (*hēsychia*) and concord (*homonoia*) were certainly important especially in the Hellenistic world after the death of Alexander the Great (about 323–30 BC),[2] but

2 On Quiet (*Hēsychia*) and Concord (*Homonoia*) personified see Stafford 2000: 12, 26–7; on concord as an opposite of internal strife or civil war (*stasis*) see Raaflaub 2007: 14.

here I will focus on *eirēnē* and, to some degree later, on friendship (*philia*), as that concept was more often mentioned in treaties and alliances. *Eirēnē* was not only an abstraction but also a personification, who came eventually to be worshipped as a goddess. I will discuss first the deity and then the concept, although it must be acknowledged that the Greeks, having no word for 'personification', would not have divorced the two ideas at all.

Eirēnē as a Goddess

The following quotation from *Cresphontes*, a fragmentary play by the Athenian tragedian, Euripides, probably dated 430–424 BC, serves to introduce *Eirēnē* the goddess and her essential characteristics of wealth, beauty, youth and festive partying.

> *Eirēnē,* deeply rich and most beautiful of the blessed gods, I am zealous for you since you are taking your time. I am afraid that old age may overwhelm me with toils before I see your graceful season, your songs for beautiful dances, and your garland-loving festivities. Come, lady, to my city, and protect the homes from hated civil war [*stasis*] and raging Strife [*Eris*], who enjoys sharpened iron. (Euripides 2008: 510–11 [fragment 453])[3]

Here she is invoked as the 'most beautiful of the blessed gods', extremely wealthy and full of feminine grace, but also absent and sorely missed. If ever *Eirēnē* comes at long last to the city, the people will celebrate with her songs and dances wearing garlands of flowers; they will enjoy peaceful pastimes once more. She will not merely fill the void left at the end of hostilities, but has the power to protect the citizens from further conflict, of internal or external origin. Euripides' words characterize the goddess for a Greek audience in the fifth century BC, but her origins go further back into the past.

The classical archaeologist, Erika Simon (1986: 700) wished to take *Eirēnē* back to a pre-Greek, Minoan vegetation goddess worshipped on the island of Crete in the second millennium BC, but a continuous link is hard to prove in the absence of literary and archaeological evidence spanning the intervening centuries (Stafford 2000: 183). What we call the personification of peace first appears in the surviving literary sources in Hesiod's poem, *Theogony*, in the seventh century BC, where 'blooming Peace' is listed (Hesiod 2006a: 74–5 [lines 901–2]) as one of three periods of time (*hōrai*) along with Good Order (*Eunomia*) and Custom/Right/Justice (*Dikē*).[4] These three Seasons, who set the time for mortal activities, are the children of Zeus (the supreme god) and Themis (the goddess of customary

---

3 See also Stafford 2000: 184–5, Smith 2005: 220–21.

4 For *Dikē* and *Eunomia* see Shapiro 1993: 39–44 and 79–85. On the *Horai* see also Gantz 1993: 53.

law and order). They are thus close sisters of the three Fates (*Moirai*), who are another set of triplets born of the same parents (Hesiod 2006a: 74–5 [lines 904–6]), and whose role is to control the birth, life and death of each person, their destiny. Subsequently, the poet, Pindar, too, in his thirteenth *Olympian Ode* of 464 BC, assigns to the Seasons the same mythological origin and positive qualities: the three sisters are 'the controllers of wealth for men, the golden children of prudent Themis; they are willing to fight off unprovoked violence (*hubris*), the bold-tongued mother of insolence' (Pindar 1997: 188–9 [lines 7–10]).

As original elements of the natural passage of time and social order the Seasons are fundamental to the Greek view of peace, even though the seasonal element of the single deity *Eirēnē* was largely incomprehensible to, and ignored by, later literary and artistic sources in the Classical period (about 480–323 BC) (Shapiro 1993: 79). Some modern scholars have, however, postulated the notion of a 'fighting season', that is summer, as opposed to a 'peace season', that is winter, from the actual practice of warfare among the Greeks (Smith 2005: 218–19). But, even if *Eirēnē* could be equated with winter in military terms, there is no corresponding mythological Season for summer called War (*Polemos*), so her seasonal aspect appears muted. Nevertheless, *Eirēnē* was ultimately conceived of and worshipped as a significant goddess, while the martial god Arēs, who was one of the 12 Olympians and who is evidenced even earlier in the Mycenaean Bronze Age, received only limited recognition in state cult before the mid to late fourth century BC (Pritchett 1979: 158–61, Burkert 1985: 169–71; 2005: 18, Larson 2007: 156–7).[5]

In Greek religion, which was distinctly polytheistic, *Eirēnē* appears as a desirable gift or companion of the other principal gods, for example, of Dionysos, the god of wine and revelry (Simon 1986: 704 nos 10–12, plate 542, Shapiro 1993: 45–7, Stafford 2000: 188–9, Smith 2005: 219). Thus, in Euripides' play *Bacchae* Dionysos loves *Eirēnē*, who is 'the giver of happiness/wealth/bliss (*olbos*), the goddess who nurses boys' (Euripides 2002a: 46–9 [lines 419–20]). But *Eirēnē* was also worshipped in her own right (Simon 1986: 700).

A major state cult, involving animal sacrifice at her altar and overseen by the military generals, was established in Athens about 375/4 BC (Parker 1996: 227–37, Stafford 2000: 173–7), following the victory won by the Athenian general Timotheus over the Lacedaemonians (Spartans) off the island of Corcyra (Corfu) (Simon 1986: 701–2, Parker 2005: 478).[6] Twenty years later about 354/3 BC, the rhetorician Isocrates recalled and justified the inauguration of this civic cult in these terms of thanks for benefits received: 'He [Timotheus] forced them [the Lacedaemonians] to agree to this peace, which made so great a change for each of the two cities that we from that day sacrifice to her [*Eirēnē*] every year, because

5 See further Pritchett 1979: 161–3 on the cults of *Eirēnē* and flight-inducing Fear (*Phobos*). On Strife (*Eris*) see Shapiro 1993: 51–61.

6 Plutarch (1914: 444–7 [*Life of Cimon* 13.6]) was aware in the second century AD that 'they say' that the altar of Peace at Athens went back to the mid-fifth century BC, but this is generally dismissed as a mistake (Wycherley 1957: 67 no. 160, Shapiro 1993: 45).

none other has been so beneficial to the city' (Isocrates 1929a: 246–7 [sections 109–10], Wycherley 1957: 66 no. 156, cf. no. 157). By the end of the Classical period epigraphic records of the income raised by selling the skins from the animals sacrificed annually (perhaps 80 oxen) indicate that the scale of her cult was comparable to the great festival of the City Dionysia, at which the famous classical dramas were performed in honour of Dionysos (*Inscriptiones Graecae* II^2 1496, lines 94, 127, dated 333/2 and 332/1 BC, Simon 1986: 701, Stafford 2000: 177; 2007: 82).

In Athens by the fourth century BC at least Eirēnē had, therefore, acquired the status of an independent goddess honoured by public ceremonies on a national scale. Later in the second century AD the travel-writer Pausanias (1918: 86–7 [1.18.3]) reported that he had seen a sculpture of *Eirēnē* in the Prytaneion (an official reception centre) in Athens next to a statue of Hestia, the goddess of the city hearth (Wycherley 1957: 168 no. 533, Thompson and Wycherley 1972: 47). Although he does not describe this statue in any detail, in line with his limited interest in Greek antiquities and works of art, it had probably been created earlier in the Classical or Hellenistic periods, between the fifth and first centuries BC, and, to judge from the sculpture's civic location next to Hestia, as Simon (1986: 702) surmised, 'E. dürfte hier den innenpolitischen Frieden verkörpert haben'.[7]

The quest for political peace was certainly a recurring literary and artistic theme in the century between 450 and 350 BC (Stafford 2000). For example, in 421 BC (just before the signing of the Peace of Nicias, which terminated the first ten years of the Peloponnesian War between Sparta and Athens) in Aristophanes' comedy called *Peace*, the Chorus of farmers and workmen rescues the goddess *Eirēnē*, along with Harvest/Fruit-time (*Opōra*) and Spectacle/Festival (*Theōria*), from their imprisonment by War (Stafford 2000: 186–7). The chorus and Trygaeus, the main character, alternately describe her as 'the greatest of all deities, who most loves the vine' (Aristophanes 1998b: 466–7 [line 308]), 'grape-giving mistress' (1998b: 494–5 [line 520]), 'fair of face' (1998b: 504–5 [line 617]), 'most holy queen, goddess, lady *Eirēnē*, mistress of dances, mistress of weddings' (1998b: 550–51 [lines 974–6]) and 'highly honoured' (1998b: 550–51 [line 978]). A sheep is sacrificed to her inside the house (off stage), because Trygaeus claims ironically 'of course *Eirēnē* does not enjoy killings, and her altar is not stained with blood' (Aristophanes 1998b: 554–5 [lines 1019–20]), (Wycherley 1957: 65 no. 152).

Similarly, in 408 BC at the end of Euripides' tragedy, *Orestes,* the god Apollo invites the characters (and the audience) to leave and honour *Eirēnē*, 'the most beautiful of the gods' (Euripides 2002b: 602–3 [lines 1682–3]). Private worship by individual citizens and their families, as implied here, may have predated the official recognition, but there is no direct proof to confirm it.

About the same time that the cult of Peace was introduced at Athens, the Greek colonial settlement of Locroi Epizephyrioi in Southern Italy issued its first silver coins (*staters*) with a head of Zeus (named) on the obverse and a female figure

7 'Here E. must have embodied the domestic peace'.

seated on an altar on the reverse (Simon 1986: 701–2 no. 1, plate 540, about 380 BC, Stafford 2000: 190). On these coins 'of the Locrians' (*Lokrōn*), she is helpfully identified by an inscription, 'Peace' (*Eirēna*). Since in the ancient world coinage was often minted to pay soldiers on a specific occasion, the reference for this image could be to another victory in war followed by sacrifices offered in thanksgiving on a Locrian altar to Peace, but one can only speculate in the absence of any historical information. Interestingly, this figure holds up a herald's staff (*kērukeion*) in her right hand. Messengers in ancient Greece carried this type of short staff with crossing snakes at the top as a symbol of their status as untouchable liaisons. In theory, they could safely travel between warring states, relaying the terms of diplomatic negotiations or announcing the truces during which the Panhellenic festivals like the Olympic Games could take place. As a distinctive attribute for a divinity, this staff is normally associated with Hermes/Mercury, the principal messenger god, in Hellenistic and later Roman art, but from this point it may also identify a female figure as *Eirēnē*, signifying her power to protect messengers and to facilitate an end to wars.

A particularly striking collocation for its novelty and aptness paired a motherly *Eirēnē* with a baby boy, Wealth (*Ploutos*). However, in the poetry of Hesiod (2006a: 80–81 [*Theogony* line 969]) Wealth is not her son, for his mother is Dēmētēr, the nurturing goddess of agriculture. Instead *Eirēnē* acts only as his nurse (*kourotrophos*) (cf. Bacchylides 1992: 258–9 [fragment 4 Maehler, line 61], Stafford 2000: 183–4), but this close bond between baby and caregiver was the ideological theme captured in the bronze statue created by the sculptor Cephisodotus and set up in the Athenian Agora (the city centre) some time around 370–60 BC (Stafford 2000: 178–84).

Unfortunately, the original work of art has not survived, but Pausanias saw and described it in the second century AD as '*Eirēnē* carrying Ploutos as a boy' (Pausanias 1918: 38–9 [1.8.2], Wycherley 1957: 66 no. 158). The basic iconography of a standing female holding a baby or child was not novel in Greek art, but this statue was soon matched by a group of Fortune (*Tychē*) and Wealth in Thebes, also seen by Pausanias (1935: 240–41 [9.16.1–2], Wycherley 1957: 67 no. 159): 'These artists [Xenophon of Athens and Callistonicus of Thebes] had the clever idea to place Wealth in the arms of Fortune as if she is his mother or nurse, and no less clever was Cephisodotus' design; for he made the statue of Peace holding Wealth for the Athenians'. We can gain some idea of its appearance and location (presumably close to the altar of Peace discussed above), and gauge its artistic and enduring psychological impact, from contemporary paintings on vases and from later Roman marble copies of Cephisodotus' sculpture (Simon 1986: 702–5 nos 6–8, plates 540–41).

Painted images are particularly informative because the stylistic dating of Athenian figured pottery is more precise than that of contemporary sculpture. Consequently, the vases in question offer a secure date by which, and probably just before which, the statue must have been set up, in connection with the establishment of the new cult of *Eirēnē*. In this case they occur on a special range of large, two-handled, storage containers, called Panathenaic amphoras. These were specially commissioned to hold the olive oil given as prizes to the athletic and equestrian winners in the quadrennial Panathenaic Games held in honour of the city's patron goddess, Athena. Because of their religious significance, an old-fashioned, black-figure decorative technique, used particularly on archaic ceramics from about 650 to 450 BC, and the traditional image of the war-goddess herself on the front side were retained with only minor stylistic changes over several centuries. However, in the fourth century it became customary to depict a variety of small-scale figures, instead of the original roosters, on the free-standing columns on either side of Athena. It was also decided to add the name of the annual magistrate (*archōn*) under whose authority the prizes were produced. Consequently, we can deduce that under the archon Callimedes in 360/59 BC the figures on the columns represent Cephisodotus' sculptural group of Peace and Wealth. Despite their miniature scale these two-dimensional pictures convey a consistent and reasonably accurate image of what the original sculpture surely looked like (for example, on Athens, National Museum inventory no. 20046: Stafford 2000, 179 figure 23, cf. Eschbach 1986: 58–70 plates 16–18).

On the vases Peace stands at rest with her weight on one leg, the other slightly bent, wearing a long dress, a three-quarter length cloak down her back and sometimes a diadem or wreath. She holds a sceptre in her raised right hand and balances a half-naked, baby boy (over painted in white) on her left arm. He holds a symbolic horn of plenty (*cornucopia*) at his left side and stretches out his right arm to her. In response she turns her head in his direction.

These characteristic features are also seen in an incomplete, Roman, marble copy, now in Munich (Glyptothek inventory no. 219, from the first half of the second century AD, Stafford 2000, 178 figure 22).[8] The height of this statue, at about two metres, presumably reproduces the impressive scale of the original bronze. Her clothing and classical stance, both old-fashioned by this time, combine with a contemporary ideal of feminine beauty, as seen especially in her soft face and long hair, to produce an appealing vision of Peace in tangible form.

Stylistically and metaphorically she blends the best of the old with the new. The sceptre signifies her queenly status as revered mistress and cult goddess, while her subtle gesture draws attention to her role as loving caregiver for the child. Wealth will grow and bring prosperity to mankind so long as Peace is there to watch over him. The human–divine relationship, founded on respect and honour shown in the hope of favours and benefits in return, is constantly renewed through the cult rituals, especially animal sacrifices, which are aimed at ensuring the interest and goodwill of the deity in human affairs. Previously other gods could bring the

8 See also another copy from the first half of the first century AD in New York, Metropolitan Museum of Art, Rogers Fund, 1906 (06.311), missing her head, both arms and *Ploutos* (Eschbach 1986: plate 19.1, Ridgway 1997: 259–60 plate 62). [Online]. Available at: http://www.metmuseum.org/toah/works-of-art/06.311 [accessed: 25 September 2011].

blessing of peace to mankind; now *Eirēnē* herself offers the promise of a future existence free of the destructive effects of war (Mikalson 2010: 21–5, 195).

In the sculptural group the abstract ideal is perfectly portrayed in an allegorical form, which transcends time and the precise, historical context that inspired it. Indeed, the latter remains unknown. Was the statue commissioned to celebrate the peace made with Sparta in 375 BC, or to coincide with the introduction of the cult of *Eirēnē* in the following year, or should it be associated with the later Panhellenic Peace of Callias of 371 BC, or the so-called Common Peace again made with Sparta in 362/1 (Stewart 1990: 173, Ridgway 1997: 259)? Whatever the exact circumstances in the 370s and 360s, when a series of unsuccessful attempts were made to conclude a permanent peace, the limited but widespread evidence for the growth of the cult of a deified *Eirēnē* in Greek religion, especially in Athens, from the eighth to the fourth centuries can be taken as a clear indication that in the background there lay a deepening political and social concern with the concept of peace.

Eirēnē as a Concept

The use of the word *eirēnē* to express a concept of peace can actually be taken back further in our sources than Hesiod's reference to a goddess. In the late eighth century BC Homer in the *Iliad* (1999 vol. 1: 120–21 [bk 2 line 797], 424–5 [bk 9 line 403], repeated in vol. 2: 462–3 [bk 22 line 156]) refers to a 'peacetime' prior to the outbreak of the Trojan War, and warriors commonly express a wishful desire to go home, yearning for an end to war marked by 'friendship and trustworthy oaths' (for example, Homer 1999 vol. 1: 132–5 [bk 3 lines 71–5], 136–7 [bk 3 lines 111–12], 152–3 [bk 3 lines 319–23]). Images of a city at peace and a city at war are described in relation to the imaginary shield of Achilles (Homer 1999 vol. 2: 322–7 [bk 18, lines 490–540]), while Hesiod (2006b: 106–7 [lines 225–47]) in his *Works and Days* similarly contrasts a just city, which is peaceful and prosperous, with its opposite, which suffers from war, hunger, disease and infertility (Raaflaub 2007: 13). In addition, the concepts of peace and quiet paired with wealth and abundance (especially that derived from agricultural prosperity) already appear at the end of Homer's *Odyssey* (1998 vol. 2: 446–7 [bk 24 line 486]), and in Hesiod's Golden Age (2006b: 96–7 [lines 109–26]), (cf. Theognis 1971: 215 [lines 885–6]).

Early poetic sources, therefore, do supply evidence that peace was seen as a common good and self-evidently preferable to war, and this view is frequently repeated in later sources like the fifth-century historians Herodotus and Thucydides, and the Athenian dramatists Euripides and Aristophanes (Zampaglione 1973). For example, Herodotus (1926: 112–13 [1.87.4]) has the Lydian King Croesus say: 'No one is so senseless as to choose war rather than peace; for in the one sons bury their fathers, and in the other fathers bury their sons'. Similarly, the Theban herald in *Suppliant Women* written by Euripides about 422 BC comments on the false hope and misplaced confidence which drive men to vote for war instead of peace:

> And yet we all know the better of the two proposals, the good and the bad, and how much better peace is than war for mortal men; she who first is dearest to the Muses, the enemy of revenge, delights in children and rejoices in wealth. Letting these go we wickedly undertake wars and enslave the weaker, men man and city city. (Euripides 1998: 60–61 [lines 486–93])

During the Peloponnesian War (431–404 BC) Aristophanes entertained, but also challenged, his Athenian audience with comedies on the theme of peace. In the *Acharnians* (425 BC), the farmer Dicaeopolis negotiates his own private peace with the enemy; the (temporary) recovery of peace is celebrated in *Peace* (421 BC); and Lysistrata in the play of that name (411 BC) motivates women from all sides to refuse to have sex until their men agree to peace.[9] While we cannot read the letters and diaries of the ordinary men and women of this time, these plays and publicly available texts convey something of their commonly held opinions about contemporary issues.

However, as Raaflaub (2007: 23) has pointed out, no ancient Greek, intellectual treatise 'About Peace' has survived or been quoted by the scholars who were based in Alexandria in Egypt in the following centuries. The text promisingly entitled *On the Peace* by Isocrates (355 BC) actually deals with the political arguments for accepting a specific peace treaty, as does Andocides' speech, *On the Peace with the Lacedaemonians* (391 BC). Should we conclude *ex silentio* that none ever existed? I think we should not, considering how many of the philosophical and literary works originally written have been lost. The survival or loss of ancient texts has been haphazard, not systematically planned, and it is quite likely that more than one of the Greek philosophers did discuss the meaning, value and pursuit of peace for both individuals and states.

On the other hand, epigraphic records do reveal the political importance of the concept of peace in association with wealth, good order and friendship (*philia*). Greek international relations have recently been analysed in more depth (see Low 2007), and the earlier scholarly criticism and dismissal of what seemed simple, even naive, diplomatic processes and language (see Sage 1996: 66) have been found to be wanting. Alonso (2007: 209–14) identifies three categories of external relations: neutral 'non-relationship' (*ameixia*), negative 'war' (*polemos*) and positive 'friendship' (*philotēs*, later *philia*), but not, literally, peace (*eirēnē*), which is instead viewed as a beneficial consequence of the accord negotiated. Complex relationships with people outside one's own *polis* or federal state, ethnic league or even Greece (Hellas) itself were soundly based on shared, internal customs and laws. The constant striving for the means or terms which would produce a lasting peaceful outcome can be seen in repeated diplomatic efforts to cease hostilities or to avoid war to begin with, by means of predictable procedures designed to resolve disputes without violence.

9 On Aristophanes' peace plays see Tritle 2007: 183–5.

Greek ambassadors negotiated truces and peace treaties, and defensive alliances, although notably the latter were usually made with the implicit or explicit expectation that war *will* occur with a third party, and that allied help will be needed against that enemy, at some time in the future (Sage 1996: 66–72, 129–34, van Wees 2004: 10–18). The swearing of oaths by the gods constituted a key component in the terms of settlements, as could clauses promoting recourse to arbitration. The optimism with which these were agreed to can be gauged from the length stipulated for a treaty to last, often 30, 50 or 100 years, or simply 'forever'.

For example, a bronze plaque was set up in the Panhellenic sanctuary at Olympia recording the terms of an alliance between the local Eleans and the people of Heraea in Arcadia, about 550–500 BC (London, British Museum GR 1824.4–99.17: Christopoulos 1975: 232 figure, Meiggs and Lewis 1988: 31–3 no. 17, Bauslaugh 1991: 58, van Wees 2004: 13 figure 1):

> THE AGREEMENT BETWEEN THE ELEANS AND THE HERAEANS
>
> There will be *an alliance for one hundred years*, beginning this year. If anything is needed, either word or deed, they shall be with one another both in all the other things and *especially in war*. But if they are not together, the violators will pay a talent of silver to Olympian Zeus for his service. If anyone damages this writing, whether a private citizen or official or people, he will be liable to the penalty written herein. [my italics]

Similar is the even briefer treaty between two cities in north–western Greece, dated to about 550 BC (Bauslaugh 1991: 57, van Wees 2004: 10):

> THE AGREEMENT BETWEEN THE ANAITOI AND THE METAPIOI
>
> *Friendship for fifty years.* Whichever of the two is not steadfast, the protectors and the prophets may take them from the altar. If they break the oath, the priests at Olympia must be informed / will adjudicate. [my italics]

A contemporary treaty relating to the Greek colony of Sybaris in Southern Italy was also dedicated at Olympia (Olympia, Archaeological Museum inventory no. B 4750: Meiggs and Lewis 1988: 18–19 no. 10, Bauslaugh 1991: 56–7, Caratelli 1996: 54 figure, 675 catalogue no. 71, van Wees 2004: 10):

> The Sybarites and their allies and the Serdaioi joined together *in friendship* faithful and sincere *forever*. Guardians: Zeus, Apollo and the other gods, and the city of Poseidonia. [my italics]

Probably to be dated in the late fifth century is a (damaged) limestone slab (*stele*) found on the Spartan Acropolis. Although it is the only one to have survived involving the Lacedaemonians (Spartans), this treaty may reflect the terms imposed by them on the members of the Peloponnesian League, which they led (Sparta, Archaeological Museum inventory no. 6265: Meiggs and Lewis 1988: 312 no. 67 bis, van Wees 2004: 14):

> TREATY WITH THE AETOLIANS
>
> On these terms there will be *friendship and peace* [*hiranan*] with the Aetolians *and an alliance* … follow wherever the Lacedaemonians lead, both by land and by sea, having the same friend and the same enemy as the Lacedaemonians. And they will not make an end without the Lacedaemonians, and not give up fighting the same opponent as the Lacedaemonian … [10] [my italics]

Of special interest here is the inclusion of the word for 'peace' (*hiranan* in the local dialect) alongside 'friendship' and 'alliance'.

This additional incentive featured in the Spartan ambassadors' (unsuccessful) proposition to the Athenians in 425 BC, according to Thucydides (1930: 242–3 [4.19.1]): 'The Lacedaemonians invite you to a treaty [*spondai*] and a cessation of war, offering peace [*eirēnē*], alliance, much other friendship and a close mutual relationship'. Van Wees (2004: 17, 257–8 n. 56) suggests that because the Spartans are 'offering "peace" when they mean *spondai*', the historian has captured the informal usage of the late fifth century, when the terminology began to change from *spondai*, literally 'libations', to 'peace treaties' (cf. Zampaglione 1973: 27–8). Previously they focussed on the liquid offerings poured out to the gods at the time oaths were sworn to guarantee an agreement or treaty, as if these ritual links with the divine meant more to them than any abstract concept of 'peace'.

It was not until the fourth century, therefore, that the Greek word *eirēnē* regularly carried a specific diplomatic meaning in legal terms. Before then *eirēnē* signified a beneficial state that results from a pact of friendship, not the actual social connection being established or maintained. In the words of Victor Alonso (2007: 212), 'technically this word neither designates the new relationship between the parties nor the legal instrument itself', and

> Not only is Greek thought incapable of conceiving of peace as a natural and universal right of all peoples (barbarians and Hellenes); as yet it cannot even conceive of peace as a legal relationship in and of itself. Peace must be enveloped and supported by a stronger bond with a bilateral character: friendship (which in this period can entail mutual assistance in warfare).

The personal links made socially between the leading individuals and their families extended politically outwards to neighbouring communities in the preceding

---

10 The terms are similar to those imposed on Athens in 404 BC (Xenophon 1918: 110–11 [*Hellenica* 2.2.20]).

Archaic and Classical periods. This basic foundation offered sufficient structure and means to organize foreign affairs and defence with fellow Greeks.

But the diplomatic terminology of friendship, alliance and truce (*spondai*) was indeed evolving by the early fourth century, as can also be seen from a speech composed by Andocides in 391 BC. After returning as a negotiator for peace with Lacedaemon (Sparta), he has to explain to the Athenian citizen assembly, which holds the final authority, that

> a peace [*eirēnē*] and a truce [*spondai*] are very different from each another. For they [the parties] make a peace with one another equally having agreed about any terms on which they differ; but, whenever they conquer in war, the stronger make a truce for the weaker out of their commands, just as the Lacedaemonians after beating us in the war [in 404 BC] ordered us to demolish the walls, hand over the ships and take back the exiles. At that time then the truce was produced from commands by force; but now you are deliberating about a peace. Consider from the letters themselves, which have been written on the stone slab for us, the terms on which now it is possible to make peace. … What do these have to do with those? So far therefore do I at least, Athenians, distinguish these: peace means safety for the people and power, but war produces the dissolution of the democracy. (Andocides 1953: 506–9 [*On the Peace* 11–12])

A gradual shift towards a distinct concept of peace as an achievable goal in itself is visible in the surviving epigraphic records as well. In 395 BC an alliance between the Boeotians and Athenians was expressed in the traditional terms for a defensive agreement (Athens, Epigraphical and Agora Museums: Rhodes and Osborne 2003: 38–41 no. 6). Each side simply promised to come to the aid of their neighbours, if they were called on to help repel an attack by a third party. Later, in contrast, in 368/7 BC an explicit clause appears after the normal expression of mutual aid in the face of external attack in the alliance between Athens and Dionysius I, the ruler of Syracuse in Sicily (Athens, Epigraphical Museum: Rhodes and Osborne 2003: 164–9 no. 34 lines 23–30):

> It is not allowed for Dionysius and his descendants to bear arms against the land of the Athenians for the purpose of doing harm either by land or by sea; nor is it allowed for the Athenians to bear arms against Dionysius and his descendants and what Dionysius rules for the purpose of doing harm either by land or by sea.[11]

In effect, the signatories agree to be friends and to live at peace with each other, but the word *eirēnē* is still not mentioned; instead the desire to secure a peaceful

11 Thucydides (1921: 34–5 [5.18.4], 90–91 [5.47.2]) had already noted similar clauses in the settlements known now as the Peace of Nicias in 421 BC and the Hundred Years Alliance between Athens, Argos, Mantinea and Elis in 420 BC.

coexistence is expressed in a lengthy pair of clauses forbidding all aggressive activity between them in the future.

Needless to say, history shows how hard it was for the Greeks to avoid conflict and abide by the terms and conditions of sworn contracts, not least because of the ambiguity and lack of definition in those agreements (Rhodes 2008).[12] An arbitration clause in the treaty known as the 30 Years' Peace of 446/5 BC failed to prevent the Peloponnesian War in 431 (Tritle 2007: 174–80), and the Peace of Nicias of 421 was soon broken because Athens refused arbitration. In 387 BC the Peace of Antalcidas, otherwise known even to the Greeks as the 'King's *Peace*', was laid down by the Persian King, since the Greeks were unable to stop fighting among themselves.

This particular peace treaty, for which the word *eirēnē* was used, appears alongside the long-standing diplomatic terms, 'the friendship, the oaths and the existing treaty (*synthēkai*)', in an inscription recording an alliance between Athens and Chios in 384/3 BC (Athens, Epigraphical Museum: Rhodes and Osborne 2003: 82–7 no. 20 lines 9–10, 18–19). Later it is also clearly referred to in a document praising Dionysius I in 369/8 BC (Athens, Epigraphical Museum: Rhodes and Osborne 2003: 160–65 no. 33 lines 23–6): '… and they [Dionysius and his sons] support the king's peace, which the Athenians, the Lacedaemonians and the other Greeks made'.

But the Athenians found it initially difficult to adapt to the novel political situation which now existed. The King's Peace, as a universal peace treaty, placed them in unfamiliar territory. This may be inferred from the cautious claim in the first of these two inscriptions that they were 'not violating anything written on the slabs (*stelai*) about the peace (*eirēnē*)' (lines 21–3). The terms and practices of the previous, bilateral or multilateral alliances were now subject to challenge, and all new agreements had to comply with the comprehensive provisions of the King's Peace.

Once the value of a single peace accord had been realized and the concept embraced in principle, a series of short-lived Common Peaces was brokered in 375, 371, 368, 366/5, 362/1 and 346, until King Philip II of Macedonia put an end to the independence of the southern city-states at the Battle of Chaeronea in 338 BC and enforced a final, shared or common peace (*koinē eirēnē*), unlimited in time and multilateral in scope (Athens, Epigraphical Museum: Rhodes and Osborne 2003: 372–9 no. 76, 338/7 BC, Tritle 2007, 180–81).

Conclusion

I have approached the question of the ancient Greek vision of peace from two angles in this chapter, keeping the evidence and ideas drawn from each distinct up to this point, but more insight may be gained by bringing them together now.

On the one hand, on the basis of contemporary literary/poetic and artistic sources I have examined peace from a religious viewpoint. This part showed how

---

12 For the handful of exceptions where Greeks stayed out of major wars in the Classical and Hellenistic periods see Alonso 2007: 208.

Eirēnē was visualised by the ancient Greeks as a female divinity who at least in Athens by the early fourth century BC had an altar in the civic centre, a prestigious sculptural image and significant cult observances. She was frequently invoked as a beautiful young woman, the bringer of wealth and the nurse of young men. In times of war *Eirēnē* offered the hope of the undoubted blessings associated with a return to a peaceful life, in which the seasonal cycle of the agricultural year could prevail.

On the other hand, on the basis of inscriptional and historical sources we have discovered a more political and secular concept. This *eirēnē* equates well with the English term for peace in a range of real-life contexts, with no suggestion of mystical personification. Perhaps surprisingly, however, the Greek word seems almost an afterthought in the human business of foreign policy making. Only after the late fifth century was peace added sporadically to the diplomatic terminology of alliances and peace treaties negotiated between the frequently combative city-states; friendship and alliance appeared earlier arguably as less elusive and more achievable goals.

To what extent the religious quality of *eirēnē* may have also and always been present in the political sphere of interstate relations is a good question. While in our secular, Western society some commentators confidently divorce the two – for example, Burkert (1985: 186) called the cult of similar personifications 'more propaganda than religion' – it is apparent that most Classical Greeks would have drawn no sharp distinction (Stafford 2000: 19–27). *Eirēnē*, the goddess, and *eirēnē*, the concept, remained one and the same. What changed over time perhaps was the balance between them. The Greeks of Homer and Hesiod's time made offerings to the gods and prayed for divine assistance, hoping to be granted the gift of Peace and all her blessings; by the fourth century peace had been appropriated as a political resource, which men (hubristically) now presumed to control and negotiate for themselves. At the same time, however, the importance of her cult grew, as appeals were still made and thanks given to the goddess *Eirēnē* herself.

In ancient Greece peace was hard to find and harder to keep. Agreements, recorded on permanent materials in civic and Panhellenic sanctuaries, were made with binding oaths sworn by the Olympian gods, who were called upon to supply the divine sanctions to enforce them, but when these were the only sanctions, something stronger was required. It was only in the fourth century BC, backed by the external authority first of the kings of Persia and then of Macedonia, that a Common Peace became more than a dream for the minor players in the ancient Greek game of war, and *Eirēnē* the goddess was worshipped in earnest.

Bibliography

Alonso, V. 2007. War, peace, and international law in ancient Greece, in *War and Peace in the Ancient World*, edited by K.A. Raaflaub. Malden, MA: Blackwell Publishing, 206–25.

Andocides 1953. On the peace with Sparta, in *Minor Attic Orators,* vol. 1 (Loeb Classical Library). Revised Edition. Translated from ancient Greek by K.J. Maidment. Cambridge, MA: Harvard University Press, 483–531.

Aristophanes 1998a. Acharnians, in *Aristophanes,* vol. 1 (Loeb Classical Library). Translated from ancient Greek by J. Henderson. Cambridge, MA: Harvard University Press, 47–217.

Aristophanes 1998b. Peace, in *Aristophanes,* vol. 2 (Loeb Classical Library). Translated from ancient Greek by J. Henderson. Cambridge, MA: Harvard University Press, 417–601.

Aristophanes 2000. Lysistrata, in *Aristophanes,* vol. 3 (Loeb Classical Library). Translated from ancient Greek by J. Henderson. Cambridge, MA: Harvard University Press, 253–441.

Bacchylides 1992. Bacchylides, in *Greek Lyric,* vol. 4 (Loeb Classical Library). Translated from ancient Greek by D.A. Campbell. Cambridge, MA: Harvard University Press, 100–317.

Bauslaugh, R.A. 1991. *The Concept of Neutrality in Classical Greece*. Berkeley, Los Angeles and Oxford: University of California Press.

Burkert, W. 1985. *Greek Religion: Archaic and Classical.* Translated from German by J. Raffan. Oxford: Blackwell Publishers.

Burkert, W. 2005. Hesiod in context: abstractions and divinities in an Aegean-Eastern koiné, in *Personification in the Greek World: from Antiquity to Byzantium*, edited by E. Stafford and J. Herrin. Aldershot: Ashgate, 3–20.

Caratelli, G.P. (ed.) 1996. *The Western Greeks: Classical Civilization in the Western Mediterranean.* London: Thames and Hudson.

Christopoulos, G.A. (ed.) 1975. *The Archaic Period. History of the Hellenic World*, vol. 2. Athens: Ekdotike Athenon.

Eschbach, N. 1986. *Statuen auf Panathenäischen Preisamphoren des 4. Jhs. v. Chr.* Mainz am Rhein: Philipp von Zabern.

Euripides 1998. Suppliant women, in *Euripides,* vol. 3 (Loeb Classical Library). Translated from ancient Greek by D. Kovacs. Cambridge, MA: Harvard University Press, 1–139.

Euripides 2002a. Bacchae, in *Euripides,* vol. 6 (Loeb Classical Library). Translated from ancient Greek by D. Kovacs. Cambridge, MA: Harvard University Press, 1–153.

Euripides 2002b. Orestes, in *Euripides*, vol. 5 (Loeb Classical Library). Translated from ancient Greek by D. Kovacs. Cambridge, MA: Harvard University Press, 399–605.

Euripides 2008. Cresphontes, in *Euripides,* vol. 7, *Fragments* (Loeb Classical Library). Translated from ancient Greek by C. Collard and M. Cropp. Cambridge, MA: Harvard University Press, 493–515.

Gantz, T. 1993. *Early Greek Myth: A Guide to Literary and Artistic Sources*. 2 vols. Baltimore, MD and London: Johns Hopkins University Press.

Heraclitus 1979. Heraclitus, in *The Art and Thought of Heraclitus: An Edition of the Fragments with Translation and Commentary*, edited by C.H. Kahn. Cambridge: Cambridge University Press.

Herodotus 1924. *The Persian Wars,* vol. 4 (Loeb Classical Library). Translated from ancient Greek by A.D. Godley. Cambridge, MA: Harvard University Press.

Herodotus 1926. *The Persian Wars,* vol. 1 (Loeb Classical Library). Revised Edition. Translated from ancient Greek by A.D. Godley. Cambridge, MA: Harvard University Press.

Hesiod 2006a. Theogony, in *Hesiod,* vol. 1 (Loeb Classical Library). Translated from ancient Greek by G.W. Most. Cambridge, MA: Harvard University Press, 1–85.

Hesiod 2006b. Works and days, in *Hesiod,* vol. 1 (Loeb Classical Library). Translated from ancient Greek by G.W. Most. Cambridge, MA: Harvard University Press, 86–153.

Homer 1998. *Odyssey*, vol. 2 (Loeb Classical Library). 2nd Edition. Translated from ancient Greek by A.T. Murray and revised by G.E. Dimock. Cambridge, MA: Harvard University Press.

Homer 1999. *Iliad,* 2 vols (Loeb Classical Library). 2nd Edition. Translated from ancient Greek by A.T. Murray and revised by W.F. Wyatt. Cambridge, MA: Harvard University Press.

Inscriptiones Graecae II^2 1496, in *Inscriptiones Graecae II et III: Inscriptiones Atticae Euclidis anno posteriores* 1927–1931. 2nd Edition, Part 2, 1–2, edited by J. Kirchner. Berlin: G. Reimer.

Isocrates 1929a. Antidosis, in *Isocrates,* vol. 2 (Loeb Classical Library). Translated from ancient Greek by G. Norlin. Cambridge, MA: Harvard University Press, 179–365.

Isocrates 1929b. On the Peace, in *Isocrates,* vol. 2 (Loeb Classical Library). Translated from ancient Greek by G. Norlin. Cambridge, MA: Harvard University Press, 1–97.

Larson, J. 2007. *Ancient Greek Cults: A Guide*. New York and London: Routledge.

Low, P. 2007. *Interstate Relations in Classical Greece: Morality and Power*. Cambridge: Cambridge University Press.

Meiggs, R. and Lewis, D.M. 1988. *A Selection of Greek Historical Inscriptions to the End of the Fifth Century B.C.* 2nd Edition. Oxford: Oxford University Press.

Mikalson, J.D. 2010. *Ancient Greek Religion*. 2nd Edition. Chichester: Wiley-Blackwell.

Parker, R. 1996. *Athenian Religion: A History*. Oxford: Clarendon Press.

Parker, R. 2005. *Polytheism and Society at Athens*. Oxford: Oxford University Press.

Pausanias 1918. *Description of Greece*, vol. 1 (Loeb Classical Library). Translated from ancient Greek by W.H.S. Jones, H.A. Ormerod and R.E. Wycherley. Cambridge, MA: Harvard University Press.

Pausanias 1935. *Description of Greece*, vol. 4 (Loeb Classical Library). Translated from ancient Greek by W.H.S. Jones, H.A. Ormerod and R.E. Wycherley. Cambridge, MA: Harvard University Press.

Pindar 1997. Olympian odes, in *Pindar*, vol. 1 (Loeb Classical Library). Translated from ancient Greek by W.H. Race. Cambridge, MA: Harvard University Press, 43–207.

Plato 1926. Laws, in *Plato,* vols 10–11 (Loeb Classical Library). Translated from ancient Greek by R.G. Bury. Cambridge, MA: Harvard University Press.

Plutarch 1914. Life of Cimon, in *Plutarch,* vol. 2 (Loeb Classical Library). Translated from ancient Greek by B. Perrin. Cambridge, MA: Harvard University Press, 403–67.

Pritchett, W.K. 1979. *The Greek State at War. Part III: Religion.* Berkeley, Los Angeles and London: University of California Press.

Raaflaub, K.A. 2007. Introduction: searching for peace in the ancient world, in *War and Peace in the Ancient World*, edited by K.A. Raaflaub. Malden, MA: Blackwell Publishing, 1–33.

Rhodes, P.J. 2008. Making and breaking treaties in the Greek world, in *War and Peace in Ancient and Medieval History*, edited by P. de Souza and J. France. Cambridge: Cambridge University Press, 6–27.

Rhodes, P.J. and Osborne, R. 2003. *Greek Historical Inscriptions 404–323 BC.* Oxford: Oxford University Press.

Ridgway, B.S. 1997. *Fourth-Century Styles in Greek Sculpture.* London: Duckworth.

Sage, M.M. 1996. *Warfare in Ancient Greece: A Sourcebook.* London and New York: Routledge.

Shapiro, H.A. 1993. *Personifications in Greek Art: The Representation of Abstract Concepts 600–400 B.C.* Zurich: Akanthus.

Simon, E. 1986. Eirene, in *Lexicon Iconographicum Mythologiae Classicae (LIMC)* III. Zurich and Munich: Artemis, vol. 1 700–705, vol. 2 plates 540–42.

Smith, A.C. 2005. From drunkenness to a hangover: maenads as personifications, in *Personification in the Greek World: from Antiquity to Byzantium*, edited by E. Stafford and J. Herrin. Aldershot: Ashgate, 211–30.

Stafford, E. 2000. *Worshipping Virtues: Personification and the Divine in Ancient Greece.* London: Duckworth and The Classical Press of Wales.

Stafford, E. 2007. Personification in Greek religious thought and practice, in *A Companion to Greek Religion*, edited by D. Ogden. Malden, MA: Blackwell Publishing, 71–85.

Stewart, A. 1990. *Greek Sculpture: An Exploration.* 2 vols. New Haven and London: Yale University Press.

Theognis 1971. *Theognidea*, in *Iambi et Elegi Graeci ante Alexandrum Cantati,* vol. 1, edited by M.L. West. Oxford: Oxford University Press, 172–241.

Thompson, H.A. and Wycherley, R.E. 1972. *The Athenian Agora. 14. The Agora of Athens: the History, Shape and Uses of an Ancient City Center.* Princeton, NJ: American School of Classical Studies at Athens.

Thucydides 1921. *History of the Peloponnesian War*, vol. 3 (Loeb Classical Library). Translated from ancient Greek by C.F. Smith. Cambridge, MA: Harvard University Press.

Thucydides 1930. *History of the Peloponnesian War,* vol. 2 (Loeb Classical Library). Revised Edition. Translated from ancient Greek by C.F. Smith. Cambridge, MA: Harvard University Press.

Tritle, L.A. 2007. 'Laughing for joy': war and peace among the Greeks, in *War and Peace in the Ancient World*, edited by K.A. Raaflaub. Malden, MA: Blackwell Publishing, 172–90.

van Wees, H. 2004. *Greek Warfare: Myths and Realities*. London: Duckworth.

Wycherley, R.E. 1957. *The Athenian Agora. 3. Literary and Epigraphical Testimonia.* Princeton, NJ: American School of Classical Studies at Athens.

Xenophon 1918. Hellenica, in *Xenophon*, vol. 1 (Loeb Classical Library). Translated from ancient Greek by C.L. Brownson. Cambridge, MA: Harvard University Press.

Zampaglione, G. 1973. *The Idea of Peace in Antiquity*. Translated from Italian by R. Dunn. Notre Dame, IN and London: University of Notre Dame Press.

Chapter 2
The Dissident Tradition of Christian Pacifism

Murray Rae

I propose in this chapter to give an account of the origins and fortunes of the tradition of Christian pacifism. As my title suggests, Christian pacifism is a dissident tradition. It has stood for most of Christian history against the mainstream of political life in the so-called Christian West. The history of Christianity and the 'Christian West' reveals clearly enough, counter-examples notwithstanding, that Christians have, in general, been as inclined to support and engage in war and violence as anyone else. Clear injunctions against the use of violence found in the teachings of Jesus have not consistently precluded Christians from engaging in or supporting violent suppression of difference or from resorting to the instruments of war in pursuit of their particular visions of a better world. Despite the prominence of a belligerent Christian tradition, however, one can also find in the 2,000 years of Christian reflection upon the subject an enduring Christian protest against the prevailing practice of warfare and violence, and sometimes heroic allegiance to the biblical injunctions to put away the sword, to love one's enemies and to turn the other cheek. This protest has been motivated, above all, by the conviction that proper faithfulness to the way of Jesus Christ involves opposition to war and the pursuit of peace, even at the cost of one's own life.

During the first three centuries of Christian history, opposition to violence and to Christian participation in the military was widespread among Christian theologians, though not applied consistently in practice. Christian writers generally supposed that the Christian gospel contained an imperative to love one's enemies, to seek peace and to refrain from killing. There is evidence in the second and third centuries of Christians refusing military service and of Christians being expelled from the military. It is clear that some Christians paid with their lives for their principled stand against involvement in the military. This tradition was rapidly eroded during the course of the fourth and fifth centuries, however, to the extent that by the mid-fifth century one had to be a Christian to serve in the Imperial Army. Following the alleged conversion to Christian faith of the Emperor Constantine and the development of 'Christendom', the pacifist voice in the Christian tradition was marginalized and sometimes suppressed. I will consider in what follows the reasons for that dramatic reversal. It did not mean that the Christian church abandoned its counsel of restraint with respect to warfare and violence; that continued. But in the era beginning around the fifth century and continuing almost until our own day it cannot be claimed that the church in the main has been pacifist in conviction. Christians throughout the era of Christendom have typically supposed that the use of force by the state and, for some, even by the church, is a legitimate and divinely sanctioned means of securing justice and peace. Christian pacifism, by which I mean absolute opposition to the use of violence and warfare, has been a minority voice.

Only in our own time has that situation begun to be reversed. Mainline Christian churches are more often to be found now on the side of those opposing warfare and signs are emerging of a resurgence of Christian commitment to non-violence. Conscientious objectors during the first and second world wars who were often vilified in their own time are increasingly regarded now as courageous upholders of Christian truth. The Christian convictions motivating Martin Luther King's advocacy of non-violent resistance in the Civil Rights movement are widely shared among Christians, while the leading role played by churches in Britain in the public protests against Britain's involvement in the invasion of Iraq in 2003 offer further evidence of a groundswell in Christian support for non-violent means of conflict resolution. But that leaves a long period from the fourth to the mid-twentieth centuries when states could rely, with intermittent but nonetheless notable exceptions, on the support of the Christian church for their belligerent pursuit of allegedly 'noble' ends. Although a comprehensive study of these historical developments lies beyond the scope of this chapter, I propose to trace in broad outline the principled opposition to violence and military service as it developed in the early church and then consider why that opposition was eroded in the era we now call Christendom. The final section of the chapter will offer a brief study of the growing Christian support for a pacifist position in our own time.

The account I will give of this tradition is that of a theologian rather than a historian. I am interested, above all, in the theological arguments offered in defence of a pacifist position. And I speak from the inside, as it were, not as one who views the Christian tradition dispassionately but rather as one who wishes to uncover and defend its conceptual roots.

Biblical Foundations

The Christian Bible comprising the Old and New Testaments is a collection of texts ranging in provenance over 2,000 years and variously telling the story of a people's encounters with God culminating, according to the New Testament accounts, in God's self-disclosure in the figure of Jesus of Nazareth. There is much scope for debate, of course, about the nature of and warrant for the Bible's claims about God, but for our purposes we have merely to observe that the Christian tradition takes the Bible to be an authoritative guide to the nature and purposes of God. Christian arguments for or against pacifism, therefore, will have to reckon with the biblical texts that bear upon this matter. Although naïve readers of Scripture often suppose that biblical authority may be adduced simply by quoting a 'proof text' in support of one's position, the mainstream of Christian tradition has long recognized that the biblical writers themselves debate, modify and contest one another's positions on a range of ethical issues. The reader of Christian Scripture is invited to participate in the debate and to consider for themselves, in conversation with others in the church, where the meandering trajectory of the biblical story might lead in terms of a particular ethical concern.

For Christian readers, as distinct from both Jewish and non-religious readers of the biblical texts, hermeneutical priority is given to the culmination of that trajectory in the life, death and resurrection of Jesus of Nazareth. Christians, that is to say, read Scripture with a Christological lens; they read 'in the light of Christ'. That means, for instance, that Christians reading the stories of conflict in the Old Testament books of Samuel or Joshua subject the claims about God's sanctioning of violence to Christological scrutiny. When Samuel conveys to King Saul his conviction that God has commanded Saul to 'go and attack Amalek, and utterly destroy all that they have; do not spare them, but kill both man and woman, child and infant, ox and sheep, camel and donkey' (The Bible, 1 Samuel 15: 2–3), a Christian reader will be inclined to 'test' that claim against the contrary indications of God's will that are found in the teaching and example of Jesus. I will return later to a consideration of how that testing might be executed in the deliberations of contemporary Christian pacifists, but for now I seek only to indicate the hermeneutical priority given in Christian ethical deliberation to the Biblical testimony concerning Jesus. It is through engagement with that testimony that Christian pacifism must be defended.

The earliest writings of the New Testament are the Pauline epistles written during the 50s, 20 to 30 years after Jesus' death. Until that time the early Christians had preserved the story of Jesus through an oral tradition, a tradition that also interpreted the story and explained its significance. Following the early epistles of Paul, the four gospels and the remaining books of the New Testament were largely complete by the end of the first century with only a very few appearing during the first decade of the second century. The writings of the New Testament thus reflect a maturing tradition of interpretation in which the presentation of Jesus' teaching and the events of his life are shaped by a great deal of theological reflection upon what those events mean. In reading the New Testament therefore, in particular the four Gospels, we learn not only about what Jesus said and did, but also about the meaning and significance of those events as understood by the early church. The writers of the New Testament presented what they considered to be the heart of the 'good news' arising from the life, death and resurrection of Jesus of Nazareth. With their heavy emphasis upon the call to discipleship, furthermore, the New Testament writers clearly considered that the teaching and example of Jesus established an imperative for those who would follow him. It is of very considerable importance for his followers therefore that, through his teaching and in the pattern of his own life, Jesus himself appears consistently to oppose violence and to reject the power of the sword.

It is a notable feature of Jesus' teaching, particularly in the 'sermon on the mount' as portrayed in Matthew's Gospel, that he frequently modifies or overrules traditional biblical stipulations concerning violence. Most famously, perhaps, Jesus says, 'You have heard that it was said, "An eye for an eye and a tooth for a tooth." But I say to you, Do not resist an evil doer. But if any one strikes you on the right cheek, turn the other also' (The Bible, Matthew 5: 38–9). Or again: 'You have heard that it was said, "You shall love your neighbour and hate your enemy." But I say to you, Love your enemies and pray for those who persecute you, so that you may be children of your father in heaven …' (The Bible, Matthew 5: 43–4).[1] In respect of the law against murder Jesus says,

> You have heard that it was said to those of ancient times, "You shall not murder"; and "whoever murders shall be liable to judgement." But I say to you that if you are angry with a brother or sister, you will be liable to judgement; and if you insult a brother or sister, you will be liable to the council. (The Bible, Matthew 5: 21–2)

Jesus typically makes more stringent the customary prohibition of violence. Again in Matthew's record of the sermon on the mount, in the segment known as the Beatitudes, Jesus promises blessing for those who make peace: 'Blessed are the peacemakers', he says, 'for they will be called children of God' (The Bible, Matthew 5: 9). That peacemakers should be called 'children of God' indicates that the way of peace is God's way and promises that God will vindicate those who make peace rather than those who make war.

The setting of these sayings of Jesus in Matthew's gospel makes clear that Jesus intended his ethical injunctions to be the hallmarks of a counter-cultural polity to be lived out by those who accepted the invitation to follow him (see Hays 1996: 321). There is very little room for argument, I suggest, against the notion that Jesus conceived the community of his followers as a non-violent community – a community distinguished not only by love of neighbour but also by love of one's enemies. It was not simply the teaching of Jesus that inspired such attitudes in the early Christians, however, it was also the logic of the divine purpose believed to have been worked out through the life, death and resurrection of Jesus. The resurrection, most especially, convinced them that God sides with the peacemakers, with the merciful and with those who trust that in the end violence and evil will be overcome not by further violence but by the exercise of love.

Christian faith grew, of course, within the fertile soil of Israel's theological tradition, a tradition that reports acts of war and violence both by and against God's chosen people but that has at its heart the establishment of a covenant in which blessing is promised to all the peoples of the earth (The Bible, Genesis

1 Of all the sayings of Jesus beginning, 'You have heard that it was said …', this is the only one where the source is not Jewish Scripture. The saying, 'You shall love your neighbour and hate your enemy', was presumably well known in the surrounding culture.

12: 3). It also includes a law that prohibits killing (The Bible, Exodus 20: 13) and a prophetic tradition that heralds a day when people will 'beat their swords into ploughshares' and will not learn war anymore (The Bible, Isaiah 2: 4, cf. the Bible, Joel 3: 1). That vision of peace appears again in Israel's hopes for a coming Messiah and in its anticipations of a kingdom of peace in which, as it is classically put, 'the wolf shall live with the lamb, the leopard shall lie down with the kid, the calf and the lion and the fatling together, and a little child shall lead them' (The Bible, Isaiah 11: 6). The vision of peace set out in Israel's Scripture extends to the whole of creation. It was to that same prophetic tradition that Jesus appealed when establishing a mandate for his own ministry. Asked to read from the book of Isaiah in the Synagogue, Jesus read the words:

> The Spirit of the Lord is upon me,
> because he has anointed me to bring good news to the poor.
> He has sent me to proclaim release to the captives
> and recovery of sight to the blind,
> to let the oppressed go free,
> to proclaim the year of the Lord's favour.

He then proclaimed, 'Today these words have been fulfilled in your hearing' (The Bible, Luke 4: 21). Thus began the three-year ministry in which Jesus became a preacher of peace, promised God's favour to those who were makers of peace, exhorted his followers to love their enemies and rejected the intervention of force when his own life came under threat. When threatened by violence himself and in response to the disciple Peter's attempt to come to Jesus' defence by drawing his sword, Jesus instructs Peter to 'put away your sword', and continues, 'Am I not to drink the cup that the Father has given me?' (The Bible, John 18: 11). The 'cup' Jesus determines to drink refers metaphorically to his suffering and crucifixion. Jesus' acceptance of this 'cup' may be taken as a form of passive resistance to violence. He does not meet violence with violence but responds with a love for his enemies that brings suffering upon himself. In this way, so the biblical testimony suggests, violence along with the sin that gives rise to it are robbed of their power. What is more, Jesus commends forgiveness for the perpetrators of evil, a forgiveness directed towards reconciliation and the establishment of peace. The resurrection of the crucified Jesus is understood by Christians to be God's vindication of this way of being.

It has to be said, however, that Christians have been endlessly resourceful in finding ways to avoid the plain sense of Jesus' teaching and example and to take up the sword rather than the cross (see Hays 1996: 320, Jeremias 1963). Among the strategies for avoidance has been the suggestion that the sermon on the mount outlines an ethic for some future kingdom of God, not for the realpolitik of our present existence (see especially Niebuhr 1941: 47–71). Others have claimed that this was an ethic of perfection for monks or clergy but not for the general run of Christians. Ambrose, a Roman church statesman of the late fourth century, extolled the virtues of military service while advising clergy to abstain (Ambrose 2002: 175 [bk 1 ch. 35]). Others suggest that the teaching of Jesus prohibits fighting on one's own behalf but does not preclude forceful intervention on behalf of others. The casuistry providing justifications for Christian participation in the violent suppression of enemies at least presumes a burden of proof upon Christians who want to indulge in war. It must be acknowledged, however, that many 'Christian nations' engaged in war appear to have been little troubled by the plain sense of Jesus' teaching.

The Early Church

The developments of later Christian tradition notwithstanding, the followers of Jesus in the centuries immediately following his death commonly took his teaching and example as an unequivocal mandate for a pacifist form of life. The salvation thought to be offered in Christ is achieved not by the sword, but through the sacrifice of the cross. Violence is met with love and, as on the lips of Jesus at his crucifixion, with the prayer for forgiveness of those who do evil (see The Bible, Luke 23: 34). Thus the earliest New Testament writer, the apostle Paul, enjoins readers of his epistle to the Romans to 'bless those who persecute you; bless and do not curse them'. And further, quoting Proverbs 25: 21–22a '"… if your enemies are hungry, feed them; if they are thirsty, give them something to drink; for by doing this you will heap burning coals on their heads." Do not be overcome by evil but overcome evil with good' (The Bible, Romans 12: 14, 20–1).[2] Such advice is repeated by the unknown author of the first epistle to Peter who writes in the face of early persecution of Christians, 'Do not repay evil for evil or abuse for abuse; but, on the contrary, repay with a blessing' (The Bible, I Peter 3: 9). Clearly, the recommendation of both authors is that Christians subjected to evil or oppression should respond with non-violent resistance.

During the first three centuries of Christian history, the refusal to engage in violence or to serve in the military was considered, virtually unanimously by Christian theologians, to be the straightforward implication of the biblical material briefly surveyed above. Although the evidence reveals some variation in practice, in general terms, the small community of Christians that preserved and retold the story of Jesus in the years following his death took that story to mean, among other things, that they ought to resign from or refuse enlistment in the military, that they ought to love and pray for their enemies rather than wage war against them and that they ought to suffer death themselves rather than give their allegiance to those political powers that wielded the instruments of war.

2 The New Testament scholar C.K. Barrett (1987: 242–3) writes, 'In view of v.21, it can scarcely be doubted that the "burning coals" are the fire of remorse. If an enemy is treated in this way he may well be overcome in the best possible fashion—he may become a friend'.

Evidence for early Christian resistance to violence and warfare comes in several forms, notably in the writings of theologians directly opposed to Christian involvement in warfare, in the taunts of opponents who deride Christians for their pacifist stance and in the documented cases of Christians who paid with their lives for their opposition to violence. Christian opposition to war gets underway very early in the tradition. Justin Martyr, for example, writing ca.150–160 AD claimed on behalf of Christians that 'we who formerly used to murder one another … now refrain from even making war upon our enemies' (Justin Martyr 1979: 176 [ch. 39]). The basis for this cessation of violence, Justin contended, lay in the fulfillment through Jesus Christ of the prophesy from Isaiah partially quoted above:

> For out of Zion shall go forth instruction,
> and the word of the Lord from Jerusalem.
> He shall judge between the nations,
> and shall arbitrate for many peoples;
> they shall beat their swords into ploughshares,
> and their spears into pruning-hooks;
> nation shall not lift up sword against nation,
> neither shall they learn war any more. (The Bible, Isaiah 2: 3)

Shortly after Justin, Clement of Alexandria (ca.150–215) took up the same theme: 'For it is not in war, but in peace, that we are trained … peace and love, simple and quiet sisters, require no arms nor excessive preparation. The Word is their sustenance' (Clement 1986: 234–5 [bk 1 ch. 12]). A pacifist stance was for Clement a universal imperative of Christian discipleship: 'Above all', he wrote, 'Christians are not allowed to correct with violence the delinquencies of sins' (cited in Maximus 2001: 581). Likewise, Hippolytus of Rome (ca.170–236), a military commander before converting to Christianity, insisted on the incompatibility of military service and Christian discipleship.

> A soldier of the government must be told not to execute men; if he should be ordered to do it, he shall not do it. He must be told not to take the military oath. If he will not agree, let him be rejected. A military governor or a magistrate of a city who wears the purple, either let him desist or let him be rejected. If a catechumen or a baptised Christian wishes to become a soldier, let him be cast out. For he has despised God. (Hippolytus 1937: 26–7 [ch. 16])

The injunctions of these theologians were taken extremely seriously, at least by some. Towards the end of the same century in which Hippolytus wrote, a young Christian from Numidia became the patron saint of conscientious objectors. Jean Bethke Elshtain offers the following version of this frequently told story: 'Called up for military service (his father had been a Roman soldier) Maximilianus told the Roman proconsul that, as a Christian, "I cannot serve as a soldier; I cannot do evil." He was executed for his persistence' (Elshtain 1987: 125).

The incompatibility between Christian faith and military service rested not only on the dominical commands not to kill but to love one's enemies, but also on the requirement of soldiers to worship the emperor. The biblical injunction, 'You shall have no other gods before me' (The Bible, Exodus 20: 3), leaves no room for obeisance to an emperor with pretensions to divinity and who required the absolute allegiance of his subjects. Christian refusal to offer such worship prompted Celsus, the Epicurean philosopher, to complain against the Christians that 'if all were to do the same as you, there would be nothing to prevent [the emperor's] being left in utter solitude and desertion, and the affairs of the earth would fall into the hands of the wildest and most lawless barbarians' (cited in Origen 1994: 665 [bk 8 ch. 68]). In his reply, the Christian theologian, Origen (ca.185–254), contended that if, 'in the words of Celsus, "they do as I do", then it is evident that even the barbarians, when they yield obedience to the word of God, will become most obedient to the law, and most humane' (Origen 1994: 666 [bk 8 ch. 68]). And further, 'if all the Romans, according to the supposition of Celsus, embrace the Christian faith, they will, when they pray, overcome their enemies; or rather, they will not war at all' (Origen 1994: 666 [bk 8 ch. 70]). Origen dismisses the legitimacy of violence and contended on behalf of Christians that 'we no longer take up "*sword against nation*", nor do we "*learn war any more*", having become children of peace, for the sake of Jesus, who is our leader' (Origen 1994: 558 [bk 5 ch. 33]).

Origen gives voice to the widespread opposition to military service among Christians but such opposition was not universal. There is evidence from the second century of the participation of Christians in the so-called Thundering Legion under Marcus Aurelius (174 AD) (see Bainton 1960: 68). Then at the beginning of the third century, the theologian Tertullian (ca.160–ca.220) considers it necessary to rebuke Christians who voluntarily enlisted in the military. Referring to Jesus' instruction to Peter to put away his sword, Tertullian wrote, 'Christ in disarming Peter unb[elt]ed every soldier' (Tertullian 1994: 73 [ch. 19]). In his treatise opposing Christian involvement in military service, *De Corona*, Tertullian reports approvingly the instance of a young soldier who, on becoming a Christian, refused to wear the laurel crown and when questioned by the tribune replies that on account of his allegiance to Christ he has no liberty to wear the crown. The crown, by contrast, indicated allegiance to Apollo or Bacchus, to Venus or Minerva and thus, in Tertullian's eyes, defiled those who wore it (Tertullian 1994b: 100–101 [ch. 12]). The Christian ought not, Tertullian (Tertullian 1994b: 102 [ch. 14]) avers, 'put the service of idolatry on his own head'. When questioned further the soldier who refused the crown sets aside also his sword and his military cloak and then, as Tertullian (1994b: 93) reports, 'girt with the sharper word of God, completely equipped with the apostles' armour, and crowned more worthily with the white crown of martyrdom, he awaits in prison the largess of Christ'. Tertullian's story shows signs of hagiographic elaboration, but it is no doubt based on many instances among Christians of a costly renunciation of their military oath. Others were expelled. Galerius around 300 AD, for example, attempted to weed Christians out of his forces having reason to question the extent of their commitment to the military cause. (Bainton 1960: 274).

Despite the extensive attention given by Tertullian to the wearing of the laurel crown, he eventually notes that the practice was 'merely accidental'. The real problem was the institution on which the practice rests. Thus he writes, 'I think we must first inquire whether warfare is proper at all for Christians. What sense is there in discussing the merely accidental when that on which it rests is to be condemned?' (Tertullian 1994b: 99 [ch. 11]) He then proceeds to ask:

> Do we believe it lawful for a human oath to be superadded to one divine, for a man to come under promise to another master after Christ … ? Shall it be held lawful to make an occupation of the sword, when the Lord proclaims that he who uses the sword shall perish by the sword? And shall the son of peace take part in the battle when it does not become him even to sue at law? And shall he apply the chain, and the prison, and the torture, and the punishment, who is not the avenger even of his own wrongs? (Tertullian 1994b: 99 [ch. 11])

Clearly Tertullian thinks that the answer to each of these questions will be no, his warrant being the teaching and example of Jesus. The straightforward inference to a pacifist position from the gospel record of Jesus' life and teaching was common among theologians of the early church. So too the biblical command, 'you shall not kill', seemed to many to settle the matter. Cyprian, a third century Bishop of Carthage (d. 258), lamented:

> Wars are scattered all over the earth with the bloody horror of camps. The whole world is wet with mutual blood. And murder–which is admitted to be a crime in the case of an individual–is called a virtue when it is committed wholesale. Impunity is claimed for the wicked deeds, not because they are guiltless, but because the cruelty is perpetrated on a grand scale! (Cyprian 1986: 277)

Although passages may be found in the writings of Tertullian that apparently tolerate Christian involvement in the military, when addressing the matter explicitly the theologians of the early church more typically condemned such involvement. The few passages that exhibit a more lenient attitude appear to be a pastoral accommodation for existing soldiers who convert to Christianity and who, presumably for economic reasons, are unable immediately to resign from their posts (see Tertullian 1994b: 100 [ch. 11]).

It is important to recognize that the church's rejection of military service was motivated not only by a commitment to non-violence, but also by a rejection of Roman piety. Military service was a focal point of imperial power and institution; service required the swearing of pagan oaths and confession of the emperor's deity, and the army marched under sacred pagan standards. Nuttall (1958: 9) claims therefore that 'the early Christians' refusal to take part in war was mainly one expression among many of their refusal to take part in the life of the world, or in the activity of the State, at all'. It is anachronistic, therefore, to claim that the pacifism of the early church was simply an unconditional rejection of violence; it rested also upon confessing the unequivocal Lordship of Jesus over and against the Caesars of Rome, and a refusal to participate in the worship of other gods. We have seen already that the wearing of a military crown and its association with idolatry was condemned in Tertullian's treatise against military service. Whatever the mix of reasons, however, opposition to Christian engagement in war was commonly upheld by church leaders through the first three centuries of the church's life.

The Erosion of Christian Opposition to Warfare

During the fourth century a dramatic reversal of the normative Christian position occurred. Whereas in the third century Christians were being dismissed from the Imperial armies on account of their lack of commitment to the military cause, by the early fifth century – under the emperor Theodosius II – one had to be a Christian in order to serve in the Imperial Legions. The dramatic turn-around was set in train by the alleged conversion of the Emperor Constantine in 312 and the subsequent adoption of Christianity as the official religion of the empire by Theodosius, emperor from 379–395. In 312, Constantine was engaged in a military campaign against his rival Maxentius. Although the details vary between the two accounts of Lactantius, who was a Christian author and advisor to Constantine, and Eusebius of Caesarea, a Christian historian, Constantine is supposed to have had a dream or vision in which he was instructed to inscribe a sign of Christ upon the shields of his soldiers, possibly a cross, or otherwise the Chi Rho symbol representing the first two letters of the word Christos. Constantine followed the instruction, subsequently won a quick and easy victory over Maxentius and marched into Rome. According to the account of Eusebius, Constantine

> ordered a lofty spear in the figure of a cross to be placed beneath the hand of a statue representing himself, in the most frequented part of Rome, and the following inscription to be engraved on it in the Latin language: BY VIRTUE OF THE SALUTARY SIGN, WHICH IS THE TRUE TEST OF VALOR, I HAVE PRESERVED AND LIBERATED YOUR CITY FROM THE YOKE OF TYRANNY. I HAVE ALSO SET AT LIBERTY THE ROMAN SENATE AND PEOPLE, AND RESTORED THEM TO THEIR ANCIENT DISTINCTION AND SPLENDOR. (Eusebius, 1986: 493 [bk 1 ch. 40])

Constantine's victory left him in no doubt that the Christian God had revealed himself as a God of war and victory! (see Harnack 1981: 99). It took little time thereafter for military service to become an acceptable vocation for Christians and for Christianity itself to take a seat close to the emperor's throne. The council of Bishops that met in Nicaea in 325 at the height of the Arian crisis offered some resistance but it had little enduring impact. Expressing its contempt for Christians who attempted to return to the military having cast aside their military girdles, the council wrote, 'They were like dogs returning to their own vomit'.[3] The Bishops prescribed a rigorous programme of repentance for such offenders. Harnack contends that this canon was directed, not against military service in general, but specifically against those who having previously left Licinius' army when he issued commands against Christians and insisted that his soldiers offer sacrifices to demons, then returned to Licinius' army in pursuit of personal gain. If Harnack (1981) is correct in his view, then opposition to military service was no longer based on a principled objection to killing and violence but rather upon the dangers of idolatry and participation in pagan worship demanded of some soldiers. If this concern could be mitigated by aligning military service to the concerns of Christian piety, as was done by Constantine and successive Roman emperors, then little remained, apparently, for the church to object to. Roland Bainton (1960: 86–7) points out that this accommodation was made more plausible by virtue of the fact that Constantine had established peace in the empire and had made possible the proclamation of the gospel throughout the empire. Christians were persuaded, very quickly it seems, to see the peace of Christ as coterminous with the Pax Romana and to see the Roman emperor as its agent.

Evidence of the rapid transformation of Christian opinion is provided in the writings of Lactantius whose own position seems to have been changed by the supposed divine support for Constantine's military endeavours. In the first decade of the fourth century Lactantius wrote in his *Divine Institutes*:

> For when God forbids us to kill, He not only prohibits us from open violence, which is not even allowed by the public laws, but He warns us against the commission of those things which are esteemed lawful among men. Thus it will be neither lawful for a just man to engage in warfare, since his warfare is justice itself, nor to accuse any one of a capital charge, because it makes no difference whether you put a man to death by word, or rather by the sword, since it is the act of putting to death which is prohibited. Therefore, with regard to this precept of God, there ought to be no exception at all; but that it is always unlawful to put to death a man, whom God willed to be a sacred animal. (Lactantius 1985a: 187 [bk 6 ch. 20])

Following the victories of Constantine and Licinius over Christianity's persecutors, however, Lactantius changes his tune and attributes these victories to the intervention of the 'Supreme God' who, says Lactantius, 'did so place their necks under the sword of their foes, that they seemed to have entered the field, not as combatants, but as men devoted to death' (Lactantius, 1985b: 319–20 [ch. 47]).[4] What seems to have brought about this change of mind was that the state's

3 Council of Nicaea, Canon XII. The reference here is to The Bible, II Peter 2: 22.

4 The unfortunate combatants referred to here are the troops of Daia who, again according to Lactantius, had vowed to 'extinguish and utterly efface the name of Christians'

instruments of war were now being deployed against Christianity's enemies. It was an easy assumption for some to make that God would approve such use of military force. That 'easy assumption' soon became widespread, thus beginning an era in which the church's alliance with state power blunted and sometimes obscured altogether Jesus' commendation of love for one's enemies and his command to set aside the sword.

Following the declaration by Emperor Theodosius in 380 that 'Catholic Christianity' was to be the only legitimate religion in the Roman Empire, those who were not Christian became enemies of the State. The instruments of the State including, eventually, military instruments thereby became legitimate tools in the suppression of non-Christians. Persecution of pagans began soon after in 381. It was clear, however, that the teaching and example of Jesus with respect to the treatment of one's enemies could not simply be forgotten. The use of force against Christianity's opponents had somehow to be reconciled with Jesus' injunctions against the use of the sword and his command to love one's enemies. Although theologians varied in their approach to this matter, a mainstream tradition developed in which the use of force was to be regarded as exceptional rather than the first resort of the state in establishing justice and peace. The 'Just War' tradition, developed especially by Augustine (354–430) in the early years of Christendom, drew upon the precedent of Greek and Roman thought, particularly that of Aristotle and Cicero, both of whom had sought to prescribe some limitations to the legitimacy of war.[5]

Augustine, for his part, had a well-developed doctrine of human sinfulness. Sin has its basis, Augustine contended, in human pride, which is to be understood in turn as the assertion of human will and power, and to the selfish appropriation of all goods (see Augustine 2010: 125; 1945: 58–9 [bk 14, ch. 28]). This led Augustine to an acute suspicion of Imperial war-mongering and the lust for domination. 'The real evils in war', he writes, 'are love of violence, revengeful cruelty, fierce and implacable enmity, wild resistance, and the lust of power, and such like …' (Augustine 1994: 515 [bk 20 ch. 74]). His understanding of human sinfulness and evil led him to acknowledge, however, the need for some means of suppressing evil and upholding justice. Following his identification of 'the real evils of war' he continues, '… it is generally to punish these things, when force is required to inflict the punishment, that, in obedience to God or some lawful authority, good men undertake wars …' (Augustine 1994: 515 [bk 20 ch. 74]). He contends further that, '… the natural order which seeks the peace of mankind, ordains that the monarch should have the power of undertaking war if he thinks it advisable, and that the soldiers should perform their military duties in behalf of the peace and safety of the community (Augustine 1994: 516 [bk 20 ch. 75]).

(Lactantius 1985b: 319 [ch. 46]).

5 For a more comprehensive account of Augustine's development of the doctrine of just war, see Russell 1975: 16–39 and Langan 1984.

The sword-wielding state was thus conceived by Augustine as an imperfect but divinely sanctioned instrument of justice and peace. In discussing the Old Testament reports of wars waged by Moses, however, Augustine approves the love that he presumes to have been Moses' motivation: 'Moses acted as he did not in cruelty but in great love' (Augustine 1994: 520 [bk 22 ch. 79]). This disposition of the heart thus becomes a condition commended to all who would wage war. It should be waged, if at all, only as a benevolent act of love for the enemy.

The importance of a disposition of love in war became a preoccupation of subsequent medieval discussion, having the salutary effect of unreservedly condemning any acts motivated by the love of violence, vengeful cruelty or greed. To the concern with loving intent, Augustine (1994: 75 [bk 22 ch. 79]) added the criteria of just cause, proper authority and just conduct within war as conditions that should be met if a war was to be considered 'just'. Note, however, that in Augustine's mind, even war justly waged remained a manifestation of human fallenness, a necessary evil that undoubtedly inflicts enduring misery upon humankind (Augustine 1998: 928–9 [bk 19 ch. 7]).

A more thorough exposition of just war criteria was offered by Thomas Aquinas (ca.1225–1274). Aquinas both reiterated and extended Augustine's criteria including in particular the criterion of proportionality. He argued against the notion, common in earlier strands of Christian pacifism, that engagement in war was always to be regarded as sinful. While it was certainly Aquinas's intention to limit the conduct of war, it could be waged legitimately, nevertheless, when conducted under proper authority, when there is a just cause, specifically when those attacked are guilty of some wrong-doing, and when conducted with the 'right intention', namely to promote the good and avoid evil' (Aquinas 1972: 81–3 [2a2ae, question 40]). Under such circumstances war could be conceived not only as a means of punishing evil but also of ensuring a political common good. Francisco de Vitoria (1485–1546) and Francisco Suárez (1548–1617), successors of Aquinas, added further conditions: all peaceful means should have been exhausted; the means of war should be proportional to the injustices being addressed; and the war should have a reasonable hope of success (Reichberg 2011, De Vitoria 1995). By now, however, the earlier Christian presumption of the incompatibility of war-mongering and Christian discipleship had largely disappeared from the mainstream Christian tradition.

That tradition was also by now thoroughly entwined with civil authority and it benefited materially from that alliance. The distinction sharply made by Jesus between that which belonged to Caesar and that which belonged to God (The Bible, Mark 12: 17, Matthew 22: 22) was no longer clear and the church had weakened its prerogative to critique the state in the name of a higher authority. It is unsurprising then that the recovery of the Christian pacifist tradition in the late Middle Ages and following the Protestant Reformation was left to a number of small sectarian movements that resisted the conflation of ecclesial and temporal power. The Waldensians in Europe, who began in the twelfth century as a reform movement within the Catholic church but later allied with the Protestants, and the

Lollards, the fourteenth century followers of John Wyclif in England, asserted a commitment to non-violence and, for the most part, sustained that commitment in the face of persecution by both church and state authorities. Their example would later find a Protestant counterpart in the Moravian Brethren and in the Anabaptists, a version of which survives in the Mennonites, a movement begun by the Dutch Anabaptist, Menno Simons. All of these were minority groups distinguished in part by a determination to live simply as Jesus had instructed his disciples to do and without recourse to the instruments of political power and warfare.[6]

There is not space in this chapter to chart the rise and development of these various movements, each of them known for a commitment to pacifism, but they are mentioned here to indicate a central point: the Christian commitment to pacifism is more easily sustained when the church is disestablished, that is, when the respective authorities of church and civil government are separated. Recognition of that point allows the further observation that in the modern secular[7] age in the West, in which ecclesial and temporal power have been progressively disentangled, the Christian church has a renewed opportunity to recover the teaching of Jesus, to commit itself again to the pursuit of peacemaking and to develop and nurture the practices of non-violent response to evil that are commended in the New Testament.

Contemporary Trends

Among Christian theologians and church leaders of the twentieth and twenty-first centuries there has been a renewed investigation of the pacifist implications of the Christian gospel. Roman Catholic statements from the second Vatican Council affirm the legitimacy of the pacifist position, while the National Conference of Catholic Bishops in America meeting in 1983 declared that both just war theory and teaching on non-violence 'share a common presumption against the use of force as a means of settling disputes' (National Conference of Catholic Bishops 1983). Among Protestant theologians, Karl Barth (1961: 455), while compelled, he believed, to set aside his pacifist convictions in the face of the evils of the Third Reich, nevertheless wrote: 'All affirmative answers to the question [of whether we should engage in war] are wrong if they do not start with the assumption that the inflexible negative of pacifism has almost infinite arguments in its favour and is almost overpoweringly strong'. While there may be exceptional circumstances in which we must set aside the biblical injunction not to kill, these are indeed exceptional and apply only *in extremis*. Barth contends that pacifism should be the normative Christian position.

6 A more detailed account of these pacifist movements can be found in Bainton 1960: ch.10, Sowle-Cahill 1994: ch.10.

7 The term 'secular' is used here to indicate the increased separation of church and state, rather than a decrease in religious belief.

Barth's position is derived straightforwardly from the sixth commandment: 'Thou shalt not kill'. We have noted already, however, that there are episodes in the Bible where God seems to break his own rule, thus giving encouragement for believers to do so as well. Notoriously, for instance, and as referred to above, Samuel conveys to King Saul the following message:

> Thus says the Lord of hosts, 'I will punish the Amalekites for what they did in opposing the Israelites when they came out of Egypt. Now go and attack Amalek, and utterly destroy all that they have; do not spare them, but kill both man and woman, child and infant, ox and sheep, camel and donkey'. (The Bible, 1 Samuel 15: 2–3)

There has been much debate in Jewish and Christian thought about what the prohibition of killing actually means. Does 'kill' mean murder, for instance, so that other kinds of non-murderous killing might be permitted? Does warfare count as a form of non-murderous killing? Christian ethics cannot proceed simply by finding a 'proof-text' and supposing that the matter is settled. Careful reflection and debate is required. According to the contemporary Christian ethicist, William Cavanaugh, the divine command to slay the Amalekites constitutes an exception to the command in the Decalogue, 'thou shalt not kill'. Cavanaugh contends further that killing in exceptional circumstances 'is permitted only if and when God commands it' (Cavanaugh 2005: 127). This might seem to play straight into the hands of those who engage in warfare and terrorism purportedly in the name of God. But the principle adduced here entails that the burden of justification should rest with those who seek to kill. The *only* possible justification for such action would be that God has commanded it. If we suppose further that the divine command has to be established beyond reasonable doubt then careful attention to that requirement will rule out most killing that actually goes on, including that perpetrated in God's name.

The principle proposed here – that killing is permitted only if God commands it – emerges from the biblical declaration that human beings are made by God and in the image of God. Historically and conceptually this biblical affirmation is the basis for the widely accepted principle of the sanctity of human life. We find an application of this principle in Genesis 9: 6: 'Whoever sheds the blood of a human, by a human shall that person's blood be shed; for in his own image God made humankind'. Precisely because God has created us in his image, Scripture contends, lifeblood belongs to God and the prerogative to take life lies with God alone (see Cavanaugh 2005: 132). The clear corollary of this principle is that the Bible denies that prerogative to us. Acceptance of the principle that killing can only be justified if God wills it saves us from the rather more troubling prospect that killing could be justified whenever the individual or the state wills it. This latter principle of justification is the one by which our world usually and tragically operates. Christian pacifists contend, however, that we need to observe far more faithfully than we do the principle that absolute authority over life and death belongs with God alone.

Acceptance of the principle that killing can only be justified if God commands it leads us then to ask what God in fact commands. As was pointed out earlier, Christian reflection on the biblical account of God's purposes takes its hermeneutical key from the New Testament witness to Jesus Christ. Cavanaugh (2005: 143) contends that as we read the biblical story we see in its overall trajectory 'a progressive broadening and deepening of the prohibition of killing', culminating in the teaching and example of Jesus and most especially in his death and resurrection. There it is revealed that God's purpose, as it was in the beginning, is that the creature should have life. The death-dealing ways of humanity are met with the passive resistance of Jesus whose teaching and example are vindicated by the God who raises him from the dead. This central conviction of Christian faith further entails that in the end death will be overcome. The biblical logic here suggests that human beings have no business taking life. In the cross of Jesus Christ, God sides not with the killers but with the one who is killed. It is that conviction, above all, that prompts among many contemporary Christians a reclamation of the early Christian rejection of military service and a renewed commitment to seek alternatives to warfare and violence in overcoming the tensions and conflicts that continue to beset our world.

Conclusion

The records of history show clearly enough that so-called Christian nations and Christians within nations have been regular participants in the conduct of war. The tacit approval of war entailed by this participation exists in considerable tension, however, with the teaching and practice of Jesus, particularly his instruction to love one's enemies and to turn the other cheek in the face of violent provocation. For this reason and also because military service in that era commonly involved participation in an imperial cult that was regarded as idolatrous, Christian theologians almost universally in the first three centuries considered military service and engagement in any kind of violence to be incompatible with Christian faith. As has been shown, that conviction was rapidly eroded among Christians following the conversion of Constantine and the resultant alliances between church and state. Through the course of the Middle Ages and into the modern era the pacifist position was marginalized and was sustained largely by minority and sectarian groups.

Only in recent decades has the Christian pacifist position regained a strong foothold among Christian theologians. The teaching and example of Jesus is the foundation of this renewed conviction. The instructions of Jesus adduced earlier leave little room for compromise. Not even in self-defence should one engage in violence. The Christian is enjoined instead to love his or her enemies, even at great personal cost. That is, afterall, the example set by Jesus himself. I have argued further that in the Christian tradition human life is understood to be a gift from God so that the taking of life is a prerogative that belongs to God alone.

Only if God commands it, therefore, could the taking of life be justified. Given their conviction, however, that God's purposes are most clearly revealed in the person of Jesus, the commands to which Christians ought to be most attentive are the commands Jesus issued to love and to forgive one's enemies, to put aside the sword and to take up one's cross rather than one's rifle and follow him.

Bibliography

Ambrose 2002. *De Officiis*, vol. 1, edited with an introduction, translation and commentary by I.J. Davidson. Oxford: Oxford University Press.

Aquinas, T. 1972. *Summa Theologiae*, vol. 35. Translated from Latin by T.R. Heath. London: Blackfriars.

Augustine 1945. *Confessions*, vol. 2. London: J.M. Dent and Sons.

Augustine 1994. Contra Faustum, in *The Nicene and Post-Nicene Fathers*, series 1 vol. 4: *Augustine, Anti-Manichaean, Anti-Donatist Writings*, edited by Philip Schaff. Grand Rapids, MI: Eerdmans, 264–592.

Augustine 1998. *The City of God Against the Pagans*, edited and translated from Latin by R.W. Dyson. Cambridge: Cambridge University Press.

Augustine 2010. *On the Free Choice of the Will, On Grace, and Other Writings*, edited by P. King. Cambridge: Cambridge University Press.

Bainton, R.H. 1960. *Christian Attitudes to War and Peace.* Nashville: Abingdon Press.

Barrett, C.K. 1987 [1957]. *Harper's New Testament Commentaries: The Epistle to the Romans*. Reprint. Peabody, MA: Hendrickson Publishers.

Barth, K. 1961. *Church Dogmatics,* vol. 4/3, edited by G.W. Bromiley and T.F. Torrance. Edinburgh: T. and T. Clark.

The Bible: new revised standard English version, 1989. Grand Rapids, MN: Zondervan.

Cahill, L.S. 1989. *Love your Enemies: Discipleship, Pacifism, and Just War Theory*. Minneapolis, MN: Fortress.

Cavanaugh, W.T. 2005. Killing in the name of God, in *I Am the Lord Your God: Christian Reflections on the Ten Commandments*, edited by C.E. Braaten and C.R. Seitz. Grand Rapids, MI: Eerdmans, 127–47.

Clement of Alexandria 1986. The instructor, in *The Ante-Nicene Fathers*, vol. 2, edited by A. Roberts and J. Donaldson. Grand Rapids, MI: Eerdmans, 207–96.

Cyprian of Carthage 1994. Epistle 1: to Donatus, in *The Ante-Nicene Fathers*, vol. 5, edited by A. Roberts and J. Donaldson. Grand Rapids, MI: Eerdmans, 275–80.

De Victoria, F. 1995. *De Indis et de iure belli*, Classics of International Law, no. 7, vol. 1. Reprint, edited by E. Nys. Buffalo, NY: W.S. Hein.

Elshtain, J.B. 1987. *Women and War.* New York: Basic Books.

Eusebius 1986. The life of Constantine, in *Nicene and Post-Nicene Fathers*, series 2, vol. 1, edited by P. Schaff. Grand Rapids, MI: Eerdmans, 471–559.

Harnack, A. 1981. *Militia Christi: The Christian Religion and the Military in the First Three Centuries*. Translated by David McInnes Gracie. Philadelphia, PA: Fortress Press.

Hays, R. 1996. *The Moral Vision of the New Testament.* San Francisco, CA: Harper.

Hippolytus 1937. *The Treatise on the Apostolic Tradition of St Hippolytus of Rome*, edited by G. Dix. London: Society for Promoting Christian Knowledge.

Jeremias, J. 1963. *The Sermon on the Mount*. Translated by Norman Perrin. Philadelphia, PA: Fortress.

Justin Martyr 1979. First apology, in *The Ante-Nicene Fathers*, vol. 1, edited by A. Roberts and J. Donaldson. Grand Rapids, MI: Eerdmans, 159–308.

Lactantius 1985a. Divine institutes, in *The Ante-Nicene Fathers*, vol. 7, edited by A. Roberts and J. Donaldson. Reprint. Grand Rapids, MI: Eerdmans, 12–497.

Lactantius 1985b. On the manner in which the persecutors died, in *The Ante-Nicene Fathers*, vol. 7. Reprint, edited by A. and J. Donaldson. Grand Rapids: Eerdmans, 301–22.

Langan, J. 1984. The elements of Augustine's just war theory, *Journal of Religious Ethics* 12(1), 19–38.

Maximus 2001. Fragment of sermon 55, in *Ante-Nicene Fathers*, vol. 2. Reprint, edited by A. Roberts and J. Donaldson. Grand Rapids, MI: Eerdmans.

National Conference of Catholic Bishops 1983. *The Challenge of Peace: God's Promise and Our Response, A Pastoral Letter on War and Peace*. Washington: United States Catholic Conference.

Niebuhr, R. 1941. *An Interpretation of Christian Ethics*. 3rd Edition. London: SCM Press.

Nuttall, G.F. 1958. *Christian Pacifism in History*. Oxford: Blackwell.

Origen 1994. Contra Celsum, in *The Ante-Nicene Fathers*, vol. 4, edited by A. Roberts and J. Donaldson. Peabody, MA: Hendrickson, 395–669.

Reichberg, G.M. 2011. Suárez on just war, in *Interpreting Suárez: Critical Essays*, edited by D. Schwartz. Cambridge: Cambridge University Press, 185–204.

Russell, F.H. 1975. *The Just War in the Middle Ages*. Cambridge: Cambridge University Press.

Tertullian 1994. On idolatry, in *The Ante-Nicene Fathers*, vol. 3, edited by A. Roberts and J. Donaldson. Peabody, MA: Hendrickson, 61–76.

Tertullian 1994b. De Corona, in *The Ante-Nicene Fathers*, vol. 3, edited by A. Roberts and J. Donaldson. Peabody, MA: Hendrickson, 93–103.

Chapter 3

Concept of Peace in Hinduism: A Historical Analysis

Kaushik Roy

Thanks to Mohandas Karamchand Gandhi (also known as Mahatma [great soul] Gandhi), Hinduism is considered a religion of peace in contrast to Islam with its baggage of jihad and Christianity with its connection to the crusades. Gandhi during the first half of the twentieth century while leading the Indian National Congress against the British *Raj* propounded his philosophy of non-violence, that is, *ahimsa*. Gandhi claimed that his *satyagraha* (love force or truth force), which is based on non-violence, is derived from the *Bhagavad Gita*. From a historical perspective, Hinduism has been anything but a religion of peace. John R. Hinnells and Richard King (2007: 2) assert that Hindu images of Durga and Kali both iconographically and metaphorically express the idea that violence and love are two sides of one reality of force. In Hinduism, Laurie L. Patton (2007: 13) claims, weaponry is seen as an extension, and sometimes as a metaphor, for sacrificial power.

Scholars differ regarding their definition of Hinduism. Hinduism is not merely a religion in the Western sense of the term but a way of life. Metaphysical beliefs and community norms, David N. Lorenzen (2004: 40) maintains, are essential components of a religion. Hinduism has the former but not the latter to the same degree as Islam. Many scholars argue that the term religion is not applicable to Hinduism, which is a way of life (*dharma*). Peter Gottschalk (2007: 207) asserts that the term Hinduism emerged in the nineteenth century. The Norwegian scholar Torkel Brekke (2002: 30) claims that the term *dharma*, which refers to a code of conduct both at the personal and collective levels, became synonymous with the Hindu religion due to the reformist activities of the Bengali intellectuals in the nineteenth century. Meera Nanda (2007: 5) writes: 'Hinduism is a monistic religion which draws no dividing lines between nature and supernatural (Brahman or the world spirit), or between natural laws and moral laws. *Dharma* is conduct which is in accord with nature of the cosmos itself'. David N. Lorenzen (2004: 16–17) claims that by about 600 BC a corpus of myths about gods and goddesses codified in the *Mahabharata*, the *Ramayana* and in the *Puranas* were more or less complete. The *Mahabharata* and the *Ramayana* are two epics; in fact, the *Mahabharata* is the longest poem in the world. The *Puranas* are quasi-historical and quasi-religious in nature. These works were composed between 600 BC and 300 AD. Most of the Hindu movements after this date were led, at least in the initial stages, by the poet saints who sang songs and told stories about these gods and goddesses. Hinduism is not a monotheistic religion but is quite amorphous. Unlike the Semitic religions, Hinduism lacks a prophet and a sacred revealed book (Thapar 2004: 335). It would be an overstatement to assert that Hinduism was a construction of the nineteenth-century British *Raj*. A more balanced assessment would be to study how the plural and multilayered Brahmanism underwent different modifications throughout the centuries and evolved as Hinduism from the early nineteenth century onwards. Peace in this chapter is conceptualized as avoidance of warfare or at least as limiting the incidence and effects of conflict on society. Peace here also relates to ethics as epitomized in the literature generated within the bounds of Hinduism. In this chapter, I examine the Hindu discourse on peace as it evolved historically over two millenniums. We will see how the rules, norms and cultural constraints of the political and military elites who shape strategic policies, that is, the strategic managers, have been shaped and influenced by the Hindu tradition. This is achieved by analysing certain classical Hindu texts and the writings of some of the larger than life religious and political figures of the subcontinent.

The traditional Hindu texts make no watertight division between the two concepts of peace (*shanti*) and war (*yuddha*/*vigraha*). The strands of thought regarding peace in Hinduism could roughly be divided into two schools: the spiritual and the Lokayata–Carvakas (realist). The spiritual school asserts that through penance and sacrifice, peace and truth (equivalent to *satya*) could be established. This strand of thought influenced the development of Gandhi's *Satyagraha* techniques that included fasting and voluntary imprisonment. The realist school within Hinduism claims that deploying force (*bala*) through authority (*danda*) is necessary for enforcing peace. Enforcement of peace might lead to warfare. Hinduism divides warfare into just or righteous war (*dharmayuddha*) and unjust war (*kutayuddha*). And long-term peace (*shanti*) could only be established after waging a successful just war. As long as chaos (*ashanti*) remains, it is justified to wage either an unjust or a just war in accordance with the changing circumstances.

Most of the ancient Sanskrit texts that contain discourses about the usefulness or uselessness of war and peace are religious in nature. They hide their true authorship in an attempt to posit their claim to be transcendentally based on absolute truth. Religious discourse is represented as the direct word of God (Doniger and Smith 1991: xxii). There are two schools of opinion about the authorship of the Sanskrit texts. One group claims that each text is the product of gradual accretions by several unknown sages over time; the other group claims that despite interpolations, each text has a core with a clear structure that is the product of a powerful personality (Olivelle 2005: 20). The role of individual authors in ancient Sanskrit literature is downplayed deliberately due to the nature of Indian philosophy. Sue Hamilton (2001: 9) claims that the term *dharma* (spelled *dhamma* in the Pali language) combines both religion and philosophy. The Indian term for philosophy is *darsana* (view) regarding the truth about the nature of reality. Indian *darsana*, Jitendra Nath Mohanty (1992) writes, is a systematic elaboration of truth, or an aspect of it that is already grasped. It is not the search for truth, but an exposition of it that entails intellectual vindication, conceptual fixation and a clarification of what has been received. In contrast, in Western philosophy, the individual thinker who is captivated by the love of wisdom plays an important role. Western philosophy derived from Greek *philosophia* is the love of wisdom, an *eros,* which by its nature generates ceaseless enquiry and a search for wisdom. But, in *darsana*, individuals play a subordinate role. Philosophers do not find a system, but carry its explication forward (Mohanty 1992: 8). Hamilton writes that the authors of sacred texts are considered merely instrumental in recording the impersonal and cosmic truth for posterity (Hamilton 2001: 20). Now, let us focus on some of the most important works of Hinduism.

Ramayana

The Valmiki *Ramayana* is an epic poem of some 50,000 lines describing the career of the legendary hero Rama, the prince of Ayodhya in north India. The poem is divided into seven major books (*kanda*s) (Goldman, 1984: 4–5). In John Brockington's view, the *Ramayana* was composed before 400 BC (Brockington 2000b: 249). In the *Ramayana,* the voice of rejection of war in favour of peace is marginalized. In this epic, Rama is portrayed as the upholder of *dharma. Dharma* stands for righteousness and proper moral values. To an extent, *dharma* also means the maintenance of the fourfold, hereditary social order that maintains the Brahmins at the top, then the Kshatriyas, the Vaishyas and finally the Sudras, and is seen to result in political stability (Bailey 2000: xiv). While the Brahmins are engaged in rituals and sacrifice, the Kshatriyas are the rulers and warriors, and the Vaishyas conduct trade and commerce. The bottom rung of the social order comprises the Sudras who are tillers of the land and engaged in other menial tasks. An account of the hierarchical caste system comes from a hymn in the *Rig Veda* composed around 1500–1200 BC: 'His mouth became the Brahmin; his arms were made into the Warrior, his thighs the People, and from his feet the Servants were born' (O'Flaherty, *Rig Veda* 1981: 31, Hamilton 2001: 26).[1]

Sita tells her husband Rama that the *raksas* without provocation should not be attacked. The term *raksas* in the *Ramayana* represents people belonging to an inferior culture, that is, the non-Aryans. Rama justifies his action of attacking the *raksas* by asserting that as a Kshatriya ruler it is his duty (*dharma*) to protect the *rishis* (Hindu sages or seers) from the attacks of the *raksas*. Broadly, the king's duty (*rajadharma*) is to take one-sixth of the subjects' produce and give the populace protection. In south India, the Aryan settlements and especially the Brahmanical sages were attacked by the *raksas* who felt that the former were penetrating into their forest habitat. The *rishis* were at the forefront of cultural and

1 My translation differs from Wendy Doniger O'Flaherty's. Instead of Warrior, I prefer the term Kshatriyas and rather than People, the apt term is the Vaishyas. The term 'Servants' refers to the Sudras.

political penetration of the Aryans against the non-Aryans in the peninsular region of the subcontinent. Spreading *dharma* is the basic objective of the *rishis*. The *rishis* were like Christian missionaries and aided in the propagation and diffusion of Aryan brahmanical culture. The Brahmins and the Kshatriyas jointly carried the banner of the Aryan culture into south India (Brockington, 2000a: 259, Sarkar 1987: 2–3, 8–9).

In retaliation for Rama's attack on the *raksas* and especially because Rama humiliated Suparnakha (the sister of Ravana, lord of the *raksas*), Ravana kidnapped Sita and took him to Lanka (probably Sri Lanka, Serandip). Rama decided to invade Lanka with the help of the *vanaras* (literally meaning monkeys; in reality it means a non-Aryan group in south India). The *Ramayana* notes that before starting war, an attempt should be made to resolve the crisis through diplomatic means. Rama sent an ambassador (*duta*) bearing the message of peace to Ravana requesting the latter to return Sita. When Ravana refused to return Rama's wife, Sita, only then the decision to wage war against Ravana was undertaken (Indra 1957: 40). As regards the establishment of the Kingdom of Rama (*ramrajya)* among the Aryans of Ayodhya in north India, Valmiki, the author of the *Ramayana*, has something positive to say. Sumitra V. Bhat (2007: 29) asserts that Valmiki interpreted *dharma* as representing truth and doing one's duty properly. The emphasis is on the value of doing one's duty (*dharmajnata*) and gratitude (*kratajnata*).

The *Mahabharata*

The *Mahabharata* epic composed between 500 BC and 400 AD describes the intra Aryan conflict between two important Aryan clans (or tribes) of north India: the Pandavas versus the Kauravas (Tripathi 1942: 66). From the perspective of the Pandavas, the conflict was a *dharmayuddha*, that is, a just war undertaken for defensive purposes when peacemaking failed. Krishna acted as a messenger of peace and a mediator (*duta*). He went to Duryodhana, the head of the Kaurava clan, and requested that the Pandavas be given five villages. When Duryodhana refused and said that he would not even grant the small amount of earth that could be held at the head of a pin, the Pandavas decided to go to war to get their due patrimony (Indra 1957: 40). Patton (2007: 13) notes: '… the ambivalence of the epics towards war is expressed in several ways. In the *Mahabharata*, war is frequently thought of as a sacrifice, where warriors are containers, not glorifiers of force. … the *Mahabharata* text in particular also repeatedly warns about the cost of such force, just as a sacrificer might be aware of the cost of sacrifice'.

The *Bhagavad Gita*

The *Bhagavad Gita* is a poem in dialogue form between Arjuna, who was the star warrior of the Pandavas, and his charioteer Krishna, who was an incarnation of

God. This dialogue took place on the first day of the war just before the onset of the conflict between two Aryan clans, the Kauravas and the Pandavas (Mohanraj 2005: 61), thus touching on the origins of the Mahabharata War. The *Bhagavad Gita* was initially composed as a separate work to the *Mahabharata*. Like all ancient Sanskrit texts, the date of composition of the *Bhagavad Gita* is still debated. In general, scholars put its composition between the fourth century BC and the beginning of the seventh century AD (Mohanraj 2005: 27, 30).

In this text, the proponents of peace occupy a marginal role. Nevertheless, it is essential to analyse the discourse of the peacemakers. The most important spokesman for avoiding war is the eldest Pandava brother, Yudhistira. In the text, he argues that the root cause of war is greed. Further, war is bad as it results in the death of one's relatives and friends (Malinar 2007: 39). Yudhistira also criticized the *kshatradharma*, that is, the code of conduct of the warriors, which according to him results in internecine struggles (Malinar 2007: 42). He goes on to say that war never results in enduring peace. Victory results in a stopgap arrangement as the defeated party harbours enmity and revenge and this in turn results in war breaking out in the near future (Malinar 2007: 43). After victory, Yudhistira claimed: 'We are the living dead' (cited in Pollock 2004: 184). Yudhistira maintains that war could be avoided by practicing asceticism. It is better to live on alms rather than to fight to gain a kingdom (Malinar 2007: 43). Interestingly, Yudhistira's response is similar to that of Gandhi who lived at least 2,000 years after the composition of the *Bhagavad Gita*. However, Yudhistira's view is a marginal one and is overpowered by the aggressive protests of his mother, Kunti, his wife, Draupadi, and Krishna (Malinar 2007: 39, 42–3).

Besides Yudhistira, Arjuna also emphasizes to Krishna that it is a sin (*adharma*) to fight relatives and friends to gain the kingdom (Mohanraj 2005: 62). *Adharma* is the opposite of duty (*dharma*). Here, the *Bhagavad Gita* portrays the opposition between *sadharanadharma* (moral duties in general and general ethics) and *svadharma* (obligations towards one's own community or caste). *Sadharanadharma* on Arjuna's part demanded showing respect and affection towards the elders and clan members. But, *svadharma* required Arjuna to fight in the fratricidal war against those elders and his clan members who were with the Kauravas (Mahulikar 2007: 40–41). Krishna made him remember his social and moral obligations as a member of the warrior caste, the Kshatriya, which is ranked second to the highest caste, the Brahmin: 'If you do not fight in this *dharmayuddha* [righteous, just war], you break your *dharma*[2] and incur sin' (Mohanraj 2005: 117).[3] Maintenance of individual *dharma* at the micro level is necessary for maintenance of the *dharma* at the macro level of the cosmic order and the functioning of the universe (Hamilton 2001: 65).

2 The emphasis is here on caste duty. It means every caste is bound to follow its prescribed duty and the duty of a Kshatriya is to fight.

3 I have modified V.M. Mohanraj's translation of the passage.

Besides Krishna, the important spokesmen of the anti-peace (or pro-war) party in the *Mahabharata* are Draupadi and Bhima.[4] The anti-peace party emphasizes the necessity of the following qualities: *paurusha* (manliness), *vikrama* (heroic deeds), *tejas* (splendour and arrogance), and *mana-abhimana* (pride plus honour). For them, performing heroic deeds in avenging past injustices (*viracharitas*) are most important. And peace resulting in inactivity against the enemy in their eyes is equivalent to being a *kliba*, which is the opposite of *paurusha* and equivalent to being either an impotent man or an effeminate one (Peterson 1991: 214–5, 221).

During the sixth century BC, the Hindu intellectual Bharavi wrote a commentary on the *Mahabharata*. He notes that a warrior must undergo asceticism or austerity (*tapas*) to enhance his mental power. *Tapas*, in general, is considered by the followers of the spiritual school as necessary for purification in thought, word and deed. It involves self-discipline and bodily purity. *Tapas* is an essential requirement for practicing non-violence (*ahimsa*). The *Bhagavad Gita* prescribes *tapas* as a component of ethics. The ascetic vow is temporary and not permanent. After undergoing *tapas* for a certain period of time, the warrior returns to the material world to perform his duty (*dharma*) (Peterson 1991: 223; Revathy 2007: 51–2). We will see later that the concept of *tapas* heavily influenced Gandhi.

Asoka and Non-Violence

As regards the advocacy of non-violence in matters of state politics, Gandhi's precursor in Indian history was the Maurya Emperor Asoka. In 256 BC, Asoka invaded the Kalinga Kingdom, Orissa. This military expedition resulted in the death of numerous non-combatants. After witnessing the horror of the war, he renounced war as a matter of state policy and enunciated the policy of non-violence. Asoka declared that in future he would only conquer by means of *dhamma*, the equivalent in the Prakrit language to the Sanskrit term *dharma,* which means right conduct, duty, religion, social justice and morality. Asoka constructed several rock edicts through which he preached the law of piety and non-violence (Sinha 2005: 289). Asoka's policy to replace conquest by sword (*digvijaya*) with conquest by the spiritual force of non-violence (*dhammavijaya*) was influenced by Buddhist doctrine (Indra 1957: 102). Buddha enunciated the concept of *dharmikdharmaraj*. It means a righteous lord who conquers not by sword but by spiritual power. For Buddha, violence leads to spiritual degradation of both the victor and the vanquished. In contrast, non-violence depends on self-control, moral courage and superior knowledge (Indra 1957: 160). Buddha stressed that the *dharmikdharmaraj* should rule with righteousness and impartiality by rejecting the swords and even

4 Here we are discussing the *Bhagavad Gita* which constitutes a dialogue between war and peace against the background of war portrayed in the *Mahabharata*. Though the *Bhagavad Gita* is a separate work, it should be read as an integral part of the *Mahabharata*.

the symbols of violence. Rigid morality should be observed not only at the personal but also at the national level (Indra 1957: 161). This concept influenced not only Asoka but also Gandhi.

Manusamhita

Manusamhita or *Manavadharmasastra* or *Manusmriti* (literally meaning the *Laws of Manu*) was probably composed around the beginning of the first century AD (Olivelle 2005: 22). The final text was completed by the following century (Kane 1968: 330). Manu's text is in response to Kautilya's realist text, *Arthasastra*, and the emergence of Buddhism and Jainism. The *sramanas* (world renouncers) were a group of Hindu thinkers who emerged around the eighth and sixth centuries BC and composed the *Upanishad*s that challenged the Vedic assumptions of the necessity of violence and related sacrifice. The *Brhadaranyaka Upanishad* emphasizes self-restraint, generosity and compassion (Dange 2007: 19, Hamilton 2001: 35). The *Satapatha Brahmana* points out that no one should be arrogant as arrogance is the cause of ruin (Dange 2007: 20). The intellectual strands of the *sramanas*, according to Doniger and Smith (1991: xxxiv), influenced the rise of heterodox religions like Ajivikas, Buddhism and Jainism (Doniger and Smith 1991). Non-violence (*ahimsa*), Romila Thapar (2004: 344) writes, was characteristic of certain *sramanic* sects and less so of Brahmanism. In contrast to the sacrifice of living beings as enunciated in the Vedic rituals, Buddhism emphasized non-violent sacrifice. In the Buddhist framework, the life of the ascetic renouncer becomes a symbol of a sacrificial victim (Gethin 2007: 69). In Buddhism, Rupert Gethin (2007) writes, *dhamma* is twofold. On the one hand, it functions as an ethic of absolute values that characterizes all forms of violence as wrong. On the other hand, *dhamma* functions as a practical moral framework of justice in which, depending on the circumstances, minimal forms of violence occasionally are considered necessary on part of the ruler (Gethin 2007: 71).

Manu partly accepted the Buddhist practical moral strand of *dhamma*. As a 'realist' he understood that even if war cannot be abolished outright it could at least be avoided for most of the time. Manu wrote that the basic objective of the rulers is to maintain peace. When conflict is unavoidable, then a ruler should depend on *sama* (conciliation or appeasement), *dana* (bribery or gift/charity/benevolence) and *bheda* (dividing the enemies), and war should be the last option (Doniger and Smith, *Laws of Manu* 1991: 148–9). *Sama*, *dana* and *bheda* are realist techniques for avoiding war which are taken from Kautilya's *Arthasastra*. Manu warns the king: 'Victory and defeat in battle are uncertain … he should therefore avoid war' (Olivelle, *Manu's Code of Law* 2005: 164). Manu realized that if it is not possible to banish war completely, at least it is important to limit the ravages of war. This, Manu intended to do by laying down certain codes of conduct for the warriors: 'Fighting in a battle, he should not kill his enemies with weapons that are concealed, barbed, or smeared with poison. … He should not kill … a man who folds his hands in supplication. … Nor anyone asleep, without armour … without a weapon, not fighting … or engaged with someone else; nor anyone whose weapons have been broken, or who is in pain, badly wounded, terrified, or fleeing … ' (Doniger and Smith, *Laws of Manu* 1991: 137–8). Thus, we have something like an ancient Geneva Convention. These theoretical works were taken seriously. One inscription dated 571 AD by the Valabhi King Dharasena says that the rules of Manu are obeyed by this monarch. Probably on the order of the monarchs various commentaries were composed on the *Manusamhita*. The earliest commentary on the *Manusamhita* is the *Bhasya of Medhatithi* composed around 900 AD (Kane 1968: 327–8).

Post-Gupta Era Hindu Treatises

After the Gupta age (post six century AD), a series of works addressed the issues of war and peace. One of the important works is the *Hitopadesa*. It is a collection of animal and human fables in prose, illustrated with numerous maxims and sayings in verse. The animal characters provide homilies on individual psychology and the rules of governance. The objective is to impart instruction in worldly wisdom and the conduct of political affairs. The aim is to teach politics and statesmanship by examples and they are often satirical. Before the *Hitopadesa* came into existence, the *Panchatantra* (literally meaning five books) was composed. Scholars still debate its date of composition. The earliest date assigned to its composition is 200 BC (Ryder 1925: 3). It was a work of *nitisastra*, that is, a textbook on *niti* which means wise conduct in life.

The structure of the *Hitopadesa* is similar to that of the *Panchatantra*. The *Hitopadesa* is translated into many vernacular languages (Haksar 1998: ix, xi–xii, xvii). The *Hitopadesa* is significantly influenced by previous Hindu works like Kamandaka's *Nitisara*, the *niti* (here means political theory) verses of *Garuda Purana* and *Nitisataka* of Bhartrhari, and also by the *Manusamhita* and the *Mahabharata*. Sometime between 800 and 950 AD, the *Hitopadesa* was composed probably in eastern India. In the view of the experts, Narayana who was a court poet of the Pala Empire in east India and a devotee of Shiva is the author of this work (Haksar 1998: ix–x, xiv).

Like Kamandaka's *Nitisara,* which criticizes overtly aggressive rulers (*ativigrahis*), the *Hitopadesa* warns the ruler against rashly going to war. As regards the pros and cons of waging war, the *Hitopadesa* tells the ruler:

> To vanquish enemies one should try
> But never by the means of war.
> For in that case, of victory,
> Neither party can be sure.
> Enemies one should influence
> By measures conciliatory,

> By gifts, or stoking dissidence;
> By one of these, or all the three
> Used together, to be sure;
> But never by resort to war … (Narayana 1998: 153)

Basically, the *Hitopadesa* is warning the ruler not to wage war unless it is absolutely unavoidable. War is the last option. And it is better to avoid war since victory and defeat, comments *Hitopadesa* like Kamandaka's *Nitisara*, is uncertain (*anitya*). Rather, diplomacy if it is possible should be used to resolve the conflict. The *Hitopadesa* concludes the section on war (*vigraha*):

> Many kings never wage a war. …
> May their enemies evermore,
> By winds of proper policy,
> To mountain caves be swept aside,
> There to take refuge and hide … (Narayana 1998: 187)

The *Panchatantra*, by contrast, takes a more 'realist' view that the world is full of people with nefarious designs and they could not be reformed. Hence, achieving security in a world driven by jealousy and hatred is of utmost necessity. Here, the *Panchatantra* treads the path of Kautilya's *Arthasastra* and differs from the *Manusamhita*, which assumes that human beings could be reformed. Unlike Kautilya's *Arthasastra*, which says that waging various forms of war (*yuddha*) is necessary, the *Panchatantra* emphasizes the use of intelligence and the policy of gaining and retaining allies for achieving security in a conflict ridden world. One of the verses of the *Panchatantra* (1925: 66) notes: 'Intelligence is power'. For gathering intelligence, the collection of enormous data is emphasized. The *Panchatantra* tells us that consciousness of the past is necessary, but knowledge about the past must be treated in a positive manner. Knowledge about the past is considered valuable for gaining wisdom in order to deal with present and future crises (Ryder 1925: 4–5, 7–8).

From the ninth century AD, the Arabs started nibbling at the Hindu dominion in Sind and Afghanistan. By the eleventh century, the Ghaznavids established themselves in Afghanistan and conducted several raids against the Hindu Rajput principalities of north India. The Ghorids of Afghanistan established the Delhi Sultanate late in the twelfth century. Early in the sixteenth century, the Delhi Sultanate was replaced by the Mughal Empire (Chagathai-Turkish rulers) and this polity continued to function till the establishment of the *Raj* by the East India Company in the mid-eighteenth century. The Delhi Sultanate and the Mughal Empire did not patronize the Brahmin intellectuals. Nor except in some rare cases did the Brahmin intellectuals enjoy power in the courts (*durbars*) of the Muslim potentates. The long era of Islamic rule did not witness any theoretical development in Hinduism about peace and war because the Hindu potentates became vassals of the Delhi Sultanate and the Mughal Empire. The powerless and subordinate Hindu chieftains lacked the resources and authority to patronize Brahmin intellectuals in their courts. Hindu reformers emerged again under British colonial rule in India.

Colonialism and Vivekananda

In colonial India, one of the foremost Hindu spiritual reformers was Swami Vivekananda (1863–1902). After the death of the mystic thinker Ramakrishna in August 1886, his disciple Vivekananda spent several years in intense spiritual practices. Initially, he was at the newly established Ramakrishna Monastery at Baranagar in Bengal and then he travelled to north India and the Himalayas and then to south India in search of spiritual solace. In 1893, Vivekananda appeared before the Parliament of Religions in Chicago (Vivekananda 2009: 5, 7).

On 11 September 1893, Vivekananda addressed the World Parliament of Religions:

> I am proud to belong to a religion which has taught the world both tolerance and universal acceptance. We believe not only in universal toleration, but we accept all religions as true. I am proud to belong to a nation which has sheltered the persecuted and the refugees of all religions and all nations of the earth. (Vivekananda 2009: 20)

Despite outward humility, Vivekananda's assertion of the superiority of the Hindu religion over all other religions is stressed in his message. The superiority of Hinduism is expressed in a subtle manner again when he says: '… the wonderful doctrine preached in the *Gita*: "Whosoever comes to Me, through whatsoever form, I reach him; all men are struggling through paths which in the end lead to Me"' (Vivekananda 2009: 21). Vivekananda's critique of Christianity is evident in the speech delivered by him in Chicago on 19 September 1893:

> The Hindus have their faults, they sometimes have their exceptions; but mark this, they are always punishing their own bodies, and never for cutting the throats of their neighbours. If the Hindu fanatic burns himself on the pyre, he never lights the fire of Inquisition. And even this cannot be laid at the door of his religion any more than the burning of witches can be laid at the door of Christianity. (Vivekananda 2009: 46)

Vivekananda is reminding his audience that if Hinduism has an evil practice like Sati, it is not the only tradition to have committed ill deeds as is evident with the Inquisition in medieval Christianity. This critique of Christianity is continued in his speech dated 20 September 1893: 'You Christians, who are so fond of sending out missionaries to save the soul of the heathen – why do you not try to save their bodies from starvation? In India, during the terrible famines, thousands died from hunger, yet you Christians did nothing' (Vivekananda 2009: 51).

For Vivekananda, the great Bengali Hindu religious reformer, the object of renunciation was not the social world but misguided thoughts, beliefs and feelings. Renunciation meant rejecting one's false ideas about the nature of reality (Brekke 2002: 37). One could argue that Gandhi followed Vivekananda's concept of renunciation. Vivekananda believed that the West was superior in economic development and technology but India was superior in the fields of religion and spirituality. Vivekananda portrayed India as the centre of humanist civilization (Brekke 2002: 49). Gandhi imbibed these ideas. Gandhi believed that while the West was superior to India in terms of science and material advancement, India had an edge over the West in the spiritual field. And the modern Western culture was a sort of 'war culture' (Johnson 2008: 102–3).

Gandhi and *Ahimsa*

Mahatma (The Great Soul) or M.K. Gandhi (1869–1948) asserted that British imperial rule in India was based on coercive force. However, challenging imperialist violence with anti-imperialist violence would result in an escalating cycle of violence. Hence, Gandhi countered British violence with his policy of non-violence (*ahimsa*) (Allen 2008: xv). Gandhi's interpretation of the *Bhagavad Gita* is opposite to that of the aggressive Hindu nationalist from Maharashtra: Bal Gangadhar Tilak (1856–1920). Tilak, who belonged to the extremist faction of the Indian National Congress, wrote a commentary on the *Bhagavad Gita* while imprisoned by the British. He stressed the rejection of passivity and justified violent activities (Brodbeck 1962: xvii–xviii). Tilak's interpretation of the ancient Hindu text is in tune with two modern commentators on Hinduism. Wendy Doniger and Brian K. Smith (1991: xxiii–xxiv) write about the *Vedas*:

> It is somewhat puzzling, however, that the world-view that informs the priestly ritual seems to be governed by values more often associated with a warrior class. In the Veda, self-aggrandisement and dominance was unabashedly embraced and unashamedly displayed – in the 'religious' sphere of ritual no less than in more 'secular' domains. Violence and power in the social realm – that is, violence and power exercised *over* another – were celebrated on their own terms, or rather, were represented as part and parcel of the natural order of things [italics in original].

Before Doniger and Smith, back in 1898, Sylvain Levi claimed Vedic ideology was brutal and materialistic (Doniger and Smith 1991: xxiv).

Gandhi saw the Mahabharata war as an allegorical representation of the tussle between the human soul and worldly temptations. On 21 December 1925, Gandhi (1993: 34) wrote:

> When, thousands of years ago, the battle of Kurukshetra was fought, the doubts which occurred to Arjuna were answered by Sri Krishna in the *Gita*; but that battle of Kurukshetra is going on, will go on, for ever within us … and our Godward impulses represented by the Pandavas will always triumph over the demoniac impulses represented by the Kauravas.

Gandhi derived inspiration about his principles of non-violence and his politics of passive resistance from the *Bhagavad Gita* (Brodbeck 2003 [1962]: xviii). One of the core concepts of Gandhian thought is *satya* (truth). For him, *satya* is equated with love, God and non-violence (*ahimsa*) (Dadhich 2008: 195). Dennis Dalton (1969: 379) writes that in South Africa, Gandhi established the inter-linkages between *brahmacharya* (the practice of living like of yogi by rejecting materialism and embracing meditation and sacrifice) and *satyagraha* (soul force/love force), that is, between self-control and political potency. Love force was to be used not only to mobilize the poor masses of India for self-rule (*swaraj*), but also to turn British opinion in favour of Indians' self-rule. Gandhi criticized Western civilization as immoral being bound up with materialism and violence. He tended to fight British imperialism – which he saw as an offshoot of Western civilization – with the principles of peace, toleration and benevolence (Rowell 2006: 36). Gandhi derived his policy of non-violence (*ahimsa*) from Hinduism, Jainism and Christian pacifism as represented by figures like Leo Tolstoy (Rowell 2006: 41). Jainism represents a reconfiguration of the warrior codes of bravery and physical control in the ascetic search for spiritual power. According to the Jaina ascetics, non-violence towards living creatures (*ahimsa*) represents the highest form of heroism (Dundas 2007: 43).

Gandhi equated vegetarianism with non-violence (*ahimsa*). In some of the early texts dealing with *dharma* (duty) as well as in some of the Ayurvedic medical treatises vegetarianism is linked with non-violence (*ahimsa*) (Doniger and Smith 1991: xxxi). In Manu's framework, *ahimsa* is listed among certain other qualities that comprise the *samanya* (universal) *dharma* and is applicable to all the castes. Those castes who follow occupations entailing little violence towards other beings and those who practice vegetarianism are ranked higher in Manu's framework compared to those who do not (Doniger and Smith 1991: xxxviii).

Two verses of the *Bhagavad Gita* found resonance with Gandhi. One verse refers to Krishna saying to Arjuna: 'Hate and lust for things in nature have their roots in man's lower nature. Let him not fall under their power' (Mascaro, *Bhagavad Gita* 1962: 20). Another is '… by constant practice and by freedom from passions the mind in truth can be trained' (*Bhagavad Gita* 1962: 34).

Gandhi conceived the Kingdom of Rama (*ramrajya*) as the rule of the people (Pollock 2004: 194). Valmiki's *Ramayana* portrays *ramrajya* as the rule of the good, just king following *dharma* (righteousness). Both *Ramayana* and *Manusmriti* stand for maintenance of the *varna-dharma* (fourfold society) (Jaiswal 2007: 80–81). Hence, Gandhi, though a social reformer, never challenged the caste system directly. In Hinduism, the two female icons of Sita and Durga represent respectively fragile, peaceful feminine qualities, and aggressive force and violence. Gandhi chose the Sita-like role for Hindu women in the freedom struggle (Hills and Silverman 1993: 749). One author states that authority was legitimized by Gandhi through appeals to the sacred, that is, by his constant reference to God, Truth and the inner voice (Dalton 1969: 378).

Hinduism, Gandhian Legacy and Peace Research in the Contemporary World

How far is Gandhi's philosophy relevant in the present day? Georg Sorensen (1992: 136) writes that peace meets our need for survival (security), freedom, welfare and respect of our identities. The main threats to these four types of needs are violence, repression, misery and alienation. The first two are material and non-material forms of direct violence. The latter two are aspects of structural violence. Sorensen continues that Gandhi advocated non-violence even in situations where it is not viable. Further, Gandhi was against developmental violence, which at times is necessary. One has in mind the uselessness of non-violent techniques against Nazi Germany. He concludes that the Gandhian heritage strengthens the utopian trend in peace research. Instead of utopianism, peace research would do better in taking a constructivist approach. Constructivism requires instead a blend between violence, which needs to be minimized, and non-violence at certain moments in certain situations (Sorensen 1992: 138–43). It is to be noted that most of the Hindu texts – *Arthasastra*, *Manusamhita*, *Panchatantra* and so on – accept the constructivist approach. To my mind, however, the bipolar division that Sorensen puts forward is a little simplistic. Gandhi at the theoretical level is an absolute pacifist but at the practical level he is willing to advocate violence rather than complete non-action. For instance, when in the summer of 1942 Gandhi launched the Quit India movement against the *Raj*, his slogan was 'do or die' ('*karenge ya marenge*').

However, Douglas Allen (2008: xv) counters by saying that Gandhi's policy has relevance for the present day. The United States' policy of countering Islamic terrorism with state sponsored counter-terrorism is resulting in an escalating cycle of violence. The use instead of the Gandhian policy of countering brute force with non-violence would make the world a better place to live in. Again, Gandhi challenged developmental violence because he believes that people cannot be treated as tools or obstacles by the state that can hinder the polity in its particular quest whether noble or narrow. To give an example from modern India, economic development requires special economic zones. This in turn necessitates forcibly uprooting lower caste poor villagers and tribes for the greater good of the country. Gandhism is against such policies. Gandhi is, after all, a liberal who is concerned with civil liberties, secularism, morality and democratic governance (Dadhich 2008: 183–4).

Sorensen is also wrong to equate Gandhian *ahimsa* with non-violence at all times. On 4 August 1920, Gandhi (1993: 337) wrote: 'I would risk violence a thousand times than risk the emasculation of a whole race'. However, Gandhi was a proponent of global disarmament and permanent peace. 'Peace can never come through war' (Gandhi 1993: 326). Further, Gandhi (1993: 324) declared: '... if we achieve freedom with non-violence, we shall defend it also with the same weapon'.

Both internal and external policies of the post-1947 Indian state have been shaped by Hindu ethos. The *Ramayana* emphasizes, according to Swarna Rajagopalan, the importance of moral principles in governance for establishing a secure state–society relationship (Rajagopalan 2006b: 50). One could argue that the emergence of the Nehruvian Indian state as a welfare state to an extent was shaped by the *dharmik* traditions of caring for the people which is a strand of *dharma* inherent in the Hindu texts especially the *Ramayana*. One of the essential components of the king's duty (*rajadharma*) is that the government or ruler must help people in distress (Rajagopalan 2006a: 11). The *dharmasutras*, which is a body of ancient Brahmanical discourses on *dharma*, say that it is the duty of the king to see that none in his realm perishes through hunger, disease or extreme heat or cold. The concept of paternal benevolence as a form of governance is present even in a realist work like Kautilya's *Arthasastra*. Kautilya states that the king should follow the policy of *sarvatracopahatanpitevanugrhniyat*, which means favouring the afflicted people like a father (Kane 1968: 250–51). C.V. Raghavulu traces this commitment of the post-1947 Indian polity to the *dharmik* traditions enunciated in ancient India's Sanskrit works. During natural disasters, like cyclones and earthquakes, the Indian state mobilizes all its possible resources including the armed forces to bring succour to the disaster victims (Raghavulu 2006: 228).

One author interprets the Rama–Sugriva (the leader of the 'monkeys' in south India) alliance to defeat Ravana of Lanka as an example of cooperative action for gaining and retaining allies in the international arena in pursuit of security. The basic policy should be the establishment of alliances in order to deter or check hostile enemies of the state (Rajagopalan 2006b: 35). One instance of establishing peace and reconciliation in the inter-state arena (*mandala*) through *sama* (conciliation or appeasement) and *dana* (bribery or gift/charity/benevolence) is the Gujral doctrine. According to this doctrine, the two concepts of *sama* and *dana* combined with a policy of divide and rule (*behda*) should be used in a holistic manner to avoid open conflagration with the hostile party. I.K. Gujral was India's Foreign Minister during 1996–1997 and when he became Prime Minister in 1997–1998, he initiated this doctrine. In accordance with this doctrine, India showed a spirit of accommodation to all its neighbours in South Asia. Further, India compromised to an extent on certain issues such as boundary and trade disputes without asking for reciprocal obligations or concessions from its neighbours (Zhengjia 2003: 161). India, for example, was willing to settle its boundary dispute with China through diplomacy and was keen on increasing trade with Pakistan.

Occasionally, due to public pressure even the Hindu hardliners were forced to tread the path of reconciliation. India's Prime Minister Atal Behari Vajpaee when leading the Bharatiya Janata Party (hereafter BJP) government initiated the 'Lahore Process' to meet with his counterpart in Pakistan and discuss outstanding issues like Kashmir, terrorism, opening the border and so on. However, the negotiations were sabotaged due to the Pakistani attack at Kargil during May–June 1999 (Zhengjia 2003: 161).

Hinduism and the Nuclear Bomb

In May 1998, India exploded several nuclear devices in the Pokhran Desert in Rajasthan. The Sangh Parivar, the umbrella association for the various Hindu nationalist organizations and the ideological father of the BJP, was always in favour of acquiring nuclear bombs well before Pakistan and China obtained them (Ramana and Reddy 2003: 1, 16). The Jana Sangha, the precursor of the BJP, was committed to a nuclear India as early as January 1965 (Ananth 2003: 325). The radical proponent of unjust war (*kutayuddha*), that is, Kautilya, influences the BJP's advocacy of aggressive techniques to defeat the enemy by all possible means. The 'Hindu' nuclear programme is conceived by the BJP as acquiring weapons of mass destruction (*brahmastra*). *Brahmastra* is described in the *Mahabharata* as necessary for establishing a 'just' Hindu order in the subcontinent by warding of all possible evils posed by hostile parties.

In contrast to the above lobby, a moderate lobby argues that possession of a limited number of nuclear weapons might be unavoidable in an international system driven by power politics. However, nuclear weapons for the Indian strategic managers are for defensive self-preservation (the *dharmayuddha* tradition). This line of thinking is in tune with Manu's injunctions that in the real world occasionally it is necessary to inflict a moderate amount of force. Swarna Rajagopalan (2006a: 9) wrote: 'The Valmiki *Ramayana* depicts an epic age and remains in the Indian imagination as a repository of metaphors and values whose political salience has been resurgent in the last two decades'. The *Ramayana* tells us that when the forces of Ravana had an upper hand, then Lakshmana told his elder brother Rama that he was going to use a weapon with ultra-destructive power (the *brahmastra*) against the *raksas* in Lanka. Rama requested Lakshmana not to use this weapon, as it would result in massive destruction of life and property. Rama continues that even when fighting an enemy like Ravana, who was an unrighteous king with *adharmic* objectives in contravention to Hindu *dharma* (duty), such weapons should still not be used as many common people would die (Sinha 2005: 292). Modern day commentators use this story to prevent civilian collateral damage by arguing against the use of weapons of mass destruction such as nuclear warheads against Pakistan's cities.

A third stream of thought is the spiritual tradition, which was originally represented by Yudhistira in the *Mahabharata*, and is now infused and operates with Gandhian ideology. On 25 April 1947, Gandhi (1993: 268) wrote: 'I hold that he who invented the atom bomb has committed the gravest sin in the world of science. The only weapon that can save the world is non-violence'. This tradition of thought rejects nuclear weapons as necessary for security. Instead of national security orientated around armed forces, this school conceptualizes national security as human security in terms of gender equality, uplifting backward communities and the provision of food, clothes and shelter for the citizens of India (Ramdas 2003: 57). The Gandhian-inspired anti-nuclear lobby criticizes the possession of nuclear weapons as immoral and impractical because there cannot be any winners in a nuclear war (Ramdas 2003: 73). This group disagrees with the *realpolitik* (*kutayuddha*) group's conceptualization of nuclear weapons as a deterrence mechanism and its advocacy of the use of tactical nuclear weapons to achieve victory in the battlefield. India's noble laureate economist Amartya Sen (2003: 187) writes: 'Nuclear restraint strengthens rather than weakens India's voice. ... But making nuclear bombs, not to mention deploying them, and spending scarce resources on missiles and what is euphemistically called "delivery", can hardly be seen as sensible policy'. The anti-nuclear lobby points out that in 1998–1999, the India government put aside Rs 9,000 crore for acquiring three nuclear submarines and only Rs 7,238 crore for rural poverty elimination programmes (Reddy 2003: 394). Following Gujral doctrine, which is a derivative of Gandhian thought, Amartya Sen (2003: 188) asserts that India's security could be strengthened if India aids its chief competitor Pakistan instead of threatening it.

Conclusion

As my survey shows, there are several traditions present in Hinduism. One school of thought, the Yudhistira–Gandhian School, supports complete abrogation of violence in pursuit of peace. The second tradition as represented by the *Manusamhita* emphasizes the application of a moderate amount of violence at times for establishing peace. And the third stream of thought, the hardliners – represented by Kautilya and in the modern day by the BJP – advocate aggressive militarism as a means to establish peace. The *Bhagavad Gita* portrays the moral dilemma faced by the two warriors Yudhistira and Arjuna over the issue of breaking the peace and going to war. The *Manusamhita* attempts to relegate warfare to the background. It would be wrong to link gender with non-violence (*ahimsa*). Not all the female characters in the epics belonged to the peace party. For instance, while Sita was a proponent of the *ahimsa* doctrine, Draupadi demanded heroic action on part of her husband to teach the Kauravas a lesson.

As in the epics, the dual traditions of just and unjust war are also present in the works on *niti* (*nitisastras*). While the *Manusamhita* followed what in modern terminology is known as the constructivist approach in international relations, Asoka and Gandhi to an extent represent the utopian trend in modern day peace research. Finally, the evolution of a welfare oriented state after 1947 to a great extent can be traced back to Hindu ethos. However, the scenario changed for the worse from the 1990s. As the subcontinent has become overtly nuclear since May 1998, an obstacle in the process of resolving the crisis between India and Pakistan is the use of religious imageries and vocabularies by hardliners in both countries. Overall, the Gandhian policy of non-violence (*ahimsa*) is still relevant for India in particular and the world in general. One scholar (Johnson 2008: 101) argues that states have more power than the non-state terrorists to inflict violence. Hence, the United States' policy of using military force against the non-state jihadi terrorists will only result in an escalating level of violence. Here Gandhi's use of non-violent techniques could be used as an alternative option.

Bibliography

Allen, D. 2008. Introduction, in *The Philosophy of Mahatma Gandhi for the Twenty-First Century*, edited by D. Allen. New Delhi: Oxford University Press, vii–xviii.

Ananth, V.K. 2003. The politics of the bomb: some observations on the political discourse in India in the context of Pokhran II, in *Prisoners of the Nuclear Dream*, edited by M.V. Ramana and C.R. Reddy. Hyderabad: Orient Longman, 315–32.

Bailey, G. 2000. Introduction: an empirical approach to the *Ramayana*, in *Epic Threads: John Brockington on the Sanskrit Epics*, edited by G. Bailey. New Delhi: Oxford University Press, vii–xxv.

The Bhagavad Gita. 1962. Translated from Sanskrit with an Introduction by J. Mascaro. London: Penguin.

Bhat, S.V. 2007. Ethical values in the *Ramayana*: a reflection, in *Ethics for Modern Man in Sanskrit Literature*, edited by K.B. Archak. Delhi: Sundeep Prakashan, 27–33.

Brekke, T. 2002. *Makers of Modern Indian Religion in the Late Nineteenth Century*. Oxford: Oxford University Press.

Brockington, J. 2000a. *Ramodharmabhrtamvarah,* in *Epic Threads: John Brockington on the Sanskrit Epics*, edited by G. Bailey. New Delhi: Oxford University Press, 250–64.

Brockington, J. 2000b. Religious attitudes in Valmiki's *Ramayana,* in *Epic Threads: John Brockington on the Sanskrit Epics*, edited by G. Bailey. New Delhi: Oxford University Press, 218–49.

Brodbeck, S. 1962. Introduction, in *The Bhagavad Gita*. Translated from Sanskrit by J. Mascaro, with an Introduction by S. Brodbeck. New Delhi: Penguin, xi–xxix.

Dadhich, N. 2008. The postmodern discourse on Gandhi: modernity and truth, in *The Philosophy of Mahatma Gandhi for the Twenty-First Century*, edited by D. Allen. New Delhi: Oxford University Press, 179–99.

Dalton, D. 1969. Gandhi: ideology and authority. *Modern Asian Studies*, 3(4): 377–93.

Dange, S.S. 2007. Ethical codes in the Vedic literature, in *Ethics for Modern Man in Sanskrit Literature*, edited by K.B. Archak. Delhi: Sundeep Prakashan, 17–26.

Doniger, W. and Smith, B.K. 1991. Introduction, in *The Laws of Manu*. Translated by W. Doniger with B.K. Smith. New Delhi: Penguin, xv–lxxviii.

Dundas, P. 2007. The non-violence of violence: Jain perspectives on warfare, asceticism and worship, in *Religion and Violence in South Asia: Theory and Practice*, edited by J.R. Hinnells and R. King. London: Routledge, 41–61.

Gandhi, M.K. 1993. *The Essential Writings of Mahatma Gandhi*, edited by R. Iyer. New Delhi: Oxford University Press.

Gethin, R. 2007. Buddhist monks, Buddhist kings, Buddhist violence: on the early Buddhist attitudes to violence, in *Religion and Violence in South Asia: Theory and Practice*, edited by J.R. Hinnells and R. King. London: Routledge, 62–82.

Goldman, R.P. 1984. General introduction, in *The Ramayana of Valmiki: An Epic of Ancient India*, vol. 1, *Balakanda*. Translated by R.P. Goldman. New Delhi: Motilal Banarasidas, 3–13.

Gottschalk, P.A. 2007. Categorical difference: communal identity in British epistemologies, in *Religion and Violence in South Asia: Theory and Practice*, edited by J.R. Hinnells and R. King. London: Routledge, 195–210.

Haksar, A.N.D. 1998. Introduction, in Narayana, *The Hitopadesa*. Translated by A.N.D. Haksar. New Delhi: Penguin, ix–xx.

Hamilton, S. 2001. *Indian Philosophy: A Very Short Introduction*. New York: Oxford University Press.

Hills, C. and Silverman, D.C. 1993. Nationalism and feminism in late colonial India: the Rani of Jhansi regiment, 1943–1945. *Modern Asian Studies* 27(4), 741–60.

Hinnells, J.R. and King, R. 2007. Introduction, in *Religion and Violence in South Asia: Theory and Practice*, edited by J.R. Hinnells and R. King. London: Routledge, 1–7.

Indra 1957. *Ideologies of War and Peace in Ancient India*. Hoshiarpur: Vishveshvarand Institute Publications.

Jaiswal, S. 2007. Social dimensions of the cult of Rama, in *Religion in Indian History*, edited with an introduction by I. Habib. New Delhi: Tulika, 71–101.

Johnson, R.L. 2008. Three 9/11s: *Satyagraha* or terrorism, in *The Philosophy of Mahatma Gandhi for the Twenty-First Century*, edited by D. Allen. New Delhi: Oxford University Press, 99–119.

Kane, P.V. 1968. *History of Dharmasastra (Ancient and Medieval Religious and Civil Law in India)*, vol. 1, revised and enlarged, Part I. Pune: Bhandarkar Oriental Research Institute.

The Laws of Manu with an Introduction and Notes. 1991. Translated by W. Doniger and B.K. Smith. New Delhi: Penguin.

Lorenzen, D.N. 2004. Introduction, in *Religious Movements in South Asia 600–1800*, edited by D.N. Lorenzen. New Delhi: Oxford University Press, 1–44.

Mahulikar, G. 2007. Ethical teachings in the *Santiparva* of the *Mahabharata*, in *Ethics for Modern Man in Sanskrit Literature*, edited by K.B. Archak. Delhi: Sundeep Prakashan, 34–42.

Malinar, A. 2007. *The Bhagavadgita: Doctrines and Contexts*. Cambridge: Cambridge University Press.

Manu's Code of Law: A Critical Edition and Translation of the Manava-Dharmasastra, 2005, edited by P. Olivelle with S. Olivelle. New Delhi: Oxford University Press.

Mohanraj, V.M. 2005. *The Warrior and the Charioteer: A Materialist Interpretation of the Bhagavadgita including a New Translation of the Poem*. New Delhi: Leftword Books.

Mohanty, J.N. 1992. *Reason and Tradition in Indian Thought: An Essay on the Nature of Indian Philosophical Thinking*. Oxford: Clarendon Press.

Nanda, M. 2007. *Breaking the Spell of Dharma and other Essays*. New Delhi: Three Essays Collective, 1–7.

Narayana, 1998. *The Hitopadesa*. Translated from Sanskrit with an introduction by A.N.D. Haksar. New Delhi: Penguin.

Olivelle, P. 2005. Introduction, in *Manu's Code of Law: A Critical Edition and Translation of the Manava-Dharmasastra*, edited by P. Olivelle with S. Olivelle. New Delhi: Oxford University Press, 3–70.

The Panchatantra 1925. Translated from Sanskrit by A.W. Ryder. Mumbai: Jaico.

Patton, L.L. 2007. Telling stories about harm: an overview of early Indian narratives, in *Religion and Violence in South Asia: Theory and Practice*, edited by J.R. Hinnells and R. King. London: Routledge, 11–40.

Peterson, I.V. 1991. Arjuna's combat with the Kirata: *Rasa* and *Bhakti* in Bharavi's *Kiratarjuniya*, in *Essays on the Mahabharata*, edited by A. Sharma. Delhi: Motilal Banarasidas, 212–50.

Pollock, S. 2006. *Ramayana* and political imagination in India, in *Religious Movements in South Asia: 600–1800*, edited by D.N. Lorenzen. New Delhi: Oxford University Press, 153–208.

Raghavulu, C.V. 2006. Disasters in India: patterns of institutional response, in *Security and South Asia: Ideas, Institutions and Initiatives*, edited by S. Rajagopalan. New Delhi and London: Routledge, 200–240.

Rajagopalan, S. 2006a. Introduction, in *Security and South Asia: Ideas, Institutions and Initiatives*, edited by S. Rajagopalan. New Delhi and London: Routledge, 1–11.

Rajagopalan, S. 2006b. Security ideas in the Valmiki *Ramayana*, in *Security and South Asia: Ideas, Institutions and Initiatives*, edited by S. Rajagopalan. New Delhi and London: Routledge, 24–53.

Ramana, M.V. and Reddy, C.R. 2003. Introduction, in *Prisoners of the Nuclear Dream*, edited by M.V. Ramana and C.R. Reddy. Hyderabad: Orient Longman, 1–24.

Ramdas, Admiral L. 2003. Nuclear Weapons and National Security, in *Prisoners of the Nuclear Dream*, edited by M.V. Ramana and C.R. Reddy. Hyderabad: Orient Longman, 53–73.

Reddy, C.R. 2003. Nuclear weapons versus schools for children: an estimate of the cost of the Indian nuclear weapons programme, in *Prisoners of the Nuclear Dream*, edited by M.V. Ramana and C.R. Reddy. New Delhi: Orient Longman, 2003, 360–408.

Revathy, S. 2007. The ethics of the *Bhagavadgita*, in *Ethics for Modern Man in Sanskrit Literature*, edited by K.B. Archak. Delhi: Sundeep Prakashan, 43–52.

The Rig Veda, An Anthology: One Hundred and Eight Hymns. 1981. Selected, translated and annotated by W.D. O'Flaherty. New Delhi: Penguin.

Rowell, J.L. 2006. Gandhi and bin Laden: religious conflict at the polar extremes. *Journal of Conflict Studies* 26, 35–54.

Ryder, A.W. 1925. Translator's introduction, in *The Panchatantra*. Translated from Sanskrit by A.W. Ryder. Mumbai: Jaico, 3–13.

Sarkar, A. 1987. *A Study on the Ramayanas*. Calcutta: Rddhi.

Sen, A. 2003. India and the bomb, in *Prisoners of the Nuclear Dream*, edited by M.V. Ramana and C.R. Reddy. Hyderabad: Orient Longman, 167–88.

Sinha, M.K. 2005. Hinduism and international humanitarian law. *International Review of the Red Cross*, 87(858): 285–94.

Sorensen, G. 1992. Utopianism in peace research: the Gandhian heritage. *Journal of Peace Research*, 29(2): 135–44.

Thapar, R. 2004. Imagined religious communities? Ancient history and the modern search for a Hindu identity, in *Religious Movements in South Asia: 600–1800*, edited by D.N. Lorenzen. New Delhi: Oxford University Press, 333–59.

Tripathi, R. 1942. *History of Ancient India*. Delhi: Motilal Banarasidas.

Vivekananda, Swami 2009. *Chicago Addresses, Swami Vivekananda*, edited by Swami Bodhasarananda, Kolkata: Advaita Ashrama.

Zhengjia, Y. 2003. China–India relations, in *Prisoners of the Nuclear Dream*, edited by M.V. Ramana and C.R. Reddy. Hyderabad: Orient Longman, 152–64.

Chapter 4
The Confucian Vision of Peace

Kam-por Yu

The word 'peace' can be used either in a weak sense or in a strong sense. 'Peace' in the weak sense is contrasted with 'war', and means basically the absence of war. It is more the absence of an undesirable state than the presence of a desirable state. In the Confucian tradition, there is also a thicker conception of peace, which means far more than the end of fighting or the non-existence of chaos and is more like harmony, happy coexistence or mutual flourishing.

'Peace' as contrasted with war is called '*ping* 平' (peace or settlement), which refers to the restoration of order and stability after the use of military force.[1] It implies both that there has been chaos or fighting and that the chaos or fighting has come to an end. '*Ping*' is contrasted with chaos (*luan* 亂), uprising (*pan* 叛) or invasion (*kou* 寇). It is not a very positive word, but just indicates the end of a negative state of affairs. By contrast, other terms such as '*taiping* 太平' (grand peace), '*heping* 和平' (harmonious peace) or '*pingzhi* 平治' (peaceful governance) refer to an ideal state that Confucius and his followers would like to promote (Legge, The Book of Filial Piety 8.4, Lau, Mencius 2B13, 4A1). It is characterized not by the absence of undesirable features but by the existence of certain desirable features; it is an ideal of high order and is rarely attained except by the sage-kings.

In the Confucian tradition, war is not always a bad thing – sometimes it can be a tool for well-being and justice. However, the Confucian tradition has no trace of certain views evident in ancient Greek civilization, such as valorizing violence and conquest, regarding strife as just and good and seeing war as ennobling the human spirit (Ni 2008: 209, 218–19).[2] The Confucian tradition also has a full-blown ethics of war. There are Confucian principles for entering into war and determining proper behaviour in a war. The Confucian tradition addresses issues of modern concern, such as pre-emptive attack, war against enemies of civilization, unilateral punitive expedition, humanitarian intervention and weapons of mass destruction (resulting in large scale indiscriminate killing) (see Yu 2010b, Bell 2008a; 2008b).

1 This usage is common in the Confucian classics, and such meaning is used repeatedly and explicitly in one of the major Confucian classics *Gongyang Zhuan*.

2 In the same vein, the American philosopher William James (1987) regards war as having fundamental positive value for human civilization and finds it necessary to look for an alternative to war (for example, competition in sports) which can do the same good to human civilization as war can do.

In this chapter I am not going to talk about the ethics of war but peace. Peace in the weak sense is a culturally thin notion and hence not so interesting as a specimen for cultural and historical study. In the following, I will focus on the exposition of the maximal conception of peace. Unlike the minimal conception of peace, the maximal conception is a culturally thick notion. It is also closely related to the Confucian ethical outlook and the Chinese way of thinking.

Before I continue, I have to make a note regarding the use of Confucian texts in this chapter. In explicating the Confucian vision, I will be relying mainly on the major Confucian classics.[3] The main Confucian classics are known as the *Five Classics,* including *The Book of Poetry, The Book of Documents, The Book of Rites,*[4] *The Book of Changes* and *The Spring and Autumn Annals*.[5] During the Song dynasty (960–1279), four elementary texts were put together as one volume, known as the *Four Books,* and since then it has been regarded as the basic text of Confucianism. *The Four Books* include *The Analects* (collected sayings of Confucius), *Mencius* (works of Mencius, 371–289 BC) and two pieces of work from *The Records of Rites,* namely, *Daxue* (*The Great Learning*) and *Zhongyong* (*Doctrine of the Mean*). There have been some disputes regarding the authorship and the authenticity of some of the texts. But such disputes are of minor importance for the present purpose, as the above texts are undeniably authoritative within the Confucian tradition and are resources that can be drawn from in working out a Confucian vision of peace.

A Thick Conception of Peace

Peace, according to the maximal conception, is not an order imposed by an authority, but a state of flourishing and development constituted by multiple divergent and competing elements. According to the Confucian ideal, the best example of *taiping* or grand peace is the rule under the sage-kings, like Shun (legendary king, third millennium BC) and King Wen (r. 1171–1122 BC), who ruled by virtue and culture. By contrast, the rule by Qin Shihuangdi (the First Emperor of China, r. 221–206 BC) – who unified China by violence and ruled it by coercion and punishment – is commonly regarded within the Confucian tradition as the antithesis of peace.

3 For a succinct and reliable introduction to Confucianism see Goldin 2011. For a discussion of Confucianism as based on human nature and human sentiments see Yu and Tao 2012. For a discussion of the *Five Classics* see Nylan 2001.

4 *The Book of Rites* consists of three works: *The Rites of Zhuo* (周禮), *The Codes of Rites* (儀禮) and *The Records of Rites* (禮記).

5 The text of *The Spring and Autumn Annals* is found in three commentaries: *Gongyang Commentary to the Spring and Autumn Annals* (春秋公羊傳), *Guliang Commentary to the Spring and Autumn Annals* (春秋穀梁傳) and *Zuo's Commentary to the Spring and Autumn Annals* (春秋左氏傳).

The order imposed by Qin Shihuangdi was unprecedented in China. It put utmost emphasis on unity, stability, conformity and solidarity. But in the views of the Confucians, it was one of the worst periods in Chinese history and its downfall was due to its lack of benevolence and righteousness.[6] According to the Confucian ideal of peace, the unification and order established by Qin was certainly not a state of peace, but quite its opposite, against which a violent revolution was justified. This notion of peace implies that order may not be good and the ultimate ground for evaluating whether a state of order and stability is good comes not from the will of the rulers or leaders but the well-being of the common people.

Harmony is one major feature of true peace. In the Chinese expression for peace, '*heping* 和平', the first Chinese character (*he* 和) means harmony. 'Harmony' (*he* 和) in Chinese is a very rich concept. In the Confucian tradition, it is to be contrasted with 'homogeneity' (*tong* 同). Harmony implies a state of diversity, peaceful co-existence, justice, good governance and truthful communication (Yu 2010a: 25–31). True peace is attained not by bringing in the best possible state for all, but by enabling multiple kinds of good to coexist and flourish. According to the Confucian view, conflicts occur not just between good and bad, but can also occur between different kinds of good. As a result, the ideal is not just to promulgate the good and to eliminate the bad but to balance different kinds of good, which are held dear by different groups of people. The real challenge is to recognize all the relevant values involved and strike the right balance among them. Hence, the Confucian vision of peace is constituted not by imposing an order or a state of stability on different parties, but by giving due recognition to all parties concerned. There are no elements that are intrinsically bad that have to be completely eradicated.

The Chinese prefer to explain the concept of harmony by analogy rather than by definition. The analogies most commonly used are cooking, music and health. In cooking, and especially in Chinese cooking, different ingredients are put together to make a dinner course. It is pointed out that by putting different ingredients together, new and rich tastes and textures can be created. In music, different instruments generate different tones such that together they can be made to constitute a coherent and enriching whole. This kind of harmonious music is possible only with the pre-existence and co-ordination of musical instruments with different natures. Another analogy that is commonly used is health. According to the view in traditional Chinese medicine, health is a matter of balance of different *qi* or energies. There is no *qi* that is intrinsically bad and should be completely eliminated. The body is in poor health if different *qi* are out of balance and health is attained when the *qi* are balanced. That is to say, sickness is not something substantial, but just a lack of balance, which can be restored by venting excessive energies and cultivating those that are inadequate. In all the above analogies, harmony is depicted not as a state of purification, but as a state of diversity and balance (Yu 2010a: 18–20).

---

6 After the downfall of Qin, the Confucian scholars explained its downfall as due to a lack of benevolence and righteousness. Confucianism became popular only after the downfall of the Qin dynasty, which had a short life of 15 years.

True peace can prevail only when there is true harmony, which requires diversity and a healthy balance that does not just aim at maintaining the status quo, but at flourishing and development. As G.E.R. Lloyd (1996: 206) points out: 'For the Chinese, the ideal is one of "free flow" interaction, intercommunication between the parts, with each fulfilling its due and proper function. That applies to the bureaucracy of the state, and the interrelation of parts of the living organism is conceived similarly bureaucratically'. True peace is not an externally imposed order, restricting the individuality of the various parts or shaping them according to certain modes into a homogeneous whole, but an order achieved through the interaction of various parts, each developing according to its nature. As it is said in *Zhongyong* (Johnson and Wang: 369): 'The ten thousand things are nurtured together, and yet do not harm each other. Different paths are simultaneously travelled, and yet are not contrary to each other'. That is to say, harmony can be achieved without giving up plurality and there is a way for the 'ten thousand things' (including humans) to coexist and to flourish together.

The above line of thinking is typical in traditional Chinese culture. Daoism, the other major school of thought in Chinese culture, goes even further than Confucianism in this regard. Daoism has a more negative view of war and the use of arms. As said in the *Lao Tzu* (Lau: 88): 'One who assists the ruler of men by means of the way does not intimidate the empire by a show of arms. … In the wake of a mighty army bad harvests follow without fail'. 'It is because arms are instruments of ill omen and there are Things that detest them that one who has the way does not abide by their use. … When victorious in war, one should observe the rites of mourning' (Lao Tzu: 89–90). Confucianism adopts a more moderate view, but Daoism puts even more emphasis than Confucianism on the importance of individuality and individual freedom, and it has a stronger distrust of institutions in general and governments in particular in terms of their intervention into individuals' lives (Schwartz 1985: 230–31). The major difference between Confucianism and Daoism is that Confucianism treasures culture and civilization but Daoism values spontaneity and non-intervention. However, the view that there is some objective evil that has to be eliminated is alien to both of these two schools.

Two Ways of Seeing Conflicts

There are different possible ways of seeing conflicts. If conflict is thought to exist between good and bad, then the ideal solution would be the triumph of the good and the elimination of the bad. However, if conflict is regarded as between two camps both with legitimate interests to some extent, then the ideal would be a happy co-existence and mutual flourishing, and the path to realize such an ideal would be a matter of weighing and balancing different considerations and concerns.

The Confucian vision of harmony or peace is closely related to the Chinese way of thinking, which sees opposites as complementing each other and the ideal state as a healthy balance of opposites. Such a way of thinking has been described as a worldview which does not recognize the objective existence of evil and does not see the world as consisting of any wrongful part that has to be eliminated; there are just excesses that have to be curbed or inadequacies that have to be fixed. This salient feature of the Chinese way of thinking has been noted by many scholars. Joseph Needham's (1956: 582) remark is typical: 'The harmonious cooperation of all beings arose, not from the orders of a superior authority external to themselves, but from the fact that they were all parts in a hierarchy of wholes forming a cosmic pattern, and what they obeyed were the internal dictates of their own natures'. This captures very well a number of important points about the Chinese conception of harmony: 1. it is not an order imposed by a superior authority; 2. it is based on the interaction of diverse parts; and 3. it does not require the parts to give up or to act against their own natures.

In addition, the Chinese conception of harmonious peace also implies that there are no intrinsic evils that have to be eradicated. In order to achieve harmonious peace, it is only necessary to put such situational evils in place, such that they do not pose as harms to other parts. There are only partial goods that have to be controlled such that they do not become excessive or interruptive when other goods are taken into consideration. The Japanese scholar Hajime Nakamura (1968: 284) puts it well:

> If the reality of all natural phenomena is absolutely upheld, then nothing imperfect can be denied existence; this idea persisted from ancient times in China. For the Chinese, the five Confucian classics are the source of ethics. They further believed that the other classics or books are also a partial revelation of the same perfect wisdom. The Chinese believed that not only can perfection exist in this world but other existence cannot be denied in spite of the fact that they are not perfect. Thus, not even a single existence is denied, and there is perfect existence which must be absolutely affirmed.

It is debatable whether the Confucians really believe that there is a perfect existence that must be absolutely affirmed. Confucius himself seems to have raised doubts about this on a number of occasions. However, the weaker claim that there is no existence that must be absolutely denied is definitely the Confucian position. As D.W.Y. Kwok (1993: 7) writes:

> This cosmology also predisposed the Chinese to view the world as without sin, at least in the Judeo-Christian sense and hence without its consequences. ... In a correlated cosmos such as China's, there was no place for wrongful or undesirable parts. Disturbances and malfunctions of the order or of the parts within it might indeed occur, but they would be temporary, and could be rectified.

Such a worldview has important practical implications. For example, according to Confucius, capital punishment is unnecessary when a capable and virtuous ruler governs a state (Lau, *The Analects* 12:19), and destroying a state is a war crime of the highest degree.[7] Confucius even goes so far as to advocate the restoration of states that have been annexed and the revival of family lines that have become extinct (*The Analects* 20: 1).

Opposites, like *yin* and *yang*, are regarded as complementing each other. The following are common Chinese expressions on the relation between opposites: 'mutually opposing and mutually accomplishing' (*xiangfan xiangcheng* 相反相成); 'mutually conflicting and mutually complementing' (*xiangchong xiangji* 相沖相濟); and 'mutually generating and mutually eliminating' (*xiangsheng xiang ke* 相生相剋). As Derk Bodde (1953: 54) notes: 'Basic among Chinese thought patterns is the desire to merge seemingly conflicting elements into a unified harmony. Chinese philosophy is filled with dualisms in which, however, their two component elements are usually regarded as complementary and mutually necessary rather than as hostile and incompatible'.

In his discussion on 'all thinkers who adopt the *yin-yang* ideology', Bodde (1953: 61) explains the relation between *yin* and *yang*:

> Never, however, is the suggestion made by them that one can or should wholly displace the other. Hence, there is no real analogy with the dualisms based on conflict (light vs. darkness, etc.) so familiar to us in the West. On the contrary, the *yin* and *yang* form a cosmic hierarchy of balanced inequality in which, however, each complements the other and has its own necessary function.

Conflicts exist not just between good and bad, but can also exist between opposites where both have some positive value. As both of the two opposites have their roles to play, the right way to handle conflict is not to uphold one and eliminate the other, but to strike a balance between the two. As Confucius (*The Analects* 2: 16, my translation) said, 'To attack another end on the basis of one end can result in nothing but harm'.

One salient feature of Confucianism is the recognition of the existence of multiple values. Confucian values usually come in pairs. For example: loyalty (*zhong* 忠) and filial piety (*xiao* 孝); temperance (*jie* 節) and righteousness (*yi* 義); human feeling (*qing* 情) and principle (*li* 理). They are opposite values, not in the sense that they are incompatible and cannot be realized at the same time, but in the sense that they point to different directions and compete for our attention and energy. Yet both of them are important positive values and should be promoted at the same time. In the Confucian classics, we can find a number of competing and complementing values, such as refinement (*wén* 文) and substance (*zhi* 質) (*The Analects* 6: 18); being respectful (*gong* 恭) and composed (*an* 安) (*The Analects* 7: 38); simplicity (*jian* 簡) and reverence (*jing* 敬) (*The Analects* 6: 2); mildness (*wēn* 溫) and strictness (*meng* 猛) (Legge, Zuo Zhuan: 684); tension (*zhang* 張) and

7 Destroying a state is regarded as an injustice much more serious than invasion and annexation of territory, and is condemned with very strong language in Confucius' *Spring and Autumn Annals* (Gongyang Zhuan: 36–7).

relaxation (*chi* 弛) (Legge, The Book of Rites: 167). The first three pairs of values are related to the nature of propriety or proper conduct (*li* 禮). While propriety has a subject matter (the realization of human nature, the promotion of well-being and the expression of sentiments, etc.), which can be called its substance, such substance has to be constructed, formulated or packaged in such a way to make it presentable as civilized, cultured or polished, which is referred to as refinement. There are also opposing demands for the codes of proper conduct. The proper codes should allow people to show respect to other people while they themselves can remain composed, natural or uncontrived as far as possible. The opposing demands for the codes of proper conduct also include being simple in essence on the one hand and being able to express reverence on the other hand. The last two pairs of values are related to good governance. Mildness should be used to remedy strictness and strictness should be used to remedy mildness. The complementarity of the two opposing values of tension and relaxation (working hard and having enjoyment) can be illustrated by the following story (The Book of Rites: 167):

> Zigong had gone to see the agricultural ceremony at the end of the year. Confucius said to him, 'Did you enjoy it?' Zigong replied, 'The whole country seemed to have gone mad. I didn't enjoy it'. Confucius said, 'After a hundred days of labour, people have one day of fun. That's not something you understand. To be tense all the time and never relax, that is too much even for King Wen and King Wu. To be relaxed all the time and never get tense, that's not what King Wen and King Wu would prefer. To alternate being relaxed and tense – that is the way of King Wen and King Wu'.

The basic idea is that all values are positive and limited. None is to be pursued in the absolute sense and all values have to be pursued in moderation with other values. The claim that there is neither absolute value nor essentially negative value has important practical implications. The belief that there is absolute value may justify the pursuit of it by all possible means, including radical measures and unlimited sacrifice, and the belief that there is essentially negative value may justify the complete annihilation of such intrinsic evil. Such a standpoint is exemplified in the opening sentences of *Zhongyong* (ch. 1, my translation): 'To follow nature is the Way. To rectify the Way is culture'. The first sentence affirms the value of nature. The second sentence immediately points out its imperfection. Following nature and rectifying nature are two opposite values that can complement each other.

Since the very early stage of the Confucian tradition, multiple competing values were recognized and they were regarded as complementing one another. When the Duke of Zhou (d. 1094 BC) acted as the regent,[8] he designed the institutions of the

8 The Duke of Zhou (d. 1095 BC) was the son of King Wu and brother of King Wen, and served as regent after the death of King Wu. All three of them were regarded as sage-rulers in the Confucian tradition. The Duke of Zhou was much admired by Confucius and was some kind of role model for Confucius (see *The Analects* 7: 5).

Zhou dynasty (1111–249 BC) on the basis of three primary values: 1. respect those who have authority (*zunzun* 尊尊); 2. maintain good relationships with those who are related (*qinqin* 親親); and 3. appoint those who are good and capable (*xianxian* 賢賢) (Wang 1973). It is not difficult to see that these three values are meant to complement one another. Each value has its contribution and limitation. 'Respect those who have authority' is essential for maintaining stability and order, but it may lead to stagnation and tyranny. 'Maintain good relationships with those who are related' is essential for fostering social cohesion, but it may lead to partiality and nepotism. 'Appoint those who are good and capable' is essential for promoting good governance, but it may lead to competition and dissatisfaction. Although these three values compete for our attention, and taken in isolation they may lead us in different directions, the real challenge is to promote all these three primary values at the same time.

Since pluralism is at the foundation of Confucianism, the interpretation of Confucianism as a kind of familism or authoritarianism is superficial and misleading (see Fan 1999; 2010, Merzger 1990: 263). It is true that there are some passages in the Confucian classics that can be interpreted as supporting familism or authoritarianism (see Fu 1993). But such evidence can only show part of the picture as it only demonstrates that care for family and respect of authority are among the values Confucianism holds dear. It in no way shows that family is the highest value or that it is the only thing that really matters. It is just one among many values recognized in Confucianism. There is considerable counter-evidence to the interpretation of Confucianism as a kind of familism. The following is just one example:

> Zigong asked, 'What must a man be like before he can be said truly to be a Gentleman?' Confucius said, 'A man who has a sense of shame in the way he conducts himself, and when sent abroad, does not disgrace the commission of his lord can be said to be a Gentleman'. 'May I ask about the grade below?' 'Someone praised for being a good son in his clan and for being a respectful young man in the village'. (*The Analects* 13: 20)

The above passage clearly indicates that a Confucian gentleman has to go beyond one's family and care about the greater human community. A gentleman (*junzi* 君子) is not yet a sage (*shengren* 聖人) or a worthy (*xianze* 賢者) and a family-centred good person is not yet good enough to be a true gentleman. Similarly, ability, unification or solidarity are recognized as valuable, but they are certainly not the only or highest values.

The Confucian classic *Zhongyong* (Legge: 408–9) talks about good governance as consisting of nine guiding principles (*jiu jing*). They are: 1. cultivate one's person; 2. honour the good and capable; 3. be devoted to one's kin; 4. respect the senior ministers; 5. understand the difficulties of the various officials; 6. love the common people; 7. attract the various artisans; 8. give preferential treatment to people from afar; and 9. pacify the feudal lords. For the present purpose, it is not necessary for me to go into a detailed explanation of these nine guiding principles for good governance. To be sure, there are different sets of such guiding principles within the Confucian tradition and sometimes they differ quite considerably from one another. It is enough for the present purpose to take note of the pluralistic nature of the guiding principles. The important message is that good governance consists of multiple concerns and all these nine aspects have to be taken care of. It would be wrong to justify one's policy just by paying attention to one or a few of the above aspects at the expense of the other aspects, which are also important and should be taken care of. These nine aspects compete for our attention and resources. The right thing is not to do this or that, but to strike the right balance among all the relevant concerns (Yu 2010c).

For Confucianism, both of the opposing values are real. The tension, and in some cases the conflict between them, is also real. Although each value is legitimate, it would not be right just to stick to one value and promote it at the expense of another. For Confucianism, there is not just one good but many goods. Different parties may have conflict with each other, not necessarily because one side is right and the other side is wrong or one side is good and the other side is evil, but because they only have a partial view and are not able to take all the relevant concerns into consideration at the same time.

The most common Confucian critique of an inferior position is not that it is totally wrong or unreasonable, but that it is partial and incomplete. As Xunzi (fl. 298–238 BC) said, 'It is a common flaw of people to be blinded by one aspect of truth and fail to see the whole truth' (Knoblock, Xunzi: 671). Confucius (*The Analects* 2: 14) puts it this way: 'A superior man is all-round in his consideration, but does not stick to a single aspect. An inferior man sticks to a single aspect, but is not all-round in his consideration'. In short, while other people might criticize their opponents as *wrong*, the Confucians would say that their opponents have only grasped a *partial truth*.

The key concepts related to this kind of all-round thinking include: *zhong* 中 (the mean), *zhongyong* 中庸 (the central way), *he* 和 (harmony), or *quan* 全 (all-roundness) (Yu 2010c: 29–32). They each imply taking all relevant values into consideration, giving all of them due respect and forming a holistic and balanced judgement as a result.

The Confucian *zhong* is different from the Aristotelian mean in that the Aristotelian mean exists between two extremes, which are both bad, whereas the Confucian *zhong* is located between two ends, which are both good. The Aristotelian mean is attained by keeping a distance from the two extremes, but the Confucian *zhong* is attained by taking the two ends into consideration and is constituted by giving both of them the right degree of affirmation. For Aristotle (1998: 39 [1107a]),

> Excellence[9] … is a state concerned with choice, lying in a mean relative to us, this being determined by reason and in the way in which the man of practical wisdom would determine it. Now it is a mean between two vices, that which depends on excess and that which depends on defect.

9 '*Αρετή*' (*aretē*) is sometimes translated as 'virtue'.

The Aristotelian mean is distinguished from the two states of excess and deficiency that are both regarded as *vices* and is attained by rejecting these two other states (see Yu 2007: ch. 3).

While the Aristotelian mean requires *rejecting* the extremes, which are both bad, the Confucian mean requires *affirming* the two opposite values, which are both good. For the Confucians, the two opposites are not to be rejected, but to be *grasped.* Commenting on a passage in *Zhongyong* which refers to 'grasping the two extremes' by the sage-king Shun, Osamu Kanaya (1996: 86) points out:

> Special note should be taken of the final words: 'grasping (*zhi* 執) these two extremes' means that instead of rejecting them he took firm hold of them. Although it is the middle that is actually adopted in government, it may be assumed that the two extremes are assimilated by and put to good use in this middle. In other words, the middle between the two extremes, inclining neither to the left nor to the right, is in fact endowed with the capacity to encompass both the left and the right.

The Confucian doctrine of the mean has the following distinctive features. First, as competing values, like loyalty and filial piety or affection and justice, both of them should be promoted as far as possible. Second, as complementing values, like leniency and strictness, or decoration and simplicity, each value should be promoted in proportion to the opposite value. Third, as competing and complementing values, like the nine canons of good governance, each value is worth pursuing in itself, but the extent to which it should be pursued should be considered together with the other values.

The above line of thinking has far reaching implications. If conflict can occur between the good, then all-round thinking instead of black and white thinking is required to look for a way out. The challenge is not just to discover what is right and what is wrong but to weigh different claims and considerations, and to strike the right balance between them.

For the Confucians, the two alternatives are not right and wrong, but one-sided and balanced. A person's standpoint is one-sided if it only incorporates part of the relevant values involved and if someone defends a position from such a partial basis. The superior view is one that is all-rounded where someone is able to identify all the relevant values and consider how best to promote them all or strike the right balance between them.

The Confucian Way to True Peace

Different ways of understanding the nature of conflict will lead to different ways of responding to conflict. If conflict is regarded as a war between good and evil, then the use of radical means can be readily justified and compromise is regarded as a sign of weakness and a lack of principles. However, if conflict is understood as existing between different perspectives that are both reasonable to some extent or between different emphases that are both good to some extent, then the hostile attitude to each other can be minimized and adjusting one's position can be regarded as an achievement rather than a frustration.

When two groups of people are in conflict and both sides regard themselves as right, it is rarely the case that one side is completely right and the other side is completely wrong. Very often, both sides have their justifications to some extent. If people regard themselves as having great grievances, then they are quite prepared to do harm to their enemy, even if that would mean further harm to themselves.

From the Confucian perspective, true peace is attained not by imposing an ideal order on the world, but by giving enough room and support to everyone, such that everyone has a part to play and contribute. As it is said in *The Book of Changes*, 'Each follows the right path of his true nature and mandate. The whole is then in grand harmony. This is conducive to benefit and perpetuation' (Legge, The I Ching: 213). There is nothing in the world that is essentially bad that has to be eradicated.

Su Shi (1037–1101) has made a perceptive observation about *The Book of Changes*. The hexagrams *dazhuang* and *guai* depict situations in which small men have a difficult time and gentlemen thrive and prosper.[10] The hexagram *tai* (泰 peaceful or healthy) depicts the situation of mutual and sincere communication whereas the hexagram *wuwang* (无妄 flawless) depicts a flawless world. But the Confucian sages who composed *The Book of Changes* approved the situation of *tai* much more than the situations of *dazhuang* and *guai*, and warned against the situation of *wuwang*. Su Shi (2005: 24, my translation) explains:

> The situation of *tai* is not as good as *dazhuang* and *guai*. In those situations the small men increasingly degenerate and the gentlemen increasingly multiply. However, the sages feel most comfortable in the situation of *tai*. This is because small men cannot be completely eliminated. Insisting to eradicate them such that they have nowhere to go will cause a lot of fighting.

The world of *wuwang* in modern terminology is the utopia. It is the ideal world where goods are realized and people all behave in the right way.

> In the world of *wuwang*, the whole world follows the right path. … In a non-ideal world, those who do not walk in the right path may have their own reasons. But in the flawless world, those who follow the right path are secure, but those who do not will have danger. (Su 2005: 46)

10 The Confucian classic *The Book of Changes* studies the logic of human affairs. The 64 hexagrams stand for 64 kinds of situation and the six lines of each hexagram stand for stages of development of a situation. The book makes observation of the potential problems and gives advice on good practices in the various situations.

Su Shi criticizes the attempt to build a flawless world and explains why such a perfectionist attempt is dangerous. In explaining why *The Book of Changes* says that 'the medicine of *wuwang* cannot be tried', Su Shi (2005: 46–7) writes:

> Those who are good in ruling the world do not seek for exhaustiveness. Seeking for exhaustiveness will lead to complete loss. *Wuwang* [flawless] means driving everyone to walk on the right path. With regard to rightness, the gentleman only seeks for the preservation of the big part. There is a way to preserve the big part, and that is not to be precise with the small part. … When there is illness in the world of *wuwang*, it is an overall upright world with minor evils. The tolerance of minor evils is necessary for the preservation of the overall uprightness. How can medicine be used? The use of *wuwang* as medicine is to poison the world. So it is said, 'the medicine of *wuwang* cannot be tried'.

It is said in *Zhongyong* (ch. 30, my translation): 'The myriad things can be nurtured without harming one another. The different ways can be followed in parallel without interfering with one another'. But the basic idea here is different from that of liberalism. Not interfering and not doing harm to others is only a 'minor virtue' and the 'major virtue' has to go beyond that. The same passage in *Zhongyong* goes on to say, 'The minor virtue is able to sustain things like a stream. The major virtue is able to make things flourish and transform'. True harmony therefore has two levels: the lower level is peaceful co-existence and the higher level is mutual enrichment and cross-fertilization. The latter is a higher ideal, but the former is a pre-condition. If it is an externally imposed or coercive 'enrichment', then it cannot be regarded as a major virtue, as it does not even meet the requirement of a minor virtue.

From the Confucian perspective, true peace is not externally or coercively imposed, but is to be generally pursued and welcomed. According to Mencius (371–268 BC), the proof that Tang's war against the tyrant Jie[11] was justified was that his army was welcomed by the people wherever they went: 'when he marched on the east, the western barbarians complained, and when he marched on the south, the northern barbarians complained. They all said, "Why does he not come to us first?" The people longed for his coming as they longed for a *rainbow* in time of severe drought' (Mencius 1B: 11), Confucius also emphasizes that the so-called good has to be appreciated and accepted by the people concerned: 'when distant subjects are unsubmissive one cultivates one's moral quality in order to attract them, and once they have come one makes them content' (*The Analects* 16: 1).

As true peace cannot be imposed and has to be generally recognized and accepted, it cannot be attained without taking the perspectives and values of the concerned parties into consideration. The key to resolve disputes, ethically and not just pragmatically, is to give due recognition to both sides, to the extent that the claim is legitimate or reasonable. The Confucian way of resolving conflict

11 Tang was the founder of the Shang dynasty (1751–1112 BC) and Jie was the last king of the Hsia dynasty (2183–1752 BC).

is sometimes taken as pragmatic in nature, seeking not the most 'reasonable' solution but a solution that is *acceptable* to both sides. Francis L.K. Hsü (1972: 367–8), for example, writes that in China an arbitrator 'does not uphold one party against another or insist that one is completely right and the other wholly wrong. His mission is to smooth ruffled feelings by having each disputant sacrifice a little, whether the sacrifice involves principles or not' (also see Creel 1987). My interpretation of Confucianism is very different from that approach. For the mediator, the question is not what is the due for each side, but how to arrive at a solution acceptable to both sides. This is very different from Confucian sage-king Shun's approach, which will be described below.

Of course, one side may be more reasonable than another, and it is sometimes justified to approve most of the claims on one side and reject most of the claims on another side. But even the side which is relatively unreasonable may still have some reasonable claims and a dispute cannot be resolved satisfactorily if the reasonable part of a contesting side is not given due recognition. True peace cannot be attained by doing injustice to one of the parties involved and people cannot live in peace if they believe that they have been victimized. On the other hand, if the justifiable part of one's claim is acknowledged, then one has lost one's ground to complain and it takes a very unreasonable person to insist to have a fight.

Another difference between the Confucian approach and the arbitration approach is that the latter emphasizes impartiality and neutrality. Value plurality is not the same as value neutrality. The Confucian approach is better described as *all-partiality* than *impartiality*. To arrive at an unbiased stance, it is not necessary to detach from all the competing values as far as possible. It is instead necessary to appreciate, appropriate, apprehend and acknowledge all the relevant (opposing) values involved.

The next step in the Confucian recipe to resolve conflict is to work out a *three* between the conflicting *two*. It is noted that if we simply take side with one of the two conflicting views, then the conflict will only escalate, but if we are able to derive an 'in-between' view from the two conflicting views, then the conflict can be resolved. This point is made in a number of Confucian texts, but is perhaps most clearly made in the ancient text the *Yi Zhoushu* (163, my translation) which is associated with *The Book of Documents* and has the status of a deuterocanonical text: 'If there is an *in-between*, it is called *three*. If there is no *in-between*, it is called *two*. *Two* struggles with each other, and results in weakness. *Three* constitutes harmony, and results in strength'.

Here 'two' refers to two opposite claims and *three* is not a claim different from the *two* that competes with the *two*, but a synthesis of the *two*. This *three* is obtained not by denying the *two*, which conflict with each other, but by affirming the *two* at the same time. It is not an unconditional affirmation of the conflicting *two*, but rather a creative synthesis of the *two*. If the *three* is not obtained by affirming the *two*, then it will compete with the *two* and true peace cannot be achieved. The *three* is constituted by the *two* – this is why the *three* is also called 'in-between'. Only when there is a *three* that is an *in-between* constituted by the *two* can the dispute be resolved and true peace be achieved. Hence it is said, if we know how to identify an *in-between*, then there is a *three,* otherwise there are only *two*. The *two* compete and fight with each other. This will lead to weakness. Here two ways of dealing with conflict are identified: 1. to exclude one by another is called struggle and leads to degeneration; 2. to accommodate both is called harmony and leads to prosperity.

The way of finding an *in-between* (*zhong* 中) has long been regarded as the secret to good governance handed down by the sage-kings from one generation to another. In the opening chapter to the last book of *The Analects* (20: 1), the legendary sage-king Yao is quoted to have said the following to his successor Shun:

> Oh! Shun,
> The succession, ordained by Heaven, has fallen on thy person.
> Holdst thou truly to the *in-between* (*zhong*).
> If the Empire should be reduced to dire straits
> The honours bestowed on thee by Heaven will be terminated forever.

It is said that the sage-king Shun also said the same thing to his successor, the sage-king Yu. The Neo-Confucian philosophers of the Song dynasty mistook this concept of *zhong* or *in-between* as a pure inner state. It was thought that if we have a pure inner state we would be able to make the right judgement. But in classical Confucianism, the right judgement is made not by projecting from the inside on the basis of a pure inner state, but by carefully inspecting the perspectives held by different parties. In *Zhongyong* (ch. 6, my translation), the sage-king Shun is said to arrive at his judgement in the following ways:

> Confucius said, 'Great indeed is the wisdom of Shun! Shun likes to ask (the views of all kinds of people) and to investigate the words of those who are close to him. He omits the bad and propagates the good. He holds fast the two ends (*duan*) and uses the *zhong* (the *in-between*) for the people. This is what makes him Shun!'

Shun does not have a preconceived solution before his investigation. He is willing to listen to diverse views, but he will also examine the views expressed to him. For every view he encounters, he is able to separate the justified from the unjustified part. He omits the unjustified part and combines the justified parts from different sources. He identifies the *in-between* on the basis of the 'two ends'. It should be noted that the 'two ends' are themselves one-sided. But the appropriate judgement is made by 'holding fast' to the two opposite ends at the same time. The *three*, which can resolve the conflict, is not constituted by denying the one-sided *two*, but by giving both of them due recognition and appropriate affirmation at the same time.

In summary, this Confucian recipe to resolve conflicts consists of six steps: 1. be fond of asking questions (*haowen* 好問): consult opinions from different perspectives; 2. be fond of careful investigation (*haocha* 好察): examine the views expressed; 3. omit what is unworthy (*yine* 隱惡): omit the unjustified part; 4. propagate what is worthy (*yangshan* 揚善): elaborate the justified part; [12] 5. hold firmly to all that is worthwhile (*zhiliang* 執兩): combine the justified parts from two opposing ends; and 6. locate the right balance and apply it (*yongzong* 用中): identify the right balance on the basis of the opposing ends.

The Confucian recipe for conflict resolution consists of the insight of locating human values through perspectives – the important human values that are at stake have to be identified by examining the perspectives people hold. As it is difficult for one person or one side alone to see the whole picture, and it is unlikely that a person or a group is not able to see at least part of the picture, so it is helpful to consult different parties concerned and learn from them, especially those who believe that they have a justified cause to fight. As a result, appropriating different perspectives and giving them due recognition are the crucial steps in getting at a more comprehensive and adequate understanding, which is necessary for arriving at a reasonable and acceptable solution. However, the Confucian approach does not see value in the subjective perspectives as such, but in the objective value that may be contained in the different perspectives.[13] The reason for valuing different perspectives is not that there is no objective truth, but that the truth is complicated and cannot be adequately grasped by a single perspective.[14]

Confucianism holds a moderate view about the objectivity and knowability of human values. On the one hand, we cannot assume that we have full knowledge of human values; on the other hand, we cannot pretend that we can start from the ground of pure neutrality, not making any value assumptions. There are some basic human values, which are commonly recognized and not really controversial. Three common objectives are repeatedly mentioned in the Confucian literature, namely, survival, flourishing and education. They are all related to the realization of human nature – to enable people to become truly human.[15] The common and uncontroversial values can serve as the basis for further quests and negotiations. Beyond the basics, however, the discussion and final conclusion has to be left open. People have something to learn from one another in understanding other people's perspectives.

---

12 This Confucian scheme is not value neutral. It assumes that there are some basic human values, such that there are some things that are really worthy and some less worthy. For the Confucians, the difference between holding and not holding such basic values is the difference with the preservation and the destruction of civilization.

13 The Confucian approach is quite unlike the 'politics of recognition' advocated by contemporary philosophers. The 'politics of recognition' aims at recognizing and including as many people as possible, as 'each of our voices has something unique to say' (Taylor 1992: 30).

14 As a result, the importance of scrutinizing and screening opinions is emphasized. See *The Analects* 15: 28, 13: 24.

15 See *The Analects* 13: 9, where the three objectives are described as 'to multiply', 'to enrich' and 'to educate' the people; and *Mencius* 3A3, where the three objectives are described as 'to clear the threats', 'to improve people's livelihood' and 'to develop culture'. The basic idea is to treat humans as humans or to help people to become fully human.

Conclusion

Conflict resolution cannot be separated from the pursuit of justice. There can be no real peace without justice. But the pursuit of justice does not mean singling out one side as just and denouncing the other side as unjust. It means rather giving due recognition to both sides. The challenge is bigger than distinguishing between right and wrong, as it also involves arbitrating among different goods or conflicting values that are represented by different perspectives. Justice is not readily appropriated by one side of the conflict. So in order to do full justice, it is necessary to learn from the perspectives of the opposing sides and make use of them judiciously. The recognition that it is impossible for anyone to monopolize values or privatize the right perspective constitutes the cornerstone of the Confucian approach to resolving conflicts and achieving peace.

Bibliography

The Analects 1992. Translated by D.C. Lau. Hong Kong: Chinese University Press.

Aristotle 1998. *The Nicomachean Ethics*, Translated by W.D. Ross. Oxford: Oxford University Press.

Bell, D.A. 2008a. Just war and Confucianism: implications for the contemporary world, in *Confucian Political Ethics*, edited by D.A. Bell. Princeton: Princeton University Press, 226–56.

Bell, D.A. 2008b. War, peace and China's soft power, in D.A. Bell, *China's New Confucianism*. Princeton: Princeton University Press, 19–37.

The book of filial piety, 1879. In *The Sacred Books of the East*, vol. 3, edited by F. Max Müller. Translated by J. Legge. Oxford: Clarendon Press, 449–88.

The Book of Rites [*Li Chi*], 1885. 2 vols. Translated by J. Legge. Oxford: Oxford University Press.

Bodde, D. 1953. Harmony and conflict in Chinese philosophy, in *Studies in Chinese Thought*, edited by A.F. Wright. Chicago: The University of Chicago Press, 19–80.

Chan, W. 1963. *A Source Book in Chinese Philosophy*. Princeton, NJ: Princeton University Press.

Creel, H.G. 1987. The role of compromise in Chinese culture, in *Chinese Ideas about Nature and Society: Studies in Honour of Derk Bodde*, edited by C. Le Blanc and S. Blader. Hong Kong: Hong Kong University Press, 133–51.

Fan, R. 1999. *Confucian Bioethics*. Dordrecht, The Netherlands: Springer.

Fan, R. 2010. *Constructionist Confucianism*. Dordrecht, The Netherlands: Springer.

Fu, Z. 1993. *Autocratic Tradition and Chinese Politics*. Cambridge: Cambridge University Press.

Goldin, P.R. 2011. *Confucianism*. Durham: Acumen Publishing.

Gongyang Zhuan vols. 20–21 of *Shisanjing zhushu*, 2000. Beijing: Peking University Press.

Hsü, F.L.K. 1972. *Americans and Chinese: Two Ways of Life*. New York: Doubleday Natural History Press.

The I Ching: The Book of Changes 1963. Translated by J. Legge. New York: Dover Publications.

James, W. 1987. The moral equivalent to war, in *Philosophical Perspectives on Peace*, edited by H.P. Kainz. Athens, OH: Ohio University Press, 213–25.

Kanaya, O. 1996. The mean in original Confucianism, in *Chinese Language, Thought, and Culture*, edited by P.J. Ivanhoe. Chicago: Open Court, 83–93.

Kwok, D.W.Y. 1993. *Ho* and *t'ung* in Chinese intellectual history, in *Cosmology, Ontology, and Human Efficacy: Essays in Chinese Thought*, edited by R.J. Smith and D.W.Y. Kwok. Honolulu: University of Hawaii Press, 1–9.

Lao Tzu: Tao Te Ching 1963. Translated by D.C. Lau. Harmondsworth: Penguin Books.

Lloyd, G.E.R. 1996. *Adversaries and Authorities: Investigations into Ancient Greek and Chinese Science*. Cambridge: Cambridge University Press.

Mencius 1984. Translated by D.C. Lau. Hong Kong: The Chinese University Press.

Merzger, T.A. 1990. Continuities between modern and pre-modern China: some neglected methodological and substantial issues, in *Ideas Across Cultures: Essays on Chinese Thought in Honor of Benjamin I. Schwartz*, edited by P.A. Cohen and M. Goldman. Cambridge, MA: Council on East Asia Studies, Harvard University, 263–92.

Nakamura, H. 1968. *Ways of Thinking of Eastern People*. Honolulu: University of Hawai'i Press.

Needham, J. 1956. *Science and Civilization in China*, vol. 2. Cambridge: Cambridge University Press.

Ni, L. 2008. The implications of ancient military culture for world peace, in *Confucian Political Ethics*, edited by D.A. Bell. Princeton: Princeton University Press, 201–25.

Nylan, M. 2001. *The Five "Confucian" Classics*. New Haven: Yale University Press.

Rosemont, H. Jr. and Ames, R.T. 2009. *The Chinese Classic of Family Reverence: A Philosophical Translation of Xiaojing*. Honolulu: University of Hawai'i Press.

Ross, W.D. 1930. *The Right and the Good*. Oxford: Oxford University Press.

Schwartz, B.I. 1985. *The World of Thought in Ancient China*. Cambridge, MA: Harvard University Press.

Su, S. 2005. *Dongpo Yizhuan*. Chang Chun: Jilin Chuban Jituan.

Taylor, C. 1992. The politics of recognition, in *Multiculturalism and 'The Politics of Recognition': An Essay*, edited by Amy Gutmann. Princeton, NJ: Princeton University Press, 25–73.

Wang, G. 1973. *Yin Zhou zhidu lun*, in G. Wang, *Guantang jilin*. Hong Kong: Zhonghua Book Co., 451–80.

Xunzi 1999. Translated by J. Knoblock. Hunan: Hunan People's Publishing House.

Yi zhoushu, 1996. In *Yi Zhoushu Jiaobu Zhushi.* Xian: Xibei Daxue Chubanshe.

Yu, J. 2007. *The Ethics of Confucius and Aristotle: Mirrors of Virtue.* London: Routledge.

Yu, K. 2010a. The Confucian conception of harmony, in *Governance for Harmony in Asia and Beyond*, edited by J. Tao et al. London: Routledge, 15–36.

Yu, K. 2010b. Confucian views on war as seen in the *Spring and Autumn Annals. Dao: A Journal in Comparative Philosophy.* Springer Netherlands, 9(1), 97–111.

Yu, K. 2010c. The handling of multiple ethical values in Confucianism, in *Taking Confucian Ethics Seriously: Contemporary Theories and Applications*, edited by K. Yu, J. Tao and P.J. Ivanhoe. Albany, NY: State University of New York Press, 27–51.

Yu, K. and Tao, J. 2012. Confucianism, in *Encyclopedia of Applied Ethics*. 2nd Edition, edited by R. Chadwick. San Diego: Academic Press, 578–86.

Zhongyong, 1971. In *Confucian Analects, The Great Learning and the Doctrine of the Mean.* Translated by J. Legge. New York: Dover Publications, 382–434.

Zhongyong, 2012. In *Daxue and Zhongyong*. Translated by I. Johnson and P. Wang. Hong Kong: The Chinese University Press, 181–397.

Zuo zhuan, 1960. In *The Chinese Classics*, vol. 5. Translated by J. Legge. Hong Kong: Hong Kong University Press.

Chapter 5

A Historical Reflection on Peace and Public Philosophy in Japanese Thought: Prince Shotoku, Ito Jinsai and Yokoi Shonan

Shin Chiba

Despite the Japanese government's repeated urge for the creation of an 'East Asian community', East Asia remains one of the few regions in the world that is shaped by the tensions and antagonisms associated with a cold war. There are, to be sure, many causes that have brought about this troublesome situation. One of the historical causes for the lingering tension in this region is the inadequate engagement of post-war Japanese governments with their responsibility towards and compensation for the victims of Japanese military conduct during the Asia–Pacific War (1931–1945). As long as these historical issues remain unresolved, the basic dissatisfaction of the victimized nations in East Asia and the Pacific region vis-à-vis the Japanese government's official recognition of its war responsibilities cannot dissipate. Thus the Japanese government's slogan of an 'East Asian community' sounds hypocritical and empty (Chiba 2008: 181–5).

But, at the same time, one can observe a number of efforts in the post-war era that have helped the region of East Asia become more peaceable and reconciliatory. Especially in the last two or three decades, the peoples of East Asia have been interacting with one another through many diverse efforts and exchanges at the level of civil society both culturally and economically. What has emerged from these interactions is a shared sense and awareness that the peoples of East Asia have been living in a similar spiritual and cultural climate long cultivated by such religions and moral codes as Confucianism, Buddhism, Daoism and various nature religions. In this connection it is important to note that the originally Confucian and later Buddhist idea of *wa* (和 *he*: peace or harmony), the Confucian ideas of *jin* (仁 *ren*: benevolence) and *jo* (恕 *shu*: commiseration or compassion) and the Buddhist idea of *jihi* (慈悲 *cibei*: mercy or compassion) are commonly shared ideas of peace and solidarity in East Asian societies. The Japanese term *heiwa* (平和) and the Chinese term *heping* (和平) – both meaning peace – etymologically originated from the term *wa*.

This Confucian–Buddhist ethos of harmony, sympathy and mutual help was manifest during the 11 March 2011 East Japan Disaster when the region was devastated by a great earthquake, tsunami and nuclear contamination. A number of countries all over the world sent supplies and relief funds to the victims in the region of East Japan. Particularly noteworthy, however, was the extent of the rescue endeavours and the amount of supplies and relief funds incessantly sent to Japan by Taiwan, South Korea and China. The rescue endeavours implemented by these neighbouring countries were impressive in their speed, size and duration. The good will and immediate assistance from the international community in general and East Asian nations in particular shall long remain etched in the memories of the Japanese. One may rightly understand that these acts displayed the ethos of benevolence and compassion found in the common cultural heritage of East Asia. Also impressive was the quiet courage, composure and patience, as well as the spirit of compassion and mutual help expressed by the victims in the North-East region of Japan to one another. I think the Confucian–Buddhist ethos of compassion and mutual help that is deeply crystallized in the psyche of East Asians suddenly revealed itself for a brief period during this great crisis.

What does *wa* mean precisely? What does a 'harmonious society' concretely entail? These are sensitive, controversial and crucial questions. Such concepts as *wa*, *jin* and *jo* constitute key values that are shared among the religio-ethical traditions of East Asia. These ideas play an important role not only in making conflict resolution and reconciliation possible in the present, but also in realizing peace in this region in the future. Behind the current reality of the tension and antagonism overshadowing East Asia there exists a potent and shared discourse of peace and harmony in this region. The purpose of this chapter is to trace historically this discourse of peace and harmony in the Japanese intellectual tradition.

Prince Shotoku and the Seventeen-Article Constitution

First, I would like to take up the ideas on *wa* as developed and elaborated by Prince Shotoku (574–622AD). Prince Shotoku, who lived in the country of Yamato (centred in today's Nara Prefecture) in the Asuka period, was a brilliant sage-leader with unusual vision. He has been legendarily called the 'Bodhisattva Prince' (菩薩大使 Buddhist saintly prince). The Asuka period was characterized by a series of severe conflicts between the two major warring political groups: the Soga and Mononobe clans. Prince Shotoku was appointed as the regent of Empress Suiko in 593AD, a year after she had been newly installed as the first woman monarch. He was considered the Empress's wise, courageous and gifted nephew.

The Twelve Cap and Rank System

Prince Shotoku's achievements included the establishment of the Twelve Cap and Rank System (603AD) and the Seventeen-Article Constitution (604AD). Both achievements were closely and organically connected. The former was the institutional embodiment of the latter's public philosophy of *wa*. And the public philosophy of *wa* expressed in the Seventeen-Article Constitution was sustained by courtesy (礼 *rei*) and trustworthiness (信 *shin*). Together they formed the two pillars of Prince Shotoku's political reform.

The turn of the sixth and seventh centuries was a time of transition when the country of Yamato was gradually emerging as an imperial and centralized, bureaucratic polity from a loosely united confederation of warring clans. The Twelve Cap and Rank System was an institutional reform necessary for the centralization of power under the imperial system. First, it served as the institutional framework in which the political power of the chief aristocrats and clans was transferred to the emperor. Second, it enabled the wide recruitment irrespective of birth and social belonging of a number of talents in various fields of social life such as politics, diplomacy, military, religion, culture, art and architecture, education, agriculture and industry, thus helping to consolidate political power at the centre.

The Twelve Cap and Rank System was the embodiment of the five Confucian virtues of benevolence (*jin*), right or justice (*gi*), courtesy (*rei*), knowledge (*chi*) and trustworthiness (*shin*). Prince Shotoku added *wa* (peace and harmony) to these five Confucian virtues as a congregating or comprehensive virtue; under the presiding virtue of *wa* all these five virtues were integrated. He then divided each of these six virtues into upper and lower levels to make 12 ranks. This Twelve Cap and Rank System with its public philosophy of *wa* was then promulgated in his Seventeen-Article Constitution.

The Seventeen-Article Constitution and the Public Philosophy of Wa

The Seventeen-Article Constitution should not be understood as a legal document despite its appellation: constitution. It was rather a series of socio-ethical precepts that were intended as governing principles for the collective life of the polity. It was addressed to the members of the imperial court, the leaders of the ruling clans, the aristocrats, the public officials and the subjects. Thus it expressed Prince Shotoku's public philosophy for the ideal state in terms of peace and harmony. Furthermore this peace manifesto was promulgated against the warring milieus of the times. In those years political disturbances followed one after another. The perpetual feuds between the Soga and Mononobe clans were followed by the murder of Prince Ananobe, the fall of the Mononobe clan and the assassination of Emperor Sushun (Chiba 2008: 186).

Thus the socio-political virtue of *wa* was the *leitmotif* of the Constitution and as such was ranked the highest presiding value in the document. Article One of the Constitution starts by proclaiming: 'Let peace (harmony) be respected among you' (de Bary et al. 2001: 51).[1] This idea of *wa* is derived from *The Analects* (論語) and *The Book of Rites* (礼記) which are among the so-called Four Books and Five Classics of Confucianism. *Wa* can be said to constitute the overarching idea of the Constitution. This virtue is, as was already explained, the presiding

1 Here I have slightly altered the translation. This practice is generally maintained throughout this chapter.

and integral virtue in which the aforementioned five Confucian virtues are orderly integrated. But *wa* has special attachment to the virtue of courtesy or *rei*. *Rei* means, amongst other things, the proper ordering of both vertical and horizontal human relationships within a community or an organization. When the officials of higher ranks and the subjects of lower ranks co-operate with one another in the spirit of *wa* and *rei*, that is, courtesy, then 'the governance of the state proceeds of itself' (de Bary et al. 2001: 52, also see Hanayama 1982: 27–9). In the teaching of Article Thirteen, the great combination of *wa* and courtesy is cemented by trustworthiness (*shin*):

> Let all persons entrusted with office attend equally to their functions. Owing to their illness or to their being sent on missions, their work may sometimes be neglected. But whenever they become able to attend to business, let them be as accommodating as if their work had cognizance of it from before and not hinder public affairs on the score of their not having had to do with them. (de Bary et al. 2001: 53)

A number of scholars have long examined and argued about the basic structure of the Constitution. According to Takeshi Umehara (1993: 335–7), who follows and elaborates upon Taro Sakamoto's interpretation, Articles One to Three represent the social virtue of *wa*. In the thought of Prince Shotoku, *wa* is the social expression of the primary Confucian virtue of benevolence (*jin*) and also incorporates the basic Buddhist virtue of mercy or compassion (*jihi*). Articles Four to Eight express the virtue of courtesy (*rei*). For instance, Article Four starts by insisting: 'The Ministers and officials should make proper behavior their leading principle. … If the superiors do not behave properly, the inferiors are disorderly; if inferiors are wanting in proper behavior, there must essentially be offenses' (de Bary et al. 2001: 51–2).

Moreover, according to Umehara, Articles Nine to Eleven represent the virtue of trustworthiness (*shin*). I have already indicated the importance of trustworthiness (*shin*) as the cementing virtue for *wa* and courtesy (*rei*). Trustworthiness further makes the virtue of right or justice (*gi*) possible. So Article Nine reads:

> Trustworthiness is the foundation of right. In everything let there be trustworthiness. … If the lord and the vassal trust one another, what is there which cannot be accomplished? If the lord and the vassal do not trust one another, everything without exception ends in failure. (de Bary et al. 2001: 52–3)

Umehara (1993: 337–8) further maintains that Articles Twelve to Fourteen manifest the virtue of right or justice (*gi*). But, *pace* Sakamoto and Umehara, I would like to propose minor revisions to their thesis by maintaining that it is more appropriate and persuasive to subsume the entire section from Articles Nine to Fourteen under the combination of the two virtues of trustworthiness (*shin*) and justice (*gi*). For both virtues are put forth inseparably in these Articles as combined and interpenetrated virtues.

Finally, Articles Fifteen to Seventeen proclaim the virtue of knowledge (*chi*). Article Seventeen is particularly important, as it points to the possibility of what we today call 'deliberative democracy' or 'deliberative politics'. It reads: 'Matters should not be decided by one person alone. They should be discussed with many others' (de Bary et al. 2001: 53, also see Chiba 2011: 60–61). There is no doubt that this order of *wa* (peace or harmony) followed by benevolence (*jin*), courtesy (*rei*), trustworthiness (*shin*), right or justice (*gi*) and knowledge (*chi*) shows a precise correspondence to the reformulated order of the five Confucian virtues as institutionally expressed in the Twelve Cap and Rank System.

The Seventeen-Article Constitution reveals a combination of Confucian and Buddhist ideas. As I have suggested, the Constitution as a whole and Article One to Three in particular clearly express the social virtue of *wa*. While *wa* is originally a Confucian concept and constituted by the Confucian idea of benevolence (*jin*), it is also informed by the Buddhist idea of mercy or compassion (*jihi*). For instance, Article Two states that 'the Three Treasures', that is, 'the Buddha, the Law and the Priesthood' should be given primary respect. For they are 'the final refuge of all beings and the supreme objects of reverence in all countries' (de Bary et al. 2001: 51). Article One also contains the following Buddhist insights: 'All men are inclined to partisanship and few are truly discerning. Hence there are some who disobey their lords and fathers or who maintain feuds with the neighbouring villages' (de Bary et al. 2001: 51). There exists – overtly or covertly – in human nature an inherent inclination towards perceptual blindness and partisanship, karma and egoism. Not only that, Prince Shotoku was reported to utter the following words at his death so as to express the vanity of this world: 'The world is all empty, false and illusory' (世間虚仮). These insights into life are expressive of a deep-seated Buddhist perception (Tamura 1964: 139–40).

Moreover, Article Ten contains a Buddhist influenced caution against anger:

> Let us cease from wrath, and refrain from angry looks. Nor let us be resentful when others differ from us. For all men have hearts, and each heart has its own leanings. Their right is our wrong, our right is their wrong. We are not unquestionably sages, nor are they unquestionably fools. Both of us are simply ordinary men. … For we are all, one with another, wise and foolish, like a ring which has no end. (de Bary et al. 2001: 53, also see Spae 1967: 18)

Prince Shotoku's philosophy of *wa* is based on his observation that the spirit of peace and harmony begets and nurtures a mutually conciliatory human attitude and concord in the discussion of all matters (de Bary et al. 2001: 51). Article Sixteen further contains a well-known passage advocating a Buddhist influenced governance of benevolence:

> Let the people be employed at seasonable times. This is an ancient and excellent rule. Let them be employed, therefore, in the winter months, when they are at leisure. But from Spring to Autumn, when they are engaged in agriculture or

> with the mulberry trees, the people should not be so employed. For if they do not attend to agriculture, what will they have to eat? If they do not attend to the mulberry trees, what will they do for clothing? (de Bary et al. 2001: 54)

As we shall see later, Ito Jinsai and Yokoi Shonan also develop a politics of benevolence. But it is distinctly Confucian in their cases. In the case of Prince Shotoku this politics of benevolence may come more substantially from his ideal of 'the Way of the Bodhisattva' (菩薩道).

Prince Shotoku's idea of *wa* does not entail a singular, homogeneous and unified peace. It is rather a way of making and maintaining peace with heterogeneous others and even with one's enemies. In the history of Japanese thought, *wa* (和) has often been misunderstood and misused to denote sameness or homogeneity (*do* 同). For example, a homogeneous idea of peace was employed by the ruling oligarchy of imperial Japan as the ideological backdrop for its aggressive war (1931–1945) against other Asia–Pacific countries. Contrary to this, Prince Shotoku's idea of *wa* means an attitude that extends to different and heterogeneous groups – and even to one's adversaries and enemies. It means having an attitude of reconciliation with a heart of mercy, benevolence and forgiveness. *Wa*'s normativity consists in its conceptual motivation and aspiration for overcoming group egoism and self-centredness. In this respect it is important to remember that Prince Shotoku's idea of *wa* was partly derived from the following Confucian idea: 'Gentle person (君子) has peace with others but does not become the same' (和而不同) (*The Analects* 13.23, Chan 1963: 41, also see Chiba 2008: 188; 2011: 60–61).

Thus Prince Shotoku's understanding of *wa* as peace and harmony is constituted of heterogeneous rather than homogeneous elements. It is consonant not merely with Confucius' teaching in *The Analects* but also with the basic teachings in other Chinese classics. Kam-por Yu (2010a) highlights two passages from ancient Chinese books which illustrate the unmistakable difference between harmony and homogeneity. One passage comes from the history book *The Guoyu* (國語) and it includes an important conversation about the reason for the decline of the Zhou dynasty, which took place between Shi Bo (史伯) and Duke Huan of Zheng (鄭桓公) in a year ca.74BC. Shi Bo said:

> Now the king rejects uprightness and openness, and pursues flattery and concealment … He deserts harmony (*he* 和) and prefers homogeneity (*tong* 同). Harmony gives rise to new things. Homogeneity will lead to stagnation. To balance one thing by another is called harmony. This is how to flourish, endure and bring things together. (Cited in Yu 2010: 16)[2]

---

2 Yu (2010: 16) continues to explain: 'Shi Bo distinguishes between two kinds of agreement: harmonious agreement and dogmatic agreement. Harmonious agreement is based on recognizing the values others have that are different from one's own. Dogmatic agreement is based on accepting others who have values that are the same as one's own'.

The second illustrative passage comes from a conversation that took place in 525BC between the ruler of the state of Qi (齊) and his Prime Minister Yanzi (晏子). This interesting conversation was recorded in *The Zuozhuan* (左伝):

> The duke said, 'Only Ju is in harmony (*he* 和) with me'. Yanzi replied, 'Ju is in complete agreement (*tong* 同) with you. How can he be in harmony with you?' The duke said, 'Are harmony and complete agreement different?' Yanzi replied, 'Different indeed! Harmony is like making soup. Water, fire, vinegar, minced meat, salt, and plum are used to cook the fish and meat. These are heated using firewood and brought into harmony by the chef, who used the different flavors to achieve a balance, providing what is deficient and releasing what is excessive. The gentle person eats the soup, and it will calm and settle his mind. The relation between a ruler and his minister is the same. … Music is like cooking … What Ju is doing is nothing like this. What you find unacceptable, Ju also says to be unacceptable. This is like adding more water to water. Who can eat that kind of food? It is like the monotonic sound made by musical instruments – who can listen to that kind of music? This is why complete agreement is unacceptable'. (Cited in Yu 2010: 17)

These two stories from ancient Chinese texts illustrate that the notion of *wa* (harmony and peace) should not be confused with the notion of *do* (sameness or homogeneity). Here there is an interesting convergence between Prince Shotoku's public philosophy of *wa* and the ancient Confucian teaching of harmony and peace.

Ito Jinsai and His Jin (Benevolence)-Based Peace Thought

Ito Jinsai[3] (1627–1705) was a unique Confucian thinker and a public philosopher in the early Tokugawa era of Japan. His uniqueness can be seen not merely in his social belonging to the merchant class. It also consists in his clear conversion to the classical Confucianism of Confucius and Mencius from his earlier upbringing as a Neo-Confucian scholar educated in the Song tradition of Zhu Xi (Chu Hsi) (de Bary et al. 2005: 177–8).[4] He called his new research method for the study of classical Confucian texts *kogigaku* (studies of ancient meanings 古義学) and he was a uniquely gifted and independent interpreter of classical Confucianism. He enlivened such classical texts as *The Analects* and *Mencius* by providing moral

3 For Japanese historical figures, I adopt the Japanese convention: surname precedes the given name. In this chapter I refer to Japanese thinkers by their given name, which is conventional in Japanese intellectual history.

4 Jinsai's criticism of the Song tradition of Zhu Xi was quite rigorous. His main objection was that Buddhist as well as Taoist ideas had been creeping into the Song scholars' interpretations of Confucius and Mencius. See Yoshikawa 1983: 9–12.

education and encouragement in an accessible manner to the people who lived in the early-Tokugawa period in Japan.[5]

Jinsai and His Hermeneutics of Retrieval

Perhaps the greatest contribution Jinsai made to the later development of Confucian thought in Japan resides in his hermeneutics of retrieval in which he deliberately and practically redeemed the classical Confucian ideas of benevolence (*jin*) and commiseration (*jo*) out of their neglect and oblivion. His *magnum opus* was entitled *Gomo Jigi* (*The Meaning of Terms in* The Analects *and* Mencius).

Jinsai certainly found the idea of commiseration or *jo* to have originated in the teachings of Confucius and Mencius. But he enriched this idea in such a stimulating manner that a moral philosophy of sympathy resulted from it. *Jo* can be rightly regarded as encapsulating 'the Confucian Golden Rule': 'Do not do to others what you do not want others to do unto you'.[6]

The idea of *jo* received a fuller and more extended treatment and reflection in *Mencius*. Mencius thinks that the ethos and feeling of benevolence (*jin*) is inherent in every human being. At a time of crisis or when an extraordinary situation arises, the ethos of benevolence prompts people to act in the interests of others by triggering and activating the bodily and practical feeling of commiseration, that is, *jo*. The following passage is widely known to readers of the Chinese classics:

> Now, when men suddenly see a child about to fall into a well, they all have a feeling of alarm and distress, not to gain friendship with the child's parents, nor to seek the praise of their neighbors and friends, nor because they dislike the reputation [of having a lack of benevolence if they did not rescue the child]. From such a case, we see that a man without the feeling of commiseration is not a man ... (Chan 1963: 65)

According to Mencius, human beings innately possess 'sprouts of virtues' or inclinational virtues such as benevolence (*jin*), justice (*gi*), courtesy (*rei*) and knowledge (*chi*). These sprouts of virtue prompt people to perform good and moral conduct (Chan 1963: 65). For instance, benevolence – which works practically and energetically as commiseration (*jo*) – prompts human beings, that is, their

---

5 Jinsai wrote: 'There is no special lineage to my scholarship. To understand Confucius and Mencius in the light of the original texts themselves. This is my only principle' (Ito 1970a: 246 [bk 3. ch. 48]. See Yoshikawa 1983: 11).

6 The well-known passage on *jo* (commiseration) appears in *The Analects* as follows: 'Zigong asked, "Is there one word that one can act upon throughout the course of one's life? What is the thing to do in one's whole life, if you express it with one word?" The Master said, "That is *jo*. Do not do to others what you do not want others to do unto you"' (Chan 1963: 44).

hands, feet and bodies, as it were, to move single-heartedly forward to save a child from falling into a well without them having any exterior motives.[7]

Jinsai's earnest search for the classical form of Confucian morality was motivated by his strong aspiration for laying a firm foundation for establishing positive interpersonal connections. Implicit in this search was his criticism of the main trends of intellectualism and inaction observable in the Japanese studies of the Song tradition of the Zhu Xi School. In those days their studies were highly introspective and tended to degenerate into a kind of self-cultivating morality. In his quest for an alternative and public moral foundation, Jinsai took seriously the significance of the classical Confucian idea of commiseration (*jo*). As Mami Tabata (2011: 97) indicates, his academic endeavour consisted in encouraging people to live a good life and to save others. As a matter of fact, Jinsai maintained: 'The virtue of a ruler is greatest when he loves people. Therefore, when gentle persons of the past talked with a ruler, they regarded loving people as the fundamental matter and saving people as the most urgent task' (Ito 1983: 97).

Jinsai's Practical Idea of Jo, Jin-based Public Philosophy and Peace Thought

Jinsai often wrote of commiseration (*jo*) as genuine commiseration (*chujo* 忠恕). He regarded as the distinct feature of genuine commiseration a sensitive, tolerant, warm and considered attitude (*sontaku* 忖度) towards others.[8] What is especially important about Tabata's argument is her acute insight into the significance of Jinsai's two notions, that is, *taisatsu* (体察: bodily sensing or judgement) and *kanyu* (寛宥: generous acceptance or forgiveness); when combined they constitute the vital core of the meaning of his conception of commiseration or *jo*. Jinsai interpreted the classic Confucian saying 'Do not do to others what you do not want others to do unto you' as a recommendation to cultivate a sensitive attitude of commiseration towards the welfare and happiness, as well as the suffering and pain of others. Therefore, *taisatsu* (bodily sensing) and *kanyu* (generous acceptance) are regarded as the *pivotal* elements and very *linchpin* that make commiseration genuinely operative and real. Other persons harbour mysteries and unfathomable depths within themselves. They are really distant and enigmatic. This is why a careful, sensitive and considered attitude (*sontaku*) is needed and postulated. And this sensitive consideration for other persons necessarily requires the act of bodily sensing (*taisatsu*) in which one encounters and tries to understand others in their very place. If they are suffering and in pain, one undergoes and shares in their suffering and pain and weeps with them. Tabata (2011: 103) explains that here a new and fresh world of compassion

---

7 See Zhang 2010: 57. Zhang (2010: 57–8) continues to argue as follows: 'We all share the innate "moral sprouts" that will generate compassionate feelings when prompted by certain instances and, when cultivated properly, will grow into a full moral character' (also see Ivanhoe 2000: 4).

8 Jinsai (1970b: 151) wrote: 'I reckon to have a full understanding and consideration for others, that is *jo* (commiseration)'. See Tajiri 2011: 88–94, Tabata 2011: 97.

and commiseration is suddenly opened up in a dynamic interpersonal relationship. The fully shared interpersonal relationship prepared by the act of bodily sensing (*taisatsu*) leads to a more dynamic and steady interpersonal communion, that is, the general acceptance and forgiveness of one another (*kanyu*).

Jinsai indicates the basic difficulty in attaining such an attitude of generous acceptance and forgiveness (*kanyu*) towards other persons. This difficulty is derived from the severe reality of the fundamental isolation that exists among human beings. He stated: 'The reason is that others and I are altogether different from one another in bodily formation and in temper or spirit. With regard to pains and itching there exists no mutual relationship' (Ito 1970a: 41). Here Jinsai seems to think that family ties, friendship and long acquaintanceship do not help much. Hence others and I are something like 'the peoples of Qin (秦人) and Jiuat (越人), that is, far-distant and isolated peoples' (Ito 1970b: 152); human beings are bound to be mutually incomprehensible mysteries to one another.

Jo's conspicuous feature is its rather direct, bodily and practical dynamism. Commiseration (*jo*) and genuine commiseration (*chujo*) in particular prompt one's heart and body to move out to help others in times of crisis or predicament. For instance, Tae-chang Kim insists that in Jinsai's thought commiseration (*jo*) activated by temper or spirit (気 *ki*) is the basic origin of the heart–body dynamism that actively relates the self to other persons (Kim et al. 2011: 123).

Thus Jinsai's public philosophy and social ethics are based upon such notions as commiseration (*jo*), genuine commiseration (*chujo*), a sensitive and considered attitude (*sontaku*), temper or spirit (*ki*), forgiveness (*kanyu*) and bodily sensing (*taisatsu*). They should be characterized as a kind of benevolence (*jin*) based public philosophy. Jinsai insists that when benevolence exists, 'it appears in instant breath, it pervades through sleeping dreams, … and one's heart entirely becomes love itself' (Ito 1970a: 70, also see Kurozumi 2003: 81).

Moreover, his public philosophy stood out in its emphasis on the practice of Confucian virtues that should be pursued in the daily life of each and every person. His public philosophy was also unique in its emphasis on academic learning including the arts of peace (*bun* 文) such as dialogue, common deliberation and learning rather than the military arts or warfare (*bu* 武). Jinsai was engaged in a kind of self-conscious and silent revolt against the garrison state (*bukoku* 武国) embodied in the Tokugawa government. His public philosophy was often described in the fashion of Mencius in terms of 'the Way of all the public world under heaven' (天下公共の道).[9] It was always oriented towards open dialogue, public-spirited fellowship and the practice of public virtues. Furthermore, it was accompanied by the creation of concrete public spaces in which his public philosophy was taught and practiced. Examples include the establishment of the free learning association called the Association of the Same Aspiration (同志会) and the opening of the Hall of the Study of Ancient Meanings (古義堂).

9 Regarding Jinsai's understanding of the Way (道) see Ito 1970b: 36–51, 66–76, de Bary et al. 2006: 180–83, Kurozumi 2003: 233–68, Koyasu 2004: 21–31, Kim 2011: 224–5.

Jinsai's public philosophy was unique and conspicuous in that it was definitely not a public philosophy solely for the Tokugawa government and the ruling samurai class, which had been the case of almost all versions of Tokugawa Confucianism in those days. His was definitely a public philosophy for the people. Jinsai was the public philosopher for the affirmation of ordinary life *par excellence*. Thus it is beyond doubt that his public philosophy harboured a number of important seeds for nurturing the public sphere and the arts of peace. The following statement by Jinsai deserves to be quoted here: 'when the arts of peace prevail over the arts of war, the state will enjoy long life; but when the arts of war prevail over the arts of peace, its life span will be shortened' (Ito 1970a: 125, also see Yoshikawa 1983: 12).

At the core of Jinsai's peace vision lays his respect for life and his rejection of killing. According to Jinsai, whereas those who fight intensely are bound to kill many people and their sin is grave, the great virtue of heaven and earth is called life. So the virtuous ruler (*oja* 王者) embodies this great virtue of life and his politics is one of benevolence (*jinsei* 仁政). Furthermore, what is important to note is that there is neither sectionalism nor parochialism on the part of Jinsai. His thought always moves beyond his own home and ancient city of Kyoto, Tokugawa Japan, and even the region of East Asia. For him, 'all the public world under heaven' (天下公共) always means a broad public sphere which naturally extends to the public world of humanity. Herein lies what can be called Jinsai's distinct 'whole–human–species–ism'. This is a fundamentally distinct perspective unique to Jinsai when compared to the main Neo-Confucian tradition. Jinsai's peace philosophy is based on *jin* (benevolence) from the beginning to the end. Here *jin* means love that is mature and complete. He once defined *jin* in the following terms:

> It is a heart of commiseration and loving-kindness which flows forth completely and penetratingly from the inner side to the world outside without any place where it does not reach to, any place it does not touch. … When learning achieves *jin*, the result will be virtuous action; all manner of good works springs from this source. (Ito 1970a: 70, 72, also see Yoshikawa 1983: 28, Spae 1971: 137–40, Minamoto 1972: 79, Koyasu 2004: 69–122)

It was Jinsai's firm conviction that a politics of benevolence (仁政) for ordinary people was greatly needed in his time. Such a politics of benevolence was in turn inspired by the model of Confucian rule manifest in the governance of the sage-kings Yao and Shun in ancient China. Jinsai thought that the distinct feature of 'the Way of Kingship' (*odo*/*wang-tao*王道) in his time and forever was bound to be 'the Way of Peace' (Ito 1970a: 98–9).

Yokoi Shonan on the Politics of Benevolence and Public Philosophy

Yokoi Shonan (1809–1869) of the Kumamoto clan was a committed Confucian samurai and thinker who sought a safe, honourable and virtuous transition from

Tokugawa Japan to the new era. While undergoing various trials and errors in the course of his life, the mature Shonan decided in 1855 to deny Japan's policy of seclusion and promote instead the opening of the country to the world, so that the Japanese people could learn about science, technology and economics from the Western powers. Shonan wrote about 'the evils of seclusion' as follows:

> Today, with all nations navigating freely and trading with one another like neighbors, if Japan alone holds on tightly to its seclusion law, it will be unable to escape the armed might of foreign enemies. When this happens, it is extremely doubtful that the state can be administered, let alone make adequate military preparations, with national power virtually lacking; nor can it rally the samurai and commoners – some resisting, others resentful – into setting up a policy of defense and driving out the foreigners. (Yokoi 1984: 311, de Bary et al. 2005: 542)

His youthful opposition to the opening of the country was drastically changed in 1855, when he carefully read Wei Yuan's (魏源) well-known 1844 work entitled *Illustrated Treatise on the Maritime Kingdoms* (海国図史) (de Bary et al. 2005: 540). The book convinced him not to repeat China's mistake and misfortune with the Opium War. He came to the conclusion that what was needed of Japan was a cautious, gradual and realistic opening of its borders to the Western world. This narrow path would be made open only by means of wise diplomacy and skilful negotiations with the great powers of the West. In domestic politics he also worked hard for, and was committed to, the movement to bring together the Tokugawa shogunate of Edo and the imperial court of Kyoto (公武合体) in order to cope with the Western powers.

To be sure, a nationalistic fervour was always present and discernible in whatever Shonan wrote and said. But, at the same time, his proposals, suggestions and ideas embodied a tolerant and open attitude towards the worldwide public under heaven and on earth. In the process of learning about the West he began to appreciate the importance of Christianity. He also began to emphasize the importance of learning about the sciences, technology, economics, military, laws, constitutionalism and politics that were developed in Western countries. Shonan was idealistic enough to think that the ideas and institutions which made up Western civilization could be learned, utilized and adapted in Japan under a Confucian worldview and morality (Matsuura 2010: 10–11). There is little doubt that Shonan throughout his entire life adhered unwaveringly to 'the Way of Yao, Shun and Confucius' (尭舜孔子之道) or 'the governing Way of Yao-Shun three generations' (堯舜三代之治道) (Tsutsumi 2009: 75–94). From time to time he excavated this ancient ideal of virtuous politics from the history of China in order to invigorate the politics and diplomacy of contemporary Japan.

Indeed, his theoretical and practical attempt based upon his Confucian ideas was not only ambitious and stimulating but also principled and realistic. His Confucianism, as with Ito Jinsai's, displayed a strong aspiration for recovering some of the ancient classical, universal elements of Confucianism. From this *universalistic* perspective, Shonan could evaluate highly the significance of Christianity for the common good it had created in Western societies. Likewise, he could entertain the highest respect for genuine statesmen such as George Washington in America, as well as for democratic politics and constitutionalism in England (Yokoi 1984: 319–20, 322–6, 447–55, de Bary et al. 2005: 545–9). One may reasonably lament his untimely assassination at the age of 61 when Shonan was a member of the Council in the newly established Meiji government.

Shonan's Politics of Benevolence

Unlike Jinsai, Shonan firmly stood in the Song Neo-Confucian tradition of Zhu Xi. But like Jinsai, Shonan was a Confucian scholar who wanted to go back to the classical stances of Confucianism as represented by Confucius and Mencius. As a faithful follower of the Confucian learning and tradition, the notion of benevolence or *jin* played a pivotal role in his political, economic and international thought. His commitment to the ethical ideals of benevolence (*jin*), benevolent justice (*jingi*) and benevolent politics (*jinsei*) permeated his writings. In a sense, Shonan tried to equip modern Japan with these Confucian public virtues. For Japan was at the threshold of opening its borders and having to cope with the new historical challenges of the imperialism and internationalism of the West.

In *Kokuze Sanron* (*Three Theses on State Policy*, 1860) Shonan insisted on the policy of a 'wealthy country, strong military' (富国強兵). The main tenet of his policy recommendations for Matsudaira Shungaku, lord of the Echizen clan, consisted in economic and military reform, and the moral cultivation of the samurai class. Shonan thought that in an age of internationalism Japan's seclusion policy was against 'the natural course of all under heaven and on earth':

> However, if we work in harmony with the natural course of all under heaven and on earth and adapt to conditions in the various nations, and if we administer the land in the interests of 'the common public Way', the obstacles everywhere will disappear, and the distressful state of affairs of the present will no longer be a problem at all. (Yokoi 1984: 312, de Bary et al. 2005: 543)

Shonan promoted free trade and commercial intercourse both at the domestic and at the international level. He also proposed social mobility across classes according to talent and skills. It would help create a tenacious public sphere as constituting the necessary condition for making the country economically and militarily strong (Yokoi 1984: 311–20, de Bary et al. 2005: 542–6, also see Yamazaki 1981: 57–113). A certain degree of military strength was considered necessary for both defending the dignity of Japan's independence and the avoidance of humiliation and disaster. He insisted that in the defence of an island country like Japan strengthening the navy was of prime importance (Yokoi 1984: 321, de Bary et al. 2005: 547).

Shonan's idea of a politics of benevolence consists partly in the development of socio-economic welfare for both the ruling samurai class and the commoners.

He indicated the great need for a number of materials and resources that many people felt to increase their production including original stock, seeds, fertilizer and even money and land. He demanded the government lend money and grain on a non-profit basis so that the people could meet their needs and increase their production. By eliminating high interest rates for their loans they would benefit a great deal (Yokoi 1984: 313–14, de Bary et al. 2005: 543).

Shonan, approvingly referring to Commodore Matthew C. Perry's astute observation of Japan on his arrival at Uraga in 1855, pointed out the 'lack of governmental administration in the country' (無政事之国) (Yokoi 1984: 318, de Bary et al. 2005: 543). The alternative that Shonan called for was a Confucian-based, enlightened politics of benevolence. He argued that Japan also had to learn about industry, technology and governmental institutions from the West because they would help promote the welfare of the people and make possible an enlightened rule. They would also help make Japan strong economically and militarily. But he insisted that the Japanese had to pursue these ends in accordance with divine virtue and sage teachings (Yokoi 1984: 320, de Bary et al. 2005: 546).

This enlightened politics of benevolence greatly needed the spiritual basis which could be supplied by 'the Way of the Samurai' (*shido* 士道). According to Shonan, the way of the samurai by no means consisted of the way of military arts (*bu* 武) alone. It was more concerned with governance informed by academic learning (*bun* 文), that is, a humane governance with deep spiritual and ethical ideals (Yokoi 1984: 329–35, de Bary et al. 2005: 549–53). He proclaimed:

> The ruler must exercise affection, respect, modesty, justice, and frankness. He must study the practice of these among the ancient sages and worthies … In carrying out these sage teachings based on their natural sentiments and moral relations, he must lead his ministers with the greatest sincerity and compassion in ruling the people. (Yokoi 1984: 334–5, de Bary et al. 2005: 552)

Thus the gist of Shonan's politics of benevolence resides not merely in his emphasis on the need for social and economic welfare at the domestic level and for international free trade. It also consists in his commitment to the Confucian public virtue of self-discipline deriving from academic learning (*bun*), the public good of benevolent justice (*jingi*) and leadership inspired by 'the Way of the Samurai' (*shido*). His unique politics of benevolence can be rightly characterized as an expression of a newly formulated public philosophy informed by his act of refashioning Confucianism in his time.

Shonan and His Public Philosophy

Shonan used such expressions as 'all the public under heaven and on earth' (天地公共) and 'practical reason of all the public under heaven and on earth' (天地公共之実理) (Yokoi 1971: 434). The implication is that the public and the entire world are penetrated by, and governed under, the operation of a certain universal and common reason. Ryoen Minamoto (2003: 129–31, 151–7; 2009: 38–9) interprets Shonan's expression 'all the public under heaven and on earth' (天地公共) as derived from the expression 'all the public under heaven' (天下公共) used by Sima Qian (司馬遷) in *The Records of the Grand Historian* (*Shiki* 史記). By changing 'all under the heaven' (*tenka* 天下) to 'all under the heaven and on earth' (*tenchi* 天地) Shonan wanted to refer to the entire public world that extends beyond the boundary of each and every state (Narahara 1998: 52). To be sure, Shonan's expression of 'all the public under heaven and on earth' (地公共) was, in fact, induced by the necessity of the times; he was seriously committed to Tokugawa Japan's 'opening of the country'. He was fully aware that in the mid-nineteenth century, the world and its international relations were fully ripe for Tokugawa Japan to stop carrying on its seclusionist policy.

But, at the same time, he only wanted to open the country on the condition that those countries with which Japan would interact would show themselves to be 'countries abiding by the Way' (有道之国). Shonan maintained that international trade and commercial intercourse should be allowed with countries that possess the appropriate virtues. But they should not be allowed with those countries that do not have them (無道之国). He defined 'virtuous countries' as those that keep trustful and peaceable relationships based on an international public good and justice, that is, in Shonan's own expression, 'practical reason of all under heaven and on earth' (天地公共之実理) (Yokoi 1984: 369–70, also see Minamoto 2002: 243–5, Yamawaki 2002: 261–3, Hiraishi 2006: 5–9). And above all Japan had to prove herself by behaving as a 'country with virtues' (有徳之国). Thus Shonan's 'politics of the public' (公共之政) encompassed not merely his incessant search for an enlightened politics of benevolence based on the social and economic welfare of all people at the domestic level. It also embodied his earnest aspiration for overcoming a narrow and selfish nationalism (割拠見) by reaching a mutually beneficial free and fair trade and world peace that were to be sought based on the universal principle of the 'public Way of heaven and earth' (天地之公道) (Yokoi 1984: 480–82, also see Minamoto 2002: 255–6).

The second pivotal aspect of Shonan's public philosophy resided in his emphasis on the importance of public debate and discussion for a 'politics of the public'. Shonan's politics of deliberation should be rightly regarded as having influenced the politics of the Meiji government. The well-known first clause of the Charter Oath (1868) reads: 'Deliberative assemblies shall be widely established and all matters shall be decided by open discussion'. Shonan's support for a politics of free speech became one of the pillars of the Meiji regime and its constitutionalism.

Shonan's politics of deliberation meant that what mattered in the politics of the public was nothing else than the forming of public opinion and policy. They, in turn, ought to be generated by the processes of open discussion among the people and their leaders. In *Shichijo* (*Seven Clauses*, 1862), Shonan stated, 'Open widely the path for discussion. And engage in politics for all in heaven and the public' (Yokoi 1971: 401, also see Minamoto 2002: 247–50, Karube 2002: 51–66; 2011: 184–97). He already had practiced this politics of deliberation back in his own Kumamoto circle in 1843, when he had initiated and conducted a debate oriented seminar with colleagues such as Shimototsu Kyuya, Nagaoka Kenmotsu and Motoda Nagazane. The common seminar was democratically conducted to induce an open debate and an exchange of opinions among participants so as to lead to reliable judgement and policy proposals.

Conclusion

We have seen the ideas and arguments of three representative Japanese thinkers: Prince Shotoku, Ito Jinsai and Yokoi Shonan. They differed from one another in the age they lived and in the thought they came to entertain. But there are some common elements observable among them. First, they were realistic and practical thinkers who reflected on the possibilities of peace, public virtues and a public philosophy for their times. Second, they can be rightly regarded as belonging to the main lineage of the 'Way of Kingship' (*odo* 王道); they rejected in one way or another 'the Way of Conquest and the Conqueror' (*hado* 覇道), to use Mencius' contrastive terminology. Their ideas on peace and public philosophy remain permanent contributions to the practical task of peace building as well as to peace research today.

In view of present-day East Asia, which still remains one of the most tension filled and turbulent regions in the world, the potential that their thought and legacies suggest for conflict resolution, reconciliation and peace building are of prime significance. It is clear that their ideas on peace, social and economic welfare, public philosophy and a politics of deliberation still possess immensely creative and relevant insights and hints – both theoretically and practically – for actualizing reconciliation and peace in this region.

Bibliography

Aston, W.G. 2011. The reign of Suiko and rule of Shotoku, in *Sources of Japanese Tradition*, vol. 1. pt. 1. *From Earliest Times to 1600.* 2nd Edition, edited by T. de Bary et al. New York: Columbia University Press: 47–8.

Chan, W.T. (ed.) 1963. *A Source Book in Chinese Philosophy*. Princeton: Princeton University Press.

Chiba, S. 2008. For realizing *wa* and *kyosei* in East Asia, in *A Grand Design for Peace and Reconciliation: Achieving Kyosei in East Asia*, edited by Y. Murakami and T.J. Schoenbaum. Cheltenham, UK and Northampton, MA: Edward Elgar, 176–97.

Chiba, S. 2011. On perspectives on peace: the Hebraic idea of *shalom* and Prince Shotoku's idea of *wa*, in *Building New Pathways to Peace*, edited by N.

Kawamura, Y. Murakami and S. Chiba. Seattle and London: University of Washington Press, 48–64.

de Bary, T. et al. (eds.) 2001. *Sources of Japanese Tradition*, vol. 1. pt. 1. *From Earliest Times to 1600*. 2nd Edition. New York: Columbia University Press.

de Bary, T. et al. (eds.) 2005. *Sources of Japanese Tradition*, vol. 2. pt. 1. *1600 to 1868*. 2nd Abridged Edition. New York: Columbia University Press.

Hanayama, N. 1982. *Shotoku Taishi to Kenpo 17 Jo*. Tokyo: Okura Shuppan.

Hiraishi, N. 2006. Bakumatsu ishin ki: Yokoi Shonan to Fukuzawa Yukichi, in *Chishikijin kara kangaeru kokyosei* (*Kokyo Tetsugaku 17*), edited by. N. Hiraishi and T. Kim. Tokyo: University of Tokyo Press, 1–19.

Ito, J. 1970a. *Doshimon* (童子問), edited by S. Shimizu. Tokyo: Iwanami Shoten.

Ito, J. 1970b. *Gomo Jigi* (語孟字義), edited by E. Kimura. Tokyo: Chikuma Shobo.

Ito, J. 1983. *Rongo Kogi* (論語古義), edited by S. Kaizuka. Tokyo: Chuo Koronsha.

Ivanhoe, P. 2000. *Confucian Moral Self-Cultivation*. 2nd Edition. Indianapolis, IN: Hackett.

Okano, M. 2003. *Shotoku Taishi*. Tokyo: Daihorinkaku.

Karube, T. 2002. 'Fushigi no sekai' no kokyo tetsugaku: Yokoi Shonan ni okeru 'koron', in *niju-ichi seiki kokyo tetsugaku no chihei*, edited by T. Sasaki and T. Kim. Tokyo: University of Tokyo Press, 47–69.

Karube, T. 2011. *Rekishi toiu hifu*. Tokyo: Iwanami Shoten.

Kim, T. 2011. Ito Jinsai wo kokyo testugaku suru, in *Ito Jinsai: Tenka kokyo no michi wo kokyushita bunjin gakusha,* edited by R. Kataoka and T. Kim. Tokyo: Tokyo University Press, 223–8.

Kim, T. et al. 2011. Toron, in *Ito Jinsai: Tenka kokyo no michi wo kokyushita bunjin gakusha,* edited by R. Kataoka and T. Kim. Tokyo: Tokyo University Press, 118–26.

Koyasu, N. 2004. *Ito Jinsai no sekai.* Tokyo: Pelican.

Kurozumi, M. 2003. *Kinsei nihon syakai to jyukyo.* Tokyo: Pelican.

Matsuura, R. 2010. *Yokoi Shonan.* Tokyo: Chikuma Shobo.

Minamoto, R. 1972. *Tokugawa gorishiso no keifu.* Tokyo: Chuo Koronsha.

Minamoto, R. 2002. Yokoi Shonan ni okeru 'kokyo' no shiso to sono kokyo tetsugaku eno kiyo, in *Nihon ni okeru ko to shi* (*Kokyo Tetsugaku 3*), edited by T. Sasaki and T. Kim. Tokyo: University of Tokyo Press, 241–61.

Minamoto, R. 2003. Yokoi Shonan ni okeru 'kaikoku' to 'kokyo' shiso no keisei, *Nihon Gakushiin Kiyo*, 57(3), 127–204.

Minamoto, R. (ed.) 2009. *Yokoi Shonan: 'Kokyo' no senkusha.* Tokyo: Fujiwara Shoten.

Murase, H. 2003. *Toyo no heiwa shiso.* Tokyo: Aoki Shoten.

Narahara, T. 1998. Kokusaikan no tenkan, in *Yokoi Shonan no subete*, edited by R. Minamoto et al. Tokyo: Shin Jinbutsu Oraisha, 49–57.

Spae, J. 1967. *Itoh Jinsai: A Philosopher, Educator and Sinologist of the Tokugawa Period.* New York: Paragon Book Print Corp.

Spae, J. 1971. *Japanese Religiosity.* Tokyo: Oriens Institute for Religious Research.
Tabata, M. 2011. Ito Jinsai ni okeru 'jo' no kanosei, in *Ito Jinsai: Tenka kokyo no michi wo kokyushita bunjin gakusha*, edited by R. Kataoka and T. Kim. Tokyo: Tokyo University Press, 97–118.
Tajiri, Y. 2011. *Edo no shisoshi.* Tokyo: Chuo Koron Shinsha.
Tamura, E. 1964. *Shotoku Taishi.* Tokyo: Chuo Koronsha.
Tsutsumi, K. 2009. *'Ko' no shisoka Yokoi Shonan.* Kumamoto: Kumamoto Shuppan Bunka Kaikan.
Umehara, T. 1993. *Shotoku Taishi,* vol. 2. Tokyo: Shueisha.
Yamawaki, N. 2002. Komento: Yokoi Shonan no konnichiteki igi, in *Nihon ni okeru ko to shi* (*Kokyo Tetsugaku 3*), edited by T. Sasaki and T. Kim. Tokyo: University of Tokyo Press, 261–3.
Yamazaki, M. 1981. *Yokoi Shonan no shakai keizai shiso*. Tokyo: Taga Shuppan.
Yokoi, S. 1971. Kokuze sanron, in *Nihon shiso taikei*, vol. 55, edited by M. Yamaguchi. Tokyo: Iwanami Shoten, 438–65.
Yokoi, S. 1984. *Kokuze Sanron* (国是三論), *Iryo Osetsu Taii* (夷虜応接大意), *Numayama Taiwa* (沼山対話), *Kokuze Junijo* (国是十二条), edited by R. Matsuura. Tokyo: Chuo Koronsha.
Yoshikawa, K. 1983. *Jinsai, Sorai, Norinaga: Three Classical Philologists of Mid-Tokugawa Japan.* Tokyo: Toho Gakkai.
Yoshikawa, K. 2008. *Rongo no hanashi.* Tokyo: Chikuma Shobo.
Yu, K. 2010. The Confucian conception of harmony, in *Governance of Harmony in Asia and Beyond*, edited by J. Tao et al. London and New York: Routledge, 15–36.
Zhang, Q. 2010. Humanity or benevolence? The interpretation of Confucian *ren* and its modern implications, in *Taking Confucian Ethics Seriously: Contemporary Theories and Applications*, edited by K. Yu, J. Tao and P.J. Ivanhoe. Albany State University of New York Press, 53–72.

Chapter 6
Visions of Peace in Medieval European Political Thought

Takashi Shogimen

Ideas of *peace* in medieval political thought may sound odd to many readers. Some might even wonder whether there was such a thing as political thought in the Middle Ages (Burns 1988). The Middle Ages remains an underappreciated field of historical research in European political thought. Classroom instruction in the history of political thought typically ignores the Middle Ages or, at best, discusses Thomas Aquinas as if his ideas 'represent' the quintessence of medieval political thinking, before turning swiftly, and gladly, to more 'proper' political thinkers such as Machiavelli and Hobbes. Medieval political thought is thus very little known beyond a circle of specialists. But even for those who are familiar with medieval political thought, ideas of peace in medieval Europe may still appear a research topic that is somewhat out of place because the Middle Ages has conventionally been seen as uncongenial to peace. The popular image of medieval Europe is often framed by the crusading movement and the idea and practice of chivalry as well as inquisition and the gory persecution of heretics and other minorities, thus amplifying the view that medieval culture was violent and belligerent.

Twentieth-century research, however, has shown that medieval intellectuals were cognizant of political thought and that medieval culture was far from being monolithically bloodthirsty. In the context of the present volume, the primary aim of this chapter is to illustrate that medieval Europe was not merely violence-oriented but also knew sophisticated conceptions and ideals of peace. Some medieval European intellectuals endeavoured to envision how to bring about peace and order in contemporary Latin Christendom, thus rendering serious criticism of the violent and belligerent aspects of medieval European culture. Such a conceptualization of peace is predicated on the idea that peace in *this* world is possible. However, one influential view of peace in the Christian tradition is that temporal peace cannot be achieved (Galtung 1981). It is widely known that Christianity was axiomatic to the medieval mental and intellectual landscape, which attributed ultimate values to the *other* world. Hence, some remarks are germane in connection with the existence of this-worldly political thinking in the Middle Ages.

These considerations dictate the sequence of the following exposition, which makes three points: first, in the later Middle Ages or, more specifically, from the late thirteenth century onwards, the medieval European intellectual world witnessed the emergence of *scientia civilis*. New ways of thinking about the human community enabled contemporary intellectuals to conceptualize peace as a possibility in *this* world. Second, one such political thinker who wrote on peace, the Florentine poet Dante Alighieri, considered the universal rule of the Roman Empire to be instrumental in realizing universal peace, although it is not clear whether his vision of peace extended beyond the borders of Christendom. Third, the medieval idea of just war, which was theologically articulated by Thomas Aquinas, was reinterpreted by the late fourteenth-century English theologian John Wyclif in a way that renders just war notionally possible but spiritually problematic and practically almost impossible. Wyclif's discussion therefore effectively constitutes a spiritual and theological critique of the justice of war, thereby asserting the Christian spiritual ideal of peace in a political and military context.

The Emergence of Peace Writings

The ideal of peace was of course not alien to medieval intellectuals before the late thirteenth century. Rufinus's (fl. the twelfth century) treatise, *On the Good of Peace* (*De bono pacis*), for example, represents one of the earliest scholarly visions of peace in medieval Europe (Rufinus 1997). However it was not until the turn of the thirteenth and fourteenth centuries that peace became a major focus in the political writings of medieval intellectuals. The Dominican friar Remigio de' Girolami (d.1319), for instance, wrote in his *On the Good of Peace* (*De bono pacis*) that the common good which is most important to the human community is peace (Girolami 1977b: 55–71, Davis 1959). The Italian physician and political philosopher Marsilius of Padua (ca.1275–1342) produced a controversial work entitled the *Defender of the Peace* (*Defensor pacis*), in which he attributed the incessant strife in Latin Christendom, in northern Italy in particular, to the papacy's claim to the plenitude of power (*plenitudo potestatis*), the universal jurisdictional power over both spiritual and temporal matters (Marsilius of Padua 1932–33; 1956; 2005). Some other works, which do not refer explicitly to peace in their titles, are still preoccupied with the issue of temporal peace in their own times: Dante Alighieri's *The Monarchy* (*De Monarchia*) (Dante 1916; 1996; 2004) and the Benedictine monk Engelbert of Admont's *On the Origin and the End of the Roman Empire* (Izbicki and Nederman 2000) envisage the realization of universal peace throughout Latin Christendom under the Roman *imperium*. Pierre Dubois's *On the Recovery of the Holy Land* (Dubois 1956) also considers the peaceful unity of Latin Christendom; however, his solution was in marked contrast to Dante's and Engelbert's in that the former repudiated the indispensability of the Roman Empire in realizing peace (Dubois 1956).

In the late fourteenth and early fifteenth centuries, some military writers began to deal with the question of peace from the viewpoint of the laws of war. The French canon lawyer Honoré Bonet explored the questions of war and peace from a juristic perspective (Coopland 1949). Drawing on Bonet, the poet Christine de

Pizan (ca.1363–ca.1430) wrote a treatise entitled *The Book of Peace* (*Livre de la paix*), which provided a secular and realistic account of the prevention of military conflicts (Pizan 2008).

What deserves attention here is that the conception of peace, which these authors discussed in the late Middle Ages, was a this-worldly one. One of the central motifs in Christian theology is the eschatological emphasis on the Christian idea of peace: the sharp distinction between peace in this world and peace in the next manifests a desire and hope for peace that will be fulfilled at the Second Coming. The eschatological idea of peace, of course, is predicated on the notion that it is God, not humans, who would implement pacification (Zampaglione 1973: 210–11). The reverse side of this is the flat rejection of the possibility of perfect peace in this world: an idea that penetrates Saint Augustine's discourse on peace (Fuchs 1965: 46).

However, Saint Augustine's idea of peace is not one-dimensional; the rejection of perfect peace in this world did not necessarily preclude the possibility of peace, however imperfect. Indeed, in his *City of God*, Saint Augustine famously defined peace as the tranquillity of order (*tranquilitas ordinis*) and opposed peace to war. While this idea had been known to medieval theologians for centuries, it entered political discourse as the new genre of *scientia civilis* was emerging in the second half of the thirteenth century. The rediscovery of Aristotle's *Politics* in the middle of the thirteenth century caused shockwaves in the intellectual world, which had significant repercussions on the discourse on peace.

Much of Aristotle's philosophical ideas were lost to Western Europe, except for some logical ideas, which were transmitted through early philosophical texts such as Boethius's *On Topical Differences* (*De topicis differentiis*), until the twelfth century. In the twelfth century, Aristotle's writings on logic, metaphysics, ethics, zoology and astronomy were rediscovered and translated into Latin. Aristotle's *Politics* was translated by William of Moerbeke and Michael Scot into Latin in the 1250s. It immediately received the attention of scholastic giants such as Albert the Great and Thomas Aquinas. The rediscovery of Aristotelian political philosophy was once hailed as the 'Aristotelian revolution' in the history of Western political thought, which allegedly marked the advent of modernity (Ullmann 1965: 159–73). Although this thesis has since been largely discredited on a number of grounds (Nederman 1988, Kempshall 1999), it still holds that the rediscovery of Aristotle's *Politics* was highly significant in the sense that it helped equip medieval intellectuals with the language to categorize and analyse the 'political'. Before the translation of Aristotle's *Politics*, *scientia civilis* was ancillary to jurisprudence. Aristotelian political science provided medieval intellectuals with a comprehensive framework by which to philosophize how the political community ought to be organized and operate – beyond the mere interpretation of legal principles. The origin and purpose of the political community and the taxonomy of constitutions, for example, were among the topics that received systematic treatment as medieval intellectuals assimilated the Aristotelian way of analysing politics.

One of the reasons why Aristotle's philosophical works including *Politics* were so enthusiastically welcomed by medieval theologians and philosophers was that they offered an alternative intellectual paradigm to the Christian theological one. Aristotelian political philosophy was obviously free from any Christian influence and provided an entirely new – and indeed rival – perspective on the human community. One area in which Aristotle and Christian theology offered two rival views was the idea of the common good as the purpose of the human community. Of course, the idea of the common good had been known to medieval intellectuals before the rediscovery of Aristotelian political science. Nonetheless, the Aristotelian idea of the common good was novel in at least two ways: one was that the Aristotelian idea serves as the touchstone by which to decipher whether or not a government in question is legitimate: serving the common good is *the* foundation of political legitimacy whether the ruler is one, a few or many. The other novelty was that Aristotle defines the common good as the attainment of the virtuous life in the community. *Vivere bene* is not good enough if it means mere material sufficiency; it requires philosophical betterment through participation in deliberations and decision-makings on public issues. In the context of the present concern, that is, the idea of peace, the latter is highly significant. The Aristotelian idea of the common good forms a sharp contrast with the Augustinian counterpart; for Saint Augustine, government is a necessary evil as the remedy for sin. Thus, his idea of the common good is restricted to the fulfilment of temporal peace and order by restraining the sinful and egoistic impulse of humans.

The Aristotelian and Augustinian ideas of the common good were recognized by late thirteenth-century intellectuals as competing, if not mutually exclusive, ideas that define the purpose of the human community, and the discussions on the topic were prompted by contemporary political events. The dispute between Pope Boniface VIII and Philip IV the Fair of France at the turn of the thirteenth and fourteenth centuries, for example, generated a number of political treatises from both pro-papal and anti-papal camps. The pro-papal authors such as Giles of Rome and James of Viterbo argued for the subjugation of temporal powers to papal power, whereas anti-papal critics such as John of Paris tried to show the independence of secular powers from papal power. In this context, the purpose of the political community came under scrutiny: pro-papal commentators argued that the natural moral purpose of the collective life is overridden by the theological purpose of the collective life, while anti-papal critics claimed that natural moral purpose was autonomous in some sense, while recognizing the superiority of the theological purpose. The discussion of the relationship between the natural and theological purposes of the human community was translated and expanded in the Aristotelian and Augustinian discourses.

Matthew Kempshall (1999) has surveyed the interplay between the two contrasting ideas of the common good in the late thirteenth and early fourteenth centuries, and concluded perceptively that the secularization of late medieval political thought, which had been attributed by Ullmann to the rediscovery of Aristotelian political science, should be ascribed to Saint Augustine. The Aristotelian common good as philosophical perfection in the communal life was teleologically consistent with the theological exaltation of spiritual perfection in the other world, thereby reinforcing the superiority of Christian theological virtues to natural moral virtues. The teleological linkage between natural moral virtues and Christian theological virtues, by implication, vindicated the contemporary papal claim of the subjection of temporal power to spiritual power. In contrast, the Augustinian idea of the common good – *mere* peace and order – provided the critics of the contemporary papacy (such as Dante, Marsilius of Padua and William of Ockham) with theoretical grounds on which to vindicate the autonomy of temporal power. In Kempshall's (2001: 331) words, 'By removing moral virtue from their theoretical definition of the goal of the political community, by insisting instead on material peace and security, all three writers [Dante, Marsilius and Ockham] were intending to remove a central support for the justification of papal intervention in temporal jurisdiction'. Paradoxical as it may seem, the pro-papal claim of the subjection of temporal power to papal power could be bolstered by an appeal to Aristotle, while the rejection of it was supported by an appeal to Augustine.

The emergence of 'peace writings' at the turn of the thirteenth and fourteenth centuries may be seen as a by-product of the debates on the relationship between Aristotelianism and Augustinianism in the sphere of political thought, prompted by contemporary political circumstances. Indeed, peace was among *political* topics that polemical writers of the period discussed explicitly, including power and government. It was not until the late thirteenth century medieval intellectuals wrote exclusively on political topics. In this intellectual climate, temporal peace as a political value was recognized and underlined especially by political thinkers who opposed the superiority of papal power over secular powers. The rediscovery of Aristotle's *Politics* generated a series of debates on, among other things, the purpose of the human community, and some intellectuals chose to assert the Augustinian idea of the common good as this-worldly peace and order.

Dante and the Renewal of Roman Peace

How did political thinkers at the turn of the fourteenth century discuss peace? Their viewpoints were diverse: the pro-papal theologian James of Viterbo, for example, envisaged the attainment of universal peace under the direction of the Roman Church, the papacy in particular, which should exercise the plenitude of power universally. Marsilius of Padua, by contrast, argued that the papal exercise of the plenitude of power was precisely the cause of strife in Latin Christendom, and more specifically in northern Italy. Hence, Marsilius conceptualized peace in the Augustinian sense, which could be achieved by stripping the Roman Church of the coercive power it claimed. Other thinkers maintained that the empire could bring about universal peace in medieval Europe. One such author was the Benedictine monk Engelbert of Admont, and another was Dante Alighieri (1265–1321).

Dante is well known as one of the greatest Italian poets, the author of the *Divine Comedy* and the *Banquet* (*Convivio*). However, early in his life, Dante pursued a political career, which began in 1295 but was aborted when he was expelled from his office due to a forged charge of corruption. Dante's misfortune was part of the factional conflict in Florence. His literary career began during his exile; he produced not only poetry but also a political work, *The Monarchy*. This work, probably written after 1314, adumbrates the imperialist position in response to the contemporary conflict between the Emperor Henry VII and Pope Clement V. The treatise, which envisaged Rome's universal rule, was condemned by the Roman Church as heretical.

One of the undercurrent themes of *The Monarchy* is the importance of universal peace. Dante (2004: 115) is unequivocal in the belief that universal peace is 'the most important of all things that are ordained for our beatitude'. Dante conceptualized the purpose of man's political life as the actualization of the intellectual potential of humanity: an idea which was markedly Aristotelian. However, Dante (2004: 114) also acknowledged that humans could attend well to the activity realizing their potential 'in quietude, or in the tranquility of peace'. In Dante's political thought, therefore, universal peace occupied an exalted status:

> From what we have said, then, it is obvious what the better, or rather, the best way is by which mankind may achieve its proper functioning. And consequently we have seen the quickest way to arrive at that to which all our actions are ordered as to a final end, that is, universal peace, which we must take as a principle for all the arguments that are to follow. (Dante 2004: 115)

What did Dante mean by 'universal peace'? Dante's peace is not merely an internal state of the human mind; it unmistakably concerns this-worldly conditions in the human community. Dante underlines the role that the Roman Empire should play in the pacification of Western Europe. In *The Monarchy* as well as in the *Banquet*, he expressed a firm belief that the Roman Empire would bring about universal peace. According to Dante, no ruler would be content with his limited territory; therefore, it is inevitable that the coexistence of various states would result in incessant wars. From this it followed that one ultimate authority was necessary to resolve conflicts. Thus Dante concluded that the Roman conquest would bring about universal peace (Shogimen 2010: 878).

Dante's conception of universal peace collided with the pro-papal vision that universal peace should be realized under the leadership of the papacy. To be sure, Dante acknowledged the duality of universal authority in Latin Christendom: papal and imperial. However, he emphasized the qualitative difference between them: while the purpose of imperial authority is the attainment of happiness through philosophical perfection in this world, the purpose of papal authority is the salvation of the souls in the next. Dante therefore refused to extrapolate the Aristotelian view of the purpose of the political community so as to justify the subjection of natural purposes to supernatural purposes. Instead he underlined different dimensions in which imperial and papal authorities operate, thereby polarizing the functions of the two authorities to the extent that it was impossible for them to overlap and collaborate with each other. Thus the Roman Empire emerged as the only conceivable agent for the realization of universal peace in this world (Davis 1959: 121).

Ascribing the task of pacification to the Roman Empire, however, was problematic in view of the Christian historical understanding of the empire. Saint Augustine, whose work was widely read throughout the Middle Ages, was highly critical of the Roman past of conquest, as he understood it as the manifestation of *libido dominandi* (the desire for domination). Dante responded to this prevailing view by arguing that the Roman conquest did not derive from *libido dominandi* but from the public concern for the benefit of humanity:

> That in subjugating the earth's globe the Roman people attended to the aforesaid good is declared, moreover, by their deeds – in which they dispelled all cupidity, which is always harmful to the common good – for by their delight in universal peace and liberty, that holy, pious, and glorious people are seen to have neglected their own best interests to look after those of the public for the welfare of mankind. (Dante 2004: 135)

This argument constitutes a significant departure from the Augustinian view of Roman history.

Dante's vision of peace was couched in his re-reading of Roman history, by appealing to ancient authorities, which included Virgil, Livy, Orosius and the Bible (Woodhouse 1997: 9). Dante (2004: 128) declared that 'we shall not find that there ever was peace throughout the world except under the immortal Augustus, when a perfect monarchy existed'. He confessed in *The Monarchy* that he had once been critical of Roman conquest; however, he underwent a change of mind (Dante 2004: 129, Davis 1957: 46–7). Thus Dante endeavoured to show that Rome conquered the world justly. His use of historical writings is selective. For example, Orosius, whose historical view was influenced by Saint Augustine and therefore did not fail to observe the 'dark side' of Roman imperialism, was referred to by Dante only in the context of the justification of conquest (Davis 1993: 76). Clearly, Dante's premeditated programme of peace dictated the use of classical sources which disregarded the intentions of the original authors.

We should not overlook, however, the fact that the ultimate source of legitimacy for Rome's wars of conquest was not human. Dante believed that the Roman conquest was providential. The Roman Empire had for the first time brought peace throughout the world in preparation for the birth of the saviour: Jesus Christ. Hence military conquest is the instrument of divine providence for the purpose of universal peace. This Christian reading of Roman history was derived from Orosius (Davis 1957: 64). The key idea that Dante inherited from Orosius was that if Roman rule had been unjust, the execution of Christ would not have been carried out by a legitimate judge, which would mean that the Passion of Christ did not redeem Adam's sin. In this way, Dante sanctified Roman rule from a Christian perspective. It is a paradoxical twist in Dante's discourse on peace that the Christian providential view of history glorified the Roman Empire's role in the pacification of Europe. Book II of *The Monarchy* is devoted to nothing but this purpose. Even when he discussed two types of happiness – temporal happiness and eternal happiness – at the conclusion of *The Monarchy*, Dante (2004: 92–3) referred to peace only in the context of temporal happiness, which was of course the goal that the 'Roman Prince' must strive to achieve.[1]

Johan Galtung (1981), a leading authority in peace studies, produced an ambitious survey of the global visions of peace, in which he identified the Roman concept of peace. The Roman idea of peace – *pax* in Latin – has two important characteristics: one is that *pax* concerns the relationship between the Roman citizens and foreigners. *Pax*, etymologically stemming from the verb *pacisci*, originally meant a 'pact' that ended a war, which led to submission, friendship or alliance (Galtung 1981: 187, Weinstock 1971: 267). The *pax*, then, is the concept of foreign policy, which forms a stark contrast with *concordia* (concord), meaning internal harmony (Galtung 1981: 187, Weinstock 1960: 45). Thus *pax* and *concordia* are twin concepts in the Roman tradition.

The other characteristic is a corollary from the first: although *pax* refers to the end of military conflict between the Romans and the foreigners, it is not conceptualized as a 'pact' between equals. Typically the *pax* as the Romans envisaged it was the unconditional surrender on the part of the non-Romans (Zampaglione 1973: 133). Therefore, Galtung (1981: 176) presents the Roman concept as pacification through conquest, and Roman peace is envisaged to expand from Rome as its one and only centre.

Galtung's 'ideal type' of Roman peace is heuristically useful in understanding Dante's vision of peace, which is markedly uni-centric. Dante's emphasis on the singularity of the centre from which peace should emanate may be discerned in his discussion of the idea of concord: 'mankind at its best forms a certain concord'. Dante discusses concord in terms of 'the unity that is within wills'. The uni-centric nature of Dante's peace becomes manifest when he wrote that concord cannot be brought about 'unless there be one single will, master and guide of all others in unity, for the wills of mortals needs direction because of the alluring delights of youth' (Dante 2004: 127). Clearly concord is a state which results not from the equilibrium of constituting members of a community but from compulsion by one powerful will. In Dante's vision, concord requires a single centre of direction.

Dante's Roman conception of peace may also be discerned in his metaphorical discussion of the body politic. His reference to thumbs, hands and arms serves to highlight the teleological relationships between the parts and the larger whole as a thumb serves the function of a greater whole, the hand, which in turn serves an even larger whole, the arm (Dante 2004: 113). Such a teleological understanding of the organic metaphor suggests the existence of a single ultimate end of the

1 This is not to say, however, that Dante did not take the Christian supremacy of eternal peace seriously; Dante viewed temporal peace as instrumental to eternal peace. On his idea of other-worldly peace see Bemrose 2005: 71–89.

community. This metaphor is clearly consistent with the uni-centric Roman idea of peace.

Although his advocacy of world monarchy, where ultimate authority was located in the Roman emperor, clearly envisaged universal peace, Dante did not explicitly argue for the expansion of Roman rule beyond the borders of Christendom. Dante's times witnessed a number of conflicts within Christendom: I have already mentioned political strife in Florence; indeed, northern Italy was in the midst of political and military struggles. The rise of national kingdoms such as England and France also resulted in confrontation between secular states and the papacy, such as the conflict between Philip IV of France and Pope Boniface VIII. Dante was clearly concerned about the political turmoil within Christendom (Mastnak 2002: 287). To overcome this, Dante insisted on the Roman emperor's centrality in the pacification of Europe: peace should emanate from the Roman centre to every corner of Christendom.

So did Dante not advocate the expansion of the Roman Empire beyond the borders of Christendom? When he discussed various types of human community, he proffered five kinds: household, village, city, kingdom and the entire humanity (Dante 2004: 115–16). Dante is unequivocal in maintaining that the whole of humanity should be subject to the authority of the emperor. However, as Andreas Osiander suggests, Dante is indifferent to political geography (Osiander 2007: 323). Indeed, Dante was not concerned about the territorial expansion of peace beyond Christendom. While he eulogized the Crusaders, for example, he did not actively promote the expansion of Christendom as a goal of the crusading movement. Indeed, his writings provide us with little evidence that he had any knowledge or interest in non-Christian worlds. In his words, in the world outside Christendom, 'all is dark' (Southern 1973: 138). It might not be far from the mark to conclude that Dante's Roman vision of peace was universal in a notional sense only, and did not entail any programme of conquest beyond the borders of Christendom.

Wyclif and the Limits of Just War Theory

If medieval political thought is to be remembered for anything by non-experts, it is probably because of the theory of just war. It has often been said that the theory of just war originates with Augustine, and was subsequently systematized by Aquinas. However, the idea of just war can be historically traced back to pagan philosophy. Cicero claimed that retaliation against harm caused by others is just. What Augustine did was, in one important respect, to Christianize the Ciceronian idea of the justice of retaliation; Augustine regarded punishment of unjust deeds as an act of charity, thereby adding a religious purpose to legitimate retaliation.

Retaliation and vengeance are obviously provoked by some kind of harm caused by others. The agents who engage in a just war are reacting to the situation where peace is violated by injurious others. The focus of just war theorists is, therefore, not the choice between war and peace, because peace has already been violated; rather, the key question for them concerns the justice of war (*jus ad bellum*) as well as the justice in war (*jus in bello*). Just war theorists subscribe to the retributive idea of justice: justice is to get what one is due. William Ian Miller (2006: ix) maintained that the idea of vengeance is the 'antitheory' of justice. Retaliation or vengeance and justice are clearly not mutually exclusive but closely related concepts.

However, peace too is, of course, associated with justice. For example, the early fourteenth-century Dominican, Remigio de' Girolami (Girolami 1977a: 3–51), argued in his short treatise, *On the Common Good*, for the inseparable relationship between peace and justice: drawing on Isaiah 32:17, Remigio asserted, 'the fruit of justice is peace' (Girolami 1977a: 4). Kempshall underscores the importance of Remigio's emphasis on the *causal* relationship between justice and peace. Indeed, 'only justice and virtue can restore harmony to the city since, without justice, no city can be ruled well' (Kempshall 1999: 324). While Remigio is remembered as a thinker who enshrined peace as the ultimate value, he did not argue for pacifism in the sense of the renunciation of violence. On the contrary, his understanding of the causal relationship between peace and justice – 'the fruit of justice is peace' – is consistent with the legitimation of the use of violence for the sake of pacification; indeed, he clearly eulogized patriotic sacrifice for the sake of the fatherland when it is under military threat (Girolami 1977a: 35). Although Remigio did not discuss just war theory explicitly, the exaltation of peace is compatible with the exercise of violence when the latter is deemed just. Clearly, exploring the medieval theory of just war is highly relevant to the understanding of medieval ideas of peace. Not only that, the conceptual constellation of the three concepts – peace, war and justice – is highly problematic.

Aquinas famously argued that a war could be just if it satisfies three conditions: 1. the war is declared by a public authority, 2. there is a legitimate reason for waging a war and 3. the war is waged with right intention (Aquinas 2002: 239–42). The first condition allows war to be commenced only if it is declared by a ruler who is in charge of the common good of a community. The second criterion specifies the circumstance in which the launch of military action is considered just; typically, fault on the other side such as invasion of one's territory. Finally, the third condition proscribes the engagement with military action motivated by private economic interest or savagery.

While Aquinas's defence of just war is widely known, John Wyclif's (ca.1320–1384) reinterpretation of it has hardly received serious attention. Wyclif's reinterpretation, I argue, deserves special attention in the history of the idea of peace because Wyclif's ostensible acknowledgement of just war theory is underpinned by serious skepticism of its viability in a spiritual sense. While the traditional Thomist theory of just war is primarily moral, Wyclif re-interpreted just war theory in the context of Christian spirituality, thereby undermining the spiritual, not moral, justice of war.

Wyclif was an Oxford theologian whose polemical work was controversially characterized by anti-clericalism. Known as the 'Morning Star of the Reformation',

Wyclif attacked the contemporary English Church in the final decade of his life; his doctrine of predestination, in particular, undermined the privileged status of the priesthood and reduced the true Church into an 'invisible' (that is, non-institutional) entity. Combined with his controversial attack on transubstatiation, his theory of the Church represents a major development in late medieval heresy.

However, Wyclif did not write on just war in the context of an ecclesiological debate. Rather, he was responding to the Hundred Years War between England and France (1337–1453). Wyclif's discussion of just war can be found in *On Civil Dominion* (*De civili dominio*), one of the major political treatises he wrote in 1376. At the time of writing, the 'Infantry Revolution' was taking place: the growing importance of common infantry in the fourteenth century had a significant impact on the cultural attitude towards war. The pikemen and archers who increasingly played an important role in warfare were generally drawn from the common populace, not from the aristocracy. One of the consequences of this was that battles became much bloodier than before. In the High Middle Ages, noble combatants, if defeated in combat, did not expect to be killed but rather captured for ransom. However, common infantry who were originally drawn from the peasantry could not afford to be ransomed. Coupled with the proximate style of combat, the battles became much more sanguinary than had been the case in previous centuries (Rogers 1999: 142–8). The changing culture of war may have prompted Wyclif to reconsider just war theory.

In discussing just war, Wyclif inherited the Thomist 'language'. Following the conventional framework faithfully, Wyclif acknowledged the three criteria which are required for a war to be just: authority, just cause and right intention. However, Wyclif raised an additional hurdle. According to Wyclif, the authority that is appropriate to declare war is political authority, authorized by Christ. Wyclif maintains that the gospel rejects the use of violence; therefore, a prince who wishes to declare war must wait for a special revelation that manifests Christ's approval of the start of military action (Wyclif 1885–1904 vol. 2: 243).

The necessity of a special revelation derives from Wyclif's own theologico-political programme. According to Wyclif, the legitimacy of political authority is predicated on dominion (*dominium*), which is sanctioned by divine grace. Wyclif's theological discussion of the origin of political authority can be boiled down to the idea that this-worldly political rule among post-lapsarian humans requires civil dominion, which is instituted by humans themselves, not God. Civil dominion is, in a nutshell, dominative relations resulting from the Fall (Shogimen 2006: 231). The Fall deprived humans of natural dominion, which was granted by God and therefore could not be exercised unjustly. Subsequent to original sin, however, humans required civil dominion of their own making, which would easily lead to strife, theft and war. This, however, did not mean to Wyclif that civil dominion could never be just; on the contrary, it could be just if divine grace justifies the holder of the dominion. This argument rests on the idea that true dominion belongs to God alone. Man-made civil dominion is, as long as it is merely man-made, not just. The holder of civil dominion must participate in divine dominion by acknowledging that his dominion is loaned by God. A civil lord is therefore no more than a steward of God (Shogimen 2006: 232–3). The theological idea of civil dominion underpins Wyclif's discussion of the public authority which can legitimately declare war: the declaration of war necessitates divine grace.

Ostensibly Wyclif's discussion of public authority declaring war is not a rejection of the traditional Thomist discourse. Rather, he examined the traditional discussion within his own theological framework, and recognized a theological possibility of declaring just war. From this point, however, Wyclif's argument swings sharply in an anti-war direction: he underscores the spiritual danger of involvement in war, in light of his reading of the New Testament and Christ's rejection of the use of violence. Drawing on Origen's exegesis, Wyclif argues that wars in the Old Testament prefigure spiritual wars in the New Testament. Thus, the Old Testament justifies no (physical) wars and under the Law of Christ, Christians must endure evil by emulating Christ's modesty and patience (Wyclif 1885–1904 vol. 2: 247, Levy 2005: 339). This 'pacifist' counsel accompanies the recognition of the theological possibility of a legitimate declaration of war.

The approval of just war theory and the recognition of the spiritual danger of war co-exist curiously throughout Wyclif's discussion of *jus ad bellum*. This is also obvious in his reflections on self-defence as one of the criteria for just war. On the one hand, he acknowledges the moral permissibility of retaliating against aggression: self-defence is indeed permitted by natural law. But, on the other hand, Wyclif added a caveat: the use of violence for self-defence needs to satisfy two conditions. One is that retaliation in response to an unjust exercise of violence must be carried out as soon as possible. The other is that the violence to be used for retaliation must not be excessive. Prompt and modest use of violence legitimizes retaliation (Wyclif 1885–1904 vol. 2: 260).

Wyclif's emphasis shifts again in an anti-war direction when he claims that self-defence is not what natural law commands; rather it only permits it in certain circumstances. No one is morally obliged to defend oneself and retaliate. Thus, Wyclif's argument points significantly towards a *spiritual* critique of self-defence. While Wyclif does not reject the possibility of just self-defence, he maintains that from the viewpoint of faith it is safer for Christians to emulate Christ in enduring even the exercise of unjust violence rather than having recourse to violence no matter how morally permissible it might be (Wyclif 1885–1904 vol. 2: 272–3). This claim of the danger to spiritual wellbeing was not divorced from the reality of human conditions. Wyclif offered a sobering critique of just war theory although he was deeply sceptical that individuals would restrict their exercise of violence for the sake of self-defence to the minimum level of necessity. His awareness of the reality that the right of self-defence was often abused compelled him to dissuade his readers from the exercise of that right.

What underlies Wyclif's ambivalence towards self-defence is the priority he gives to the rigorous practice of Christ's humility and charity. Clearly Wyclif's expectation in the practice of Christian ethics was high for lay believers, and even higher for the clergy. Indeed, while Wyclif tolerates the lay believers' exercise of violence for self-defence, he recommends the clergy to flee without confronting violent enemies. It is spiritually risky, Wyclif avers, that clergymen resist enemies by means of violence. It is permissible that clergymen somehow manage to suppress enemies without killing them and persuade them to stop exercising violence by means of Christian virtue. However, the best course of action, according to Wyclif, is non-resistance to enemies. The clergy ought to continue persuading enemies to stop using violence, but they should be ready to be killed (Levy 2005: 341).

From what I have outlined above, it should be clear that the third condition of just war – right intention – was highly significant for Wyclif. The Law of Christ preached humility, charity and fraternal love. Committing oneself to war in pursuit of political dominion or temporal wealth would make war unjust. Wyclif's political thought is predicated on the idea that political dominion, which is a loan from God, was a 'burden' that no one should desire to bear. Nonetheless, reality was precisely the opposite: wars were fought incessantly in order to seek greater political power and material wealth. Wyclif thus reasserted that no prince ought to take a spiritual risk of waging war unless such action was commanded by God through a new revelation. No matter how just the intention might be, waging war was less preferable to the practice of humility and charity, which might change the hostile attitude of enemies. For Wyclif, war damaged both invaders and the invaded by implanting such vices as anger and arrogance in those who were involved in the war. In a spiritual sense, therefore, Wyclif observed that there were no winners in war (Wyclif 1885–1904 vol. 2: 238–9, Levy 2005: 336).

Clearly Wyclif undermined the justice of war on spiritual grounds. For him, war might be a morally permissible instrument for political conflicts; however, it was not seen as an instrument for peace because war was antithetical to Christian humility and charity; rather war was first and foremost a serious danger to the spirituality of all those involved. Wyclif therefore claimed that the pursuit of peace must begin with the spiritual battle with original sin. Wyclif's reading of just war theory was therefore not political. Rather it was a theological reinterpretation of just war theory. Frederick H. Russell (1975) showed that just war theory was an innovation of medieval canon lawyers, which Aquinas incorporated into his theological system. While Aquinas discussed the justice of war on moral grounds, Wyclif re-examined it in a spiritual context. Wyclif's theologico-spiritual response to just war theory may be integral to his ideological opposition to lawyers. Indeed, Wyclif was one of the theologians who were weary of canon lawyers' influence on ecclesiastical affairs (Shogimen 2006). As major ecclesiastical offices were increasingly monopolized by canon lawyers, theologians asserted the superiority of theology over canon law, thereby criticizing the penetration of juristic thinking in ecclesiastical governance. Wyclif's radical re-reading of just war theory may be seen as part of this ideological trend: war is not merely a matter of law or morality, but also of spirituality, which could be addressed not by canon lawyers but by theologians.

Conclusion

I have outlined how and why political writings on peace emerged at the turn of the thirteenth and fourteenth centuries before I examined Dante's 'Roman' vision of peace and Wyclif's 'spiritual' critique of just war theory. I have not singled out the two thinkers because they represent medieval thinking about war and peace. Indeed, there was no such thing as *the* medieval conception of peace; there were diverse visions of it. The present chapter has shown such diversity through two case studies, which approached the question of peace from very different perspectives.

The emergence of peace writings in this period suggests a wide recognition of the possibility of this-worldly peace as well as a desire for such peace. Dante's 'Roman' peace is clearly an alternative to the Roman Church's claim for universal peace under the direction of the papacy. Dante's vision of pacification is secular in the sense that it concerns the actual arrangement of the social and political order, to which, Dante claims, the Roman Church cannot contribute, although he sees the emperor's role as the guarantor of peace in the context of Christian history. Dante's perspective on peace is consequentialist in that his focus is on the actual realization of peace, which is entrusted to the emperor. Wyclif's vision of peace is, by contrast, not political in that it concerns not so much the actual conditions of a political community as the spiritual aspirations of individual Christians. If Dante's vision can be labelled a 'macro' theory, Wyclif's is a 'micro' theory. Wyclif is demanding the renunciation of violence by individual believers for the sake of Christian spirituality; he is not advancing an argument for the political value of peace in this world. Finally, Wyclif's perspective on peace is, unlike Dante's, intentionalist: each believer's adherence to his religious conviction is his primary focus, not the actual fulfillment of peace. Despite the differences in time, context, perspective and motivation, the two thinkers shared a desire for peace in this world.

Yet neither Dante's universal vision nor Wyclif's spiritual counsel brought about peace in fourteenth-century Western Europe. Wyclif stood at the threshold of a 'military revolution'. In the fifteenth century, firearms were introduced to the European battlefield. The scale of human loss and physical destruction became ever greater. Their limited contributions to the pacification of Europe in the fourteenth century does not necessarily mean they have no relevance in fertilizing our conceptions of peace in the twenty-first century. The visions of peace proposed by Dante, Wyclif and other medieval thinkers remain a source of ideas that have yet to be excavated. While their conclusions are certainly of historical interest, perhaps the key point is that their perspectives and methods in problematizing just war and envisaging peace are more instructive to our own conceptualization of peace. Both Dante and Wyclif placed a thick question mark on the predominant ideological assumptions of their day, that is, the universal domination of the Roman Church and the legitimacy of just war theory respectively. Radical scepticism towards our tacit assumptions may be a lesson we can learn from medieval European theorists of peace.[2]

Bibliography

Aquinas, T. 2002. *Political Writings*. Translated from Latin by R.W. Dyson. Cambridge: Cambridge University Press.

Bemrose, S. 2005, *Gaudium et Pax*: what being in heaven means for Dante. *Forum for Modern Language Studies,* 41(1), 71–89.

Burns, J.H. 1988. Introduction, in *The Cambridge History of Medieval Political Thought*, edited by J.H. Burns. Cambridge: Cambridge University Press, 1–8.

Coopland, G.W. 1949. *The Tree of Battles of Honoré Bonet*. Liverpool: Liverpool University Press.

Dante 1916. *De Monarchia*, edited by E. Moore. Oxford: Clarendon Press.

Dante 1996. *Monarchy*. Translated from Latin by P. Shaw. Cambridge: Cambridge University Press.

Dante 2004. Monarchia, in A.K. Cassell, *The* Monarchia *Controversy*. Washington DC: Catholic University of America Press, 111–73.

Davis, C.T. 1957. *Dante and the Idea of Rome*. Oxford: Clarendon Press.

Davis, C.T. 1959. Remigio de' Girolami and Dante: a comparison of their conceptions of peace. *Studi Danteschi*, 36, 105–36.

Davis, C.T. 1993. Dante and empire, in *The Cambridge Companion to Dante*, edited by R. Jacoff. Cambridge: Cambridge University Press, 67–79.

Dubois, P. 1956. *The Recovery of the Holy Land.* Translated from Latin by W.I. Brandt. New York: Columbia University Press.

Fuchs, H. 1965. *Augustin und der antike Friedensgedanke*. Berlin and Zurich: Weidmannsche Verlagsbuchhandlung.

Galtung, J. 1981. Social cosmology and the concept of peace. *Journal of Peace Research,* 18(2), 183–99.

Girolami, R. de' 1977a. De bono communi, in M.C. de Matteis, *La 'teologia politica comunale' di Remigio de' Girolami*. Bologna: Patro Editore, 3–51.

Girolami, R. de' 1977b. De bono pacis, in M.C. de Matteis, *La 'teologia politica comunale' di Remigio de' Girolami*. Bologna: Patro Editore, 55–71.

Izbicki, T. and Nederman, C.J. 2000. *Three Tracts on Empire*. Bristol: Thoemmes Press.

Kempshall, M.S. 1999. *The Common Good in Late Medieval Political Thought*. Oxford: Clarendon Press.

Kempshall, M.S. 2001. Ecclesiology and politics, in *The Medieval Theologians*, edited by G. R. Evans. Oxford: Blackwell, 303–33.

2 This chapter is part of my research project supported by the Marsden Fund of the Royal Society of New Zealand. Special thanks are due to Stephen Conway for his help.

Levy, I.C. 2005. John Wyclif: Christian patience in a time of war. *Theological Studies*, 66(2), 330–57.

Marsilius of Padua 1932–1933. *Defensor Pacis*, edited by R. Scholz. Hannover: Hahn.

Marsilius of Padua 1956. *The Defender of Peace*. Translated from Latin by A. Gewirth. New York: Columbia University Press.

Marsilius of Padua 2005. *The Defender of the Peace*. Translated from Latin by A.S. Brett. Cambridge: Cambridge University Press.

Mastnak, T. 2002. *Crusading Peace: Christendom, the Muslim World, and Western Political Order*. Berkeley, CA: University of California Press.

Miller, W.I. 2006. *Eye for an Eye*. Cambridge: Cambridge University Press.

Nederman, C.J. 1988. Nature, sin and the origins of society: the Ciceronian tradition in medieval political thought. *Journal of the History of Ideas*, 49(1), 3–26.

Osiander, A. 2007. *Before the State: Systemic Political Change in the West from the Greeks to the French Revolution*. Oxford: Oxford University Press.

Pizan, C. de 2008. *The Book of Peace*, edited and translated from French by K. Green, C.J. Mews and J. Pinder. University Park, PA: Pennsylvania State University Press.

Rufinus 1997. *De Bono Pacis*, edited and translated from Latin by R. Deutiger. Hannover: Hahn.

Russell, F.H. 1975. *The Just War in the Middle Ages*. Cambridge: Cambridge University Press.

Shogimen, T. 2006. Wyclif's ecclesiology and political thought, in *A Companion to John Wyclif: Late Medieval Theologian*, edited by I.C. Levy. Leiden: Brill, 199–240.

Shogimen, T. 2010. European ideas of peace in the late thirteenth and early fourteenth centuries. *The European Legacy*, 15(7), 871–85.

Southern, R.W. 1973. Dante and Islam, in *Relations between East and West in the Middle Ages*, edited by D. Baker. Edinburgh: Edinburgh University Press, 133–45.

Ullmann, W. 1965. *A History of Political Thought: The Middle Ages*. Harmondsworth: Penguin Books.

Weinstock, S. 1960. 'Pax' and the 'Ara Pacis'. *Journal of Roman Studies,* 50(1–2): 44–58.

Weinstock, S. 1971. *Divus Julius*. Oxford: Clarendon Press.

Woodhouse, J. 1997. Dante and governance: contexts and contents, in *Dante and Governance*, edited by J.R. Woodhouse. Oxford: Clarendon Press, 1–11.

Wyclif, J. 1885–1904. *De Civili Dominio*, 4 vols, edited by J. Loserth. London: Wyclif Society.

Zampaglione, G. 1973. *The Idea of Peace in Antiquity*. Translated from Italian by R. Dunn. Notre Dame, IN: University of Notre Dame Press.

Chapter 7
Enlightenment Perspectives on War and Peace

Bruce Buchan

When actions, unadorn'd, are faint and weak,
Cities and countries must be taught to speak;
Gods may descend in factions from the skies,
And rivers from their oozy beds arise;
Fiction may deck the truth with spurious rays,
And round the hero cast a borrow'd blaze. (Addison 1710: 16)[1]

The European Enlightenment has long been viewed as a pivotal era characterized by the consolidation of modern ideas of personal rights and freedom, the wider dissemination of humanitarian and reformist sentiments, the emergence of civil societies with more responsive governments and commercial economies whose dynamics were deemed explicable by the rational standards of political economy. Though recent scholarship has seriously revised this traditional interpretation, and indeed has questioned the usefulness of speaking of a unitary European Enlightenment, the idea of a unified Enlightenment is still regularly heralded as an era in which the wanton or at least unregulated cruelty of war was increasingly subjected to rational and pacifying principles and statutes (Bacevich 2008, Lawrence 1999). Indeed, for one recent writer (Gittings 2012: 10, 18), 'the first step towards' international plans to limit war and realize peace was taken by 'the Enlightenment' that lauded 'glorious peace' in preference to 'glorious warfare'. A little more soberly, Antony Adolf (2009: 127–8) traced the emergence of modern efforts to pursue peace through multinational organizations and 'a legal framework in which wars and warfare could be contained or even eliminated' to the utopian schemes of Enlightenment intellectuals. This celebratory narrative needs to be contextualized. As I will show, many of Europe's Enlightenment luminaries believed that the prospects of peace were tied to the practice of war, albeit war that exemplified principles of 'humanity'. Humanity here meant not only virtues of clemency and civility, as well as sentiments of pity and compassion, but also the cool calculation of self and national interests (Hanley 2011: 208). These principles, interests and sentiments of humanity have played a key part in the celebratory self-image of the Enlightenment as an age, if not quite of peace, then

1 Addison wrote *The Campaign* in the wake of British victory at the battle of Blenheim in 1704.

at least of an increasingly civilized, more strictly limited and therefore less bloody warfare, in which peace became a serious object of European diplomacy (Buchan 2013, Heuser 2010a: 98).

This self-image built upon the conviction that François de Callières (1645–1717) expressed in his *The Art of Negotiating With Princes* when he wrote,

> that all the States of *Europe* have necessary Ties and Commerces one with another, which makes them to be look'd upon as Members of one and the same Commonwealth, and that there can hardly happen any considerable change in some of its Members, but what is capable of disturbing the Quiet of all the others. (Callières 1716: 7)

For Callières (1716: 16–17, 106–7), it was the job of the diplomat to nudge and entice his sovereign to avoid costly wars, to embrace peace and seek the honour of mediating other's disputes. In this chapter, I will argue that the European Enlightenment's apparent veneration for peace was underwritten by a much more complicated discourse on the relationship between war, peace and civilization. For some, Europe was in the process of giving rise to a more peaceful mode of limited and civilized war. Nonetheless, these sentiments were often hedged by claims that European warfare was also becoming a more sophisticated technical practice, the scientific mastery of which promised to give European war-makers unparalleled power and reach. Uncovering the connection between these two claims, about civilized and limited but scientific and overwhelming war-making, reveals how closely war and peace were linked in European self-imagining during the Enlightenment period. This self-imagining, I argue in the first section, was heavily laced with fictional accounts of the civilized and pacific qualities of modern war. In the second and third sections, I contend that notions of a European accomplishment of peace were taken up, in particular, by Scottish Enlightenment intellectuals who attempted to provide a more coherent account of European war-making as both an agent of peace and an index of historical development. As I argue in the fourth section, the corollary of their normative histories was that the emergence of increasingly civilized norms of conduct in Europe was tied to the development of sovereign states, effectively consigning peoples without such states to a parlous status awaiting supposedly superior European civilization and superior European military power.

Civil and Military Fictions

At the dawn of the eighteenth century, the Baron de Lahontan (1666–ca.1715) provided some reflections on the nature of European war-making in comparison to the war-making of Canada's indigenous Huron and Iroquois warriors. Lahontan's reflections were an early attempt at a satirical reverse ethnography, for he used a fictional indigenous interlocutor to reflect back on the identity and conventions of his French and European readers. In speaking of the 'Military Art of the Savages', which had hitherto largely been portrayed by Europeans as an unremitting scene of savage cruelty, one of Lahontan's invented interlocutors, a Huron warrior named 'Rat', articulates a savage indictment of European war-making. 'Prithee, my Brother', says Rat,

> I do not know any Animal that wages war with others of its own Species, excepting Man, who upon this score is more Unnatural than the Beasts. ... this Reason which Man boasts so much of is the greatest Instrument of his Misery ... if Men were without the Faculty of Thinking, Arguing and Speaking, they would not imbarque in mutual Wars as they now do, without any regard to Humanity or Sacred Promises. (Lahontan 1703: 495–6)

'Such, Sir, are the Moral Thoughts of a Savage', Lahontan continued, 'who pretends to Philosophise upon the Custom that we have of killing Men with Justice and Honour'. Lahontan's 'Rat' here voiced a familiar anthropocentric complaint that war was the blight of humankind, but Lahontan gave this complaint a less familiar edge. The horror of war was a fault not so much of an unredeemed savage human nature, but of refined and civilized accomplishments of reason, thinking, arguing and speaking. The implication that contemporaries must have drawn was that contrary to commonplace Hobbesian assumptions about the endemic uncertainty and potentially ceaseless violence of the *savage* state of nature, wars would be more frequent where *civilized* accomplishments were most developed.

Not content with this unsettling of common assumptions, Lahontan broadened his attack in a significant way. Unlike the beasts, he suggested, human beings launch wars in flagrant breach of the most fundamental principles of humanity and religion. The very same civilized faculties that allowed human beings to register these principles were the same media for their cynical abrogation. Lahontan, this time in his own rather than Rat's voice, appeared to flatter his audience with a knowing wink, the 'moral thoughts of a savage' can only be an ignorant pretence, but he acknowledged that they still indicted *our* 'custom' of 'killing men with justice and honour'. The import of Lahontan's phraseology could easily be missed, for the idea that Europeans (the 'we' he invokes from his readership) waged civilized war in a rational manner in conformity with civilized principles of humanity, justice and honour was rapidly becoming a hallmark of European belief in its own civilization. For many Europeans, especially in the late eighteenth century, European civilization consisted, in part at least, in waging 'civilized' war in contrast to more barbarous or even savage non-European ways of war. Importantly, the European idea of civilized war was propagated by thinkers engaged above all in intra-European reflection. Civilized war thus became an identifier not simply of a civilized Europe in contrast to barbarous or savage peoples and lands beyond Europe. Rather, civilized war was an identifier of the partial nature of civilization within Europe.

This feature of the idea of civilized war was on full display in François-Marie Arouet's (Voltaire) (1694–1778) account of France's victory over British and allied forces at the battle of Fontenoy on 11 May 1745. Fontenoy has been seen as a classic example of Enlightened warfare in which highly disciplined military forces met in open battle under apparently strict rules of engagement, where the opposing forces approached within musket shot before saluting their opponents and inviting them to fire first (Weigley 1993: 203–7). As colourful as this tale is, there was no mention made in primary accounts of the battle of this exchange of civilities between the British and French officers (see Buchan 2009). The story originates with Voltaire (1859: 261–74), whose national sentiment had been so stirred by news of the victory that he penned his poetic elegy to the sacrifice of the fallen. Among Voltaire's reasons for writing the poem were his close connections to the Marquis d'Argenson, for whom, as Louis XV's foreign minister, victory at Fontenoy vindicated France's participation in the war of the Austrian Succession (1742–1748). Voltaire's poem celebrated the achievements of French arms in the service of the peace, security and civilization of Europe, in direct contrast to the earlier efforts of Joseph Addison (1672–1719) to make the same claims for British victory over the French at Blenheim in 1704.

Addison's *The Campaign* (1710: 11) hit all the right notes of British national sentiment triumphing over French tyranny, 'the Dread of *Europe*'. Much of the success of the poem lay in Addison's politically useful portrayal of Louis XIV as a vainglorious tyrant seeking European domination, and Britain's Queen Anne as the agent of Divine providence responding to European fear and despair, 'To Britain's Queen the Nations turn their Eyes,/ On her Resolves the Western World relies' (Addison 1710: 4). The battle itself, 'Big with the Fate of *Europe*' (Addison 1710: 5), was portrayed in terms that would resonate in Britain throughout the eighteenth century, as a contest between righteous British courage and indignation at the prostration of Europe before the dreadful and terrifying hosts of the French tyrant (Pocock 1999: 219). This was not simply a battle against France, Addison suggested, but a struggle for the peace, stability and security of Europe. Addison pictured Britain's involvement in the campaign alongside the forces of Holland and the Holy Roman Emperor as confirmation of a European system of alliances 'Polish'd in Courts, and harden'd in the Field' (Addison 1710: 6). British and allied victory was loudly proclaimed, as was the utter rout and confusion of French defeat amid 'Floods of Gore that from the Vanquish'd fell' (Addison 1710: 13). The 'rescued States' of Europe are able to rejoice that the 'fate of Europe' had been decided by crushing victory over Louis's 'thirst of universal sway' (Addison 1710: 13, 16). Significantly, Addison ended his poem with a final reflection of what he had done. Specifically, he reflected on the use, and the need, for fiction,

> Thus would I fain Britannia's wars rehearse,
> In the smooth records of a faithful verse; …
> When actions, unadorn'd, are faint and weak,
> Cities and countries must be taught to speak;

> Gods may descend in factions from the skies,
> And rivers from their oozy beds arise;
> Fiction may deck the truth with spurious rays,
> and round the hero cast a borrow'd blaze. (Addison 1710: 16)

Curiously, it was in the use of artful exaggeration, or in Addison's own terms, the 'spurious rays' and 'borrow'd blaze' of 'fiction', that Voltaire was to celebrate French victory at Fontenoy on precisely the same grounds as Addison had celebrated Blenheim. For Voltaire (1859: 252), Fontenoy was an opportunity not only to rebut Addison's epic charges that the French fled from Blenheim by swimming the Danube, but also to picture France as the bulwark of European peace and security, and the source of an even more valuable European civilization. Voltaire's poem did little to establish this claim, for in it he mostly commemorated the bravery and courage of the French monarch and dauphin (both present on the field) and the various aristocratic French officers who demonstrated cultivated sang-froid and an almost casual courage. Voltaire used his prose preface to the poem to establish the significance of this point. 'The French', Voltaire (1859: 254) maintained, 'can never be denied the glory of valor and politeness'. In speaking of politeness, Voltaire pointed to the cultivated manners, refined tastes and education of the aristocracy of France as the embodiment and the source of Europe's civilization. This civilization consisted in the peaceful 'principles of humanity' that 'are not to be found in the other quarters of the world; they [Europeans] are better united with each other; they have certain laws, which are common to them all; all their royal families are related; the inhabitants of each kingdom travel among their neighbors' (Voltaire 1859: 253).

By these means, Voltaire argued, the nations of Europe (or at least their upper classes) 'keep up a reciprocal connection', even in war. In words that almost seemed to echo those of Callières, Voltaire (1859: 253) maintained that although European nations fight frequent wars: 'in the midst of these dissensions, they generally observe so much decorum and politeness, that it often happens, that a Frenchman, an Englishman, and a German meeting, seem to be natives of the same city'. It was this desire to celebrate the aristocratic civilization of French and other European officers that coloured Voltaire's later description of the legend of battlefield civility at Fontenoy in his *History of the War of 1741* which makes a centre-piece of the supposed encounter. At the climactic moment, when the opposing forces were no more than 'fifty paces' apart, Voltaire (1756: 215) recounts the following exchange:

> The English officers saluted the French by taking off their hats. The Count de Chabannes and the Duke de Biron advanced forward, and returned the compliment. My Lord Charles Hay, captain of the English guards, cried out, 'Gentlemen of the French guards, give fire'. The Count d'Antroche, then lieutenant and since captain of grenadiers, made answer with a loud voice, 'Gentlemen, we never fire first; fire you first'. Then the captain said to his men, in English, *Fire*.

Voltaire's account of this civilized encounter has become an emblem of eighteenth-century European war-making. For many contemporary Europeans, the distinctive feature of European war-making was its order and discipline, enabling its practitioners, so it was argued, to limit its destructiveness. The idea that European warfare in the eighteenth century was (or was becoming) civilized, though widely shared by contemporary theorists and practitioners, was as illusory as Voltaire's legend of battlefield civilities. Addison's and Voltaire's military fictions sought to elevate the horrors of war to a higher plane of pan-European and even global significance by claiming that war embodied civilized values of humanity and peace. In doing so, these European thinkers were engaged in the task, relatively new in European thought, of seeing themselves not simply as a 'new' but a 'modern' age characterized by a greater respect for the values of 'humanity', that is, of pacifying considerations of clemency, honour, magnanimity and decency. In constructing genealogies of a more civilized and peaceful modernity, a variety of mid and later eighteenth century European thinkers aimed to convince their readers not by means of poetic fiction, but by supposed historical objectivity. As we will see in the following section, their narratives established the idea of civilized war as an index of Europe's modernity and of its aspiration towards peace.

War and Peace in the 'Age of Negotiation'

The perception that the nations of Europe, or at least some of them, were at the forefront of a modern age emerged in the sixteenth century in response to the series of changes ushered in by the Protestant Reformation and Catholic Counter-Reformation of the sixteenth century. Both events, it has been argued (Fasolt 2004: 18–21), shattered whatever consensus existed at the time that human history was developing along a divinely ordered trajectory. This transformation led to the effort to place European peoples and nations within a temporal scheme that did not hinge on a divine dispensation, but sought to demonstrate that scientific, geographic and technological advances validated a European 'genius'. This genius and the very special advances that seemed to flow from it pointed to a process of historical development driven by human thought and action. This process might not be a unidirectional Christian eschatological historical scheme, but neither was it a perennial Polybian cycle of historical greatness and decline. It was a process whose causes and driving forces Europeans felt increasingly confident in being able to unravel. It was above all a progressive model of history, one that could accommodate reversals and stagnations, and promised through diligent study of historical cause and effect, to explain not only how Europe's modern civilization emerged but also why it was superior to those it succeeded.

By the eighteenth century, Europeans had come to define their 'modernity' in terms of the creation of an apparently 'new' social order based on the cultivation of 'new' manners and interests. As Henry St John, Lord Bolingbroke (1678–1751) put it:

> New interests beget new maxims of government, and new methods of conduct. These in their turns, beget new manners, new habits, new customs. … Such a period therefore is … an epoch or era … from which you reckon forward. … The end of the fifteenth century seems to be just such a period as I have been describing, for those who live in the eighteenth, and who inhabit the western parts of Europe. … [At that time] all those revolutions began, that have produced so vast a change in the manners, customs, and interests of particular nations … (Bolingbroke 1972: 82–3)

What Bolingbroke also signalled here was the emergence of a modern Europe incorporating a new domestic social order centred on individual interests and a new international political order based on peaceful national interests. This was a post-Westphalian order based on a 'balance of power' between sovereign states premised on the dispassionate pursuit (by each member state) of their own national interests. Far from unleashing further conflict, Bolingbroke saw this development as a further step towards greater regularity and peace – the cold-blooded calculation of national interest maximization replacing the hot-blooded pursuit of religious zealotry or dynastic ambition.

It was in this vein that Bolingbroke (1748: 219–22) had depicted ancient Athens as a model that contemporary Britain should emulate. Moderate in its manners, so Bolingbroke claimed, Athens was militarily secure but without ambition for extensive territorial conquests, and it pursued a policy of naval supremacy and benign protection of weaker states. When threatened by Sparta, the Athenians wisely resorted to all diplomatic means to avoid war and it was then, Bolingbroke (1748: 230) argued, that 'the Age of *Negotiation*' between states began. Britain's Advocate General, James Marriott (1730–1803), later echoed Bolingbroke's sentiments very closely when he characterized his as an age in which European diplomatic practice had been 'civilized' (Marriott 1765). In effect, he suggested that modern Europe was more 'civilized' than previous eras due in large part to the calculated pursuit of self-interest:

> When I speak of the present Age, I mean an interval of Time from the Treaty of Westphalia down to the last definitive Treaty of Versailles, which may be called the Age of Negotiation, of which kind of Intercourse and Connections the Greeks and Romans contending always with barbarous Nations, had very partial Notions, drawn however from and adapted to the Condition of their Rivals, and the rest of Mankind in those Ages. (Marriott 1765)

Here the logic of Marriott's argument turned on the fundamental assumption that European nations had succeeded in civilizing war by directing it towards peace, interest and the values of humanity.

> In the present Age as War is commenced on different Principles from the Wars of Antiquity, so it ends with different Principles, in both more to the Honour of

> Humanity. The public law of Europe abhors the sanguinary Object of antient [sic] Wars, universal Slavery, or Extirpation – Every War in these Times is considered but as an Appeal to the rest of the powers of Europe, and is but a temporary Exertion of Force to decide a Point of Interest. (Marriott 1765)

The premise of Bolingbroke's and Marriott's contentions was that history had a direction, leading away from the almost ceaseless violence of Europe's savage past towards the rational pursuit of peace in Europe's modern age. A key to unravelling the direction of historical development was the transformation of the rude virtues of savage life (based on simplicity, hardiness and a warrior ethos) into the polite and cultivated manners of civilized societies that reflected the peaceful values of humanity (Smith 1976: 205–9).

In emphasizing manners, Scottish historians of civilization argued that civilized, if mundane interests and the laudable virtues of honour and clemency, coupled with the desire to win the approbation of others, gradually replaced the savage virtues of courage and intrepidity as well as the savage desire for revenge (Smith 1976: 144–5, Hume 1985c: 406–7). According to Adam Ferguson (1723–1816), in earlier stages of social development, exemplars of which included the 'barbarous' Ancient Greeks and the 'savage' American Indians, revenge was a constant source of conflict and a drain on the population (Ferguson 1995a: 98). The ungovernable desire for revenge and extermination of one's enemies was opposed, in Ferguson's (1995a: 201–3) view, to considerations of clemency, gallantry and above all, the principle of honour among combatants which, he thought, had become a hallmark of European 'civilization'. In the practice of 'civilized' war in particular, 'honourable' conventions (such as sparing the lives of prisoners and wounded) were thought to limit the extent of violence on the battlefield, and to direct war solely to the dispassionate pursuit of national interests. As David Hume (1711–1776) put it, 'where honour and interest steel men against compassion as well as fear … combatants divest themselves of the brute, and resume the man' (Hume 1985a: 274).

Civilized societies were those characterized by the interdependent development of both flourishing commercial economies and effective state sovereignty. These 'civilized' states, such as Britain, France and Holland, confronted one another in a new international order of sovereign states in Europe. In this way, the domestic development of civilized manners was tied to the civilization of international relations by the influence that those civilized manners had on the mechanisms of international conduct – war, diplomacy and treaties. As Marriott (1765) put it, 'The System of Nations concerning their reciprocal Rights, whether by Usage or Treaty depends upon their Manners'. Perhaps nowhere were these sentiments more forcefully expressed than in Scottish Enlightenment histories of civilization in which war and diplomacy were treated as crucial indexes of social progress.

Artillery and Pacification in the 'System of Europe'

Many of the Scottish intellectuals of the eighteenth century took their lead from Montesquieu (1689–1755). He had already celebrated the civilization of war in Europe (that he referred to as the European 'right of nations in war'), due to the softening influence of Christianity, which 'leaves to the vanquished ... life, liberty, laws, goods' (Montesquieu 1985: 461–2). Characteristically, however, Scottish Enlightenment thinkers emphasized the essentially unintentional effects of civilization (Hume 1985a: 271).[2] Accordingly, even the destructiveness of European war-making could produce benefits, one of which was the intensification of considerations of national interest among European states leading to greater peace within the 'system of Europe'.[3] This 'system' consisted in a rough military balance between European states who agreed to pursue their individual interests by means, first of all, of diplomacy and treaties, and by war if necessary, though even here the pacifying influence of interest predominated. In Hume's *History* for example, even the invention of devastatingly lethal artillery showed the influence of civilization by reinforcing the calculation of national interests. This 'furious engine', Hume (1983 vol. 2: 148) wrote:

> Though it seemed contrived for the destruction of mankind, and the overthrow of empires, has in the issue rendered battles less bloody, and has given greater stability to civil societies. Nations by its means have been brought more to a level: Conquests have become less frequent and rapid: Success in war has been reduced nearly to be a matter of calculation: And any nation overmatched by its enemies, either yields to their demands, or secures itself by alliances against their violence and invasion.

The extension of Hume's argument was that the practice of war in Europe showed not only the effect of civilization, but even drove it forward. The crucial point was that this kind of warfare reinforced the intimate connection between peace and civilized war conducted according to dictates of interest and civilized manners.

Few Scottish Enlightenment thinkers spent more time reflecting on the historical connection between war and peace than William Robertson (1721–1793). Robertson began his *History of the Reign of Charles V* with an extended discourse on the period from the collapse of the Roman Empire to the sixteenth century entitled, 'A View of the Progress of Society in Europe'. According to Robertson (1827 vol. 3: 8), the rapid conquests of 'barbarian' peoples in Europe were accompanied by 'horrible devastations and incredible destruction of the

---

2 As Hume argued here, technological advances ('industry') stimulated the growth of '*knowledge*, and *humanity*' by opening up more avenues for sociability, leading to greater knowledge and refinement of manners.

3 The phrase 'system of Europe' was Hume's (1983 vol. 3: 126), but his analysis, as Pocock (1999: 310) has argued, closely mirrored that of Robertson (see below).

human species'. This barbaric violence he directly opposed to the 'cool reflection' of carefully weighed self-interest with which the 'Civilized nations' of Europe in his own day 'carry on their hostilities with so little rancour or animosity' where war 'is disarmed of half its terrors'. Uncivilized barbarians by contrast prosecute their wars with unrestrained and passionate ferocity. Their objectives are to exterminate or to terrorize their opponents, and it is precisely in this form that the 'savage tribes in America' in his day make war. Robertson traced the gradual emergence of more civilized principles of war to a variety of causes, among them the survival of Roman law and the consolidation of feudal land tenure that linked military service to a central authority. Among these causes, however, one of the most important was the elimination of 'the private right of war' to redress civil wrongs (Robertson 1827 vol. 3: 40).

Importantly, this development was linked to a range of other crucial advances. In his terms, the right of private war, or 'judicial combat', made sense in a 'rude' society where reading and writing were uncommon accomplishments rendering laws inconsistent and justice uncertain. For these reasons, Robertson (1827 vol. 3: 43–7) argued, contest by violence was deemed consistent with the only certain source of justice, the judgement of God. The consolidation of written legal codes from the twelfth century, Robertson (1769 vol. 3: 62–4) argued, went hand in hand with the professionalization of law and jurisprudence which in turn consolidated property ownership and secured greater internal peace and social order, all of which facilitated greater specialization of other professions and the ascription of honour and social prestige to more peaceful activities than the art of war. In common with his Scottish Enlightenment contemporaries, Robertson emphasized the development and change of manners. Manners did not refer exclusively to mores of polite conduct, but the full range of attitudes, beliefs and values that rendered social practices and institutions comprehensible (Robertson 1827 vol. 3: 240–69).[4] Change in manners could be used to chart historical social progress, for change in manners was both a response to as well as a driver of the larger scale impersonal historical forces of economic production, the rise and decline of empires and even war.

In this vein, Robertson traced the emergence of civilized war in Europe to the ending of the chaotic wars of religion in the sixteenth century. By this time, European states had developed larger professional military forces capable of sustaining wars for longer periods than had been the case throughout the medieval period, when armies were composed of temporary feudal levies whose campaigns were limited by the seasons (Robertson 1827 vol. 4: 131). These changes resulted, Robertson maintained, in wars of longer duration, fought between larger armies

4 In Robertson's extensive notes in relation to the abolition of the right of private war in Europe he indicates the complex interplay of monarchical self-interest, the imposition of legal statutes and the gradual change of attitudes. In this context, the imposition of fines in place of trial by combat was as important a cause of change as the investment of honour in seeking peaceful reconciliation between litigants.

that were less decisive but more expensive, requiring more extensive governmental infrastructure, administration and taxation. In this seemingly unpropitious context, ideas of civilized war emerged alongside the development of the notion of religious toleration and in direct response to the horrors of almost incessant sectarian war and violence across Europe (Robertson 1827 vol. 5: 255–7).

In the wake of the Protestant Reformation of the early sixteenth century, the calamitous consequences of religiously inspired violence both within and between the nations of Europe were played out across Italy, France and especially Germany. By dint of mutual exhaustion of the various states of Germany riven by sectarian and confessional divides, the 'pacification' of the peace of Augsburg was negotiated in 1555. Robertson's account of this 'pacification' amounted to a mutual agreement among the different states of Europe to put confessional divisions aside and to seek to maintain a more general peace in the form of a rough balance of power. This balance of power formed the crucial foundation for the civilization of war in Europe, and his description closely mirrors Hume's reflections on the pacifying effects of artillery,

> when nations are in a state similar to each other, and keep equal pace in their advances towards refinement, they are not exposed to the calamity of sudden conquests. … The fate of states in this situation depends not on a single battle. … Nor are they [states] themselves alone interested in their own safety, or active in their own defence. Other states interpose, and balance any temporary advantage which either party may have acquired. After the fiercest and most lengthened contest, all the rival nations are exhausted, none are conquered. At length they find it necessary to conclude a peace which restores to each almost the same power and the same territories of which they were formerly in possession. (Robertson 1827 vol. 5: 347)

Robertson's *History* thus culminated in the creation of independent, militarily powerful sovereign states in Europe, each based on largely pacified civil societies, capable of regulating their international relations on the basis of a rough military balance of power. A strikingly similar view informed Hume's (1985b: 338–41) contention that Britain's national interest invited a prudent participation in continental warfare against France in order to maintain a balance of power in Europe. Above all, Hume and Robertson portrayed the emergence of a formalized structure of interaction between sovereign states in Europe as a model of largely peaceful modernization in which war was gradually subjected to more limitations in which pacific manners, such as honour and clemency dictated civility even in the midst of hostility, and in which war itself served the pacifying interests of humanity. Waging war according to the 'principles of humanity' would lead to abstention from 'slaughter as much as possible' and to winning the 'approbation and esteem of mankind' (Burlamaqui 1776: 38, 209, 214). Considerations of interest also played a role in leading to finer calculations of the benefits of securing a peace favouring future commercial prosperity, and thereby 'the Effusion of

Blood is spar'd' (Brewster 1740: 7, also see Hutcheson 1747: 232–4). As Adam Ferguson (1995: 190, 189) put it, the nations of Western Europe were now able to 'carry the civilities of peace into the practice of war' enabling them to 'mingle … politeness with the use of the sword'. Civilized war was now waged 'with little national animosity' and combatants were 'almost in the very heat of a contest, ready to listen to the dictates of humanity or reason' (Ferguson 1975: 295). In arguing so Ferguson and his contemporaries explicitly tied the civilization of war to state sovereignty. Although sovereign states had consolidated the means of military violence, they were also keenly subjected to civilizing calculations on how best to use those means. As we will see in the following section, however, this association of civilization with sovereign states placed those without states in an uncertain position, potentially outside the limitations of civilized war.

The 'mechanical device of providence'

In European thought, the historical development of states had long been construed in terms of protection for person and property. A central feature of European Natural Law traditions, for example, was a conception of the individual as a rational self whose agency was tied to property ownership and accumulation. The individual and its property, however, both required protection. Europe's experience of civil strife and religious war in the sixteenth century in particular, resulted in later Natural Law thinkers placing a premium on the provision of protection by sovereign states (Grotius 1925: 39, 43, 53, Pufendorf 2003: 55–6). In seeking to show how that protection could be secured and sovereign states legitimated, Natural Law thinkers developed theories of historical development based on the harnessing of productive labour (in manufacture and agricultural cultivation) and engagement in economic exchange or trade (typically involving money) as concomitants in the development of sovereign states as protective institutions (Grotius 1925: 186–90, Pufendorf 2003: 129, Salter 2001: 544–5, Pagden 2003: 180). The rights of particular members of these societies were held to be secure precisely because they lived within societies based on private property and protected by systems of written law enforced by sovereign states (Keal 2003: 26).

The centrality of sovereignty in European thought in the sixteenth and seventeenth centuries was also reflected in the way in which warfare came to be defined as an armed contest between sovereign states, as opposed to armed violence between private individuals. As the sixteenth century jurist Alberico Gentili (1552–1608) defined it (1933: 12), war 'is a just and public contest of arms'. What constituted the international realm of activity was precisely the interaction of 'public' authorities or sovereign states. The international status of 'private' individuals depended on their being 'subjects' of a sovereign state. European attitudes to people without states were thus shaped by the assumption that such peoples had only tenuous claims to consideration. Indeed for Immanuel Kant (1724–1804), though himself a critic of European empires and wars of conquest, the often bloody international interaction of European states was infinitely preferable to the condition exemplified by 'state-less', 'savage' peoples (Kant 1970d: 102–3).

Kant anticipated a gradual convergence of similarly sovereign states in a 'pacific federation' committed to the elimination of war. This federation would be held together not only by ties of mutual self-interest – in fostering trade and avoiding the perils and costs of war – more importantly, each state would enable the fulfilment of nature's plan for humanity, the moral awareness Kant described as the 'Kingdom of Ends'. This awareness consisted in the universal realization of freedom founded on the individual accomplishment of autonomous moral reasoning in line with the categorical imperative to treat others as ends in themselves and never as a means to one's own ends. Statehood performed a vital role in this process of development by embodying the necessary sources of discipline by which human nature could be curbed and moral imperatives could assert themselves over base appetites. Statehood thus signified that a people had attained the appropriate level of development that accorded them an entrance into the possibilities of the pacific federation (Kant 1970c: 90).

In his *Anthropology from a Pragmatic Point of View*, a work based on a series of lectures he delivered between the early 1770s to the late 1790s, Kant (1996: 238) summarized his philosophy of human development. For him, only the individual human being had the rational capability to 'perfect ... himself according to purposes which he himself adopts'. This purposive self-development was driven, he argued, not simply by human reason, but by the genius of nature: 'Nature has planted in the species the seed of discord, and ... nature has willed that the common species, through its reason, turn discord into concord or at least a constant approximation of it' (Kant 1996: 238).

In other words, competition and conflict between human beings (individuals, communities and nations) spurs the use of reason to search for ever better solutions to conflict, leading inevitably to the development of 'culture', civil society and states. For Kant (1996: 240), this process of 'becoming civilized through culture' involved personal moral development 'from the crudity of mere self-reliance to a well-mannered (but not yet moral) being bent on concord'. Importantly, it also involved social development because the 'destiny' of human beings is to realize fully the capacity not just of civilized ('well-mannered') conduct, but for moral conduct in which all action is undertaken in accord with the autonomous awareness of the categorical imperative to treat others as ends in themselves. Not only does this process require 'instruction as well as correction (discipline)', but would also involve 'an endless sequence of many generations' of the entire species (Kant 1996: 241).

The key part of this process, as Kant (1996: 240–41) implied by his reference to 'instruction and correction', was that reason would incline individuals to live in society in which 'he has to cultivate himself, civilize himself, and apply himself to a moral purpose' by means of education in 'the arts and sciences'. By civilization, Kant meant something different to his Scottish Enlightenment contemporaries.

For Kant, civilization meant the cultivation of conduct through education and correction. It was an inferior but very necessary stage in the process of human development. Civilization itself did not constitute the moral awareness of the Kingdom of Ends, but merely the preliminary step of curbing and controlling natural impulses. Kant (1996: 247), however, was very clear that not all forms of social life were worthwhile, arguing that human development required not simply a 'herd like' gathering, but an industrious 'hive community' or *civil society* based on property ownership, industrious activity and a precise regimen of disciplined conduct. Most importantly, Kant (1970a: 58–9) also tied human development to political development, in particular to state formation under monarchical government.

Just as Kant (1970b: 48) identified striving between individuals as the motor force behind the emergence of greater concord through society and culture, so striving between states, by which he meant war, would lead to greater international concord. Kant (1996: 247–8) went on to describe this process in terms of his 'herd and hives' analogy:

> many such hives next to each other will soon carry on feuds as robber bees do (war). But robber bees do not do this for the same reason as men, namely, to strengthen themselves by uniting with others – for here the comparison ends – but, rather, merely to use by cunning or force the industry of others for themselves. Each people seeks to strengthen itself by the subjugation of its neighbours, either through the desire to expand or the fear of being swallowed up by the other … Therefore civil or foreign war in this species [humans], as great an evil as it may be, is yet at the same time the mainspring for the transition from the crude state of nature to the civil state.

It was for this reason that Kant would describe warfare as 'the mechanical device of Providence', a means by which 'struggling forces weaken each other through friction' and thereby gradually come to a greater awareness of the need to avoid conflict and seek peace but also ever greater political integration.

By means of this conflict, Kant argued, individuals would be driven to seek integration into larger collectives (families, communities, nations and states). By means of war, states would be driven to seek their own integration within international collectives, culminating in his projected 'pacific federation'. In driving individuals towards civil societies and states, and in driving states towards a pacific federation, war may be described as the 'mechanical device of providence', but war was at best a blunt and bloody instrument; 'a regrettable expedient for asserting one's rights by force within a state of nature' (Kant 1970d: 96). For so long as the international realm remained a veritable 'state of nature', there would be no source of authority to curb war. As a result, there would be only one way of deciding disputes, and that by the 'outcome of the conflict'. Consequently, 'a war of extermination, in which both parties and right itself might all be simultaneously annihilated, would allow perpetual peace only on the vast graveyard of the human race'.

This then is Kant's ultimate point. Humans must be prepared to put aside the 'mechanical device of providence' and seek more peaceful means of instituting the pacific federation. Modern, civilized warfare is a double-edged weapon. On the one hand, it strengthens the hand of states and thus consolidates their position vis-à-vis the state of nature; on the other hand, it makes longer, larger and bloodier wars possible. Kant was hardly alone among European Enlightenment thinkers to make this observation (see Buchan 2006). But even with the obvious cost of war between states, Kant nonetheless held that they were at least able to come to minimal agreements to regulate their interaction and warfare. These minimal or 'preliminary articles of a perpetual peace between states' could then provide the foundation for later substantive principles, that Kant called the 'definitive articles of a perpetual peace between states', aimed at finally eliminating war. Among these crucial 'preliminary articles' were agreements to avoid 'dishonourable stratagems' in war, such as espionage, poisoning or assassination (Kant 1970d: 96). In arguing so, Kant gave voice to a widespread view in Enlightenment European thought that, for all its destructiveness, 'honour' was becoming the hallmark of the civilized, and potentially civilizing, European way of war.

Conclusion

In celebrating the civilization of a supposed European way of war, the writers canvassed here paradoxically portrayed war as an agent of peace and an essential means to uphold a potentially pacific system of states. The kind of war they celebrated was 'conventional warfare'. Conventional warfare was ordered by chains of command, theoretically subject to laws and limitations, and waged by and between sovereign militaries. The persuasive allure of this image of civilized war derived from multiple sources including poetic fictions, theoretical arguments and convoluted historical analyses. Few if any of these sources ever explicitly addressed the troubling implications of 'unconventional warfare' waged by or against partisan or guerrilla forces and fought in frank denial of civilized limitations. The eighteenth century witnessed a wide array of such conflicts both within Europe and beyond. One of the only Enlightenment luminaries to address unconventional war was Adam Ferguson. His opposition to the 'rebellion' of Britain's American colonies (1776–83) led to his appointment in 1777 as secretary to the Carlisle Commission that was sent to Philadelphia to negotiate a return of the colonies to the imperial fold (see Buchan 2009). It was in this context that Ferguson (1995b: 561–4) appeared to endorse, on behalf of the Commission, the 'extremes of war' being unleashed upon the rebels. He later argued that the 'Rules of War' designed to protect 'Innocent Subjects' and to limit warfare to the 'just measure of Hostilitys', did not apply to American 'Subjects in Arms against Their Sovereign & in Alliance with his enemys'. Although at first sight inconsistent with his arguments about conventional civilized war, Ferguson's views on unconventional war were an extension of the same set of ideas. For

Ferguson, the idea of civilized war depended on the sovereignty of the states that waged it. It was inconceivable that wars waged by anything other than sovereign states could be described as 'civilized'. They were rather savage or barbarous wars characterized by rancour and cruelty and an incessant cycle of revenge. It was into this category that Ferguson placed the War of Independence in America, for it threatened or usurped the sovereignty of the British state and thus challenged the mores, manners and conventions of civilization that came to fruition only within sovereign states. Wars of this kind, he seemed to suggest, simply could not be fought by civilized standards, but they had to be won.

Ferguson's dilemma reverberates still in the way Western discourse on war continues to consign unconventional war to a moral netherworld outside the civilized and civilizing reach of conventional war. Ironically it was the Nazi jurist, Carl Schmitt (1975: 52, 82), who perhaps best articulated this sentiment in his characterization of 'partisan war' as an unlimited form of war without recognition of legal or moral constraint. Partisan war stands outside the 'bracketing' of conventional war within accepted rules and laws, and thus denies the possibility that war can be waged within humanitarian limits and in the name of peace (Schmitt 1975: 90). This analysis continues to shape the interpretation of unconventional war today as 'a relic of pre-modern times', a kind of 'primitive' war more akin to the horrors of terrorism than to the rational pursuit of conventional warfare (Rink 2010: 11, 12, Gat 2009: 579). In seeing unconventional war as an atavistic and anachronistic survival or 'throw back', as Heuser (2010b: 141–4) suggests, or even by consigning it to the darkened realms beyond the limits of conventional war, we merely reiterate the narrative of European civilized war that Lahontan cheekily satirized. The sting in the tail of Lahontan's satire is that our faith in the rationality and humanity of modern conventional war blinds us to the imbrication of terror and brutality in all forms of war, even in those supposedly 'civilized' wars waged in the names of humanity and peace.[5]

Bibliography

Addison, J. 1710. *The Campaign: a Poem, to His Grace the Duke of Marlborough*. London: printed and sold by H. Hills.

Adolf, A. 2009. *Peace: A World History*. Cambridge: Polity.

Bacevich, A. 2008. Peace at last: the pacification of the West. *World Affairs Journal*, 171(1), 98–105.

Bolingbroke, H.St.J. 1748. On the policy of the Athenians, in *A Collection of Political Tracts*. London: s.n., 215–41.

5 Research for this chapter was conducted as part of my Future Fellowship project on the conceptual history of asymmetric warfare funded by the Australian Research Council and hosted by the Centre for Excellence in Policing and Security, Griffith University.

Bolingbroke, H.St.J. 1972 [1752]. Letters on the study and use of history, in *Lord Bolingbroke, Historical Writings*, edited by I. Kramnick. Chicago, IL: University of Chicago Press, 3–149

Brewster, S. 1740. *Jus feciale Anglicanum, or a Treatise on the laws of England relating to war and rebellion: with an account of the laws of capitulations and surrenders at mercy and discretion: to which is prefix'd and expostulatory preface to the Right Honourable the Lord Parker, Lord Chief Justice of England.* 2nd Edition. London: Printed for T. Cooper and T. Gardner.

Buchan, B. 2006. Civilization, state sovereignty and war: the Scottish Enlightenment and international relations. *International Relations*, 20(2), 175–92.

Buchan, B. 2009. Adam Ferguson, the 43rd and the fictions of Fontenoy, in *Adam Ferguson: Philosophy, Politics and Society*, edited by E. Heath and V. Merolle. London: Pickering and Chatto, 25–44.

Buchan, B. 2013. Pandours, Partisans, and Petite Guerre: two dimensions of Enlightenment discourse on war. *Intellectual History Review*, 23(3), 23(3), 329–47.

Burlamaqui, J.J. 1776. *The Principles of Politic Law: Being a Sequel to the Principles of Natural Law*, vol. 2. Dublin: Printed for J. Sheppard and G. Nugent.

de Callières, F. 1716. *The Art of Negotiating With Princes*. London: Printed for Geo. Strahan.

Fasolt, C. 2004. *The Limits of History*. Chicago: University of Chicago Press.

Ferguson, A. 1975 [1792]. *Principles of Moral and Political Science*, vol. 2. Hildesheim: Georg Olms Verlag.

Ferguson, A. 1995a [1767]. *An Essay on the History of Civil Society*, edited by F.O. Salzburger. Cambridge: Cambridge University Press.

Ferguson, A. 1995b. Notes on the enquiry into General Sir William Howe's conduct in the American war, 10 May 1779, in *The Correspondence of Adam Ferguson*, vol. 2, edited by V. Merolle. London: Pickering and Chatto, 561–4.

Gat, A. 2009. So why do people fight? Evolutionary theory and the causes of war. *European Journal of International Relations*, 15(4), 571–99.

Gentili, A. 1933 [1612]. *De Iure Belli Libri Tres*, edited by J.C. Rolfe. Oxford: Clarendon Press.

Gittings, J. 2012. *The Glorious Art of Peace: From the Iliad to Iraq*. Oxford: Oxford University Press.

Grotius, H. 1925 [1625]. *The Law of War and Peace*. Translated by. F.W. Kelsey. Indianapolis, IN: Bobbs–Merrill.

Hanley, R.P. 2011. David Hume and 'politics of humanity'. *Political Theory*, 39(2), 205–33.

Heuser, B. 2010a. *The Evolution of Strategy: Thinking War from Antiquity to the Present*. Cambridge: Cambridge University Press.

Heuser, B. 2010b. Small wars in the age of Clausewitz: the watershed between partisan war and people's war. *Journal of Strategic Studies*, 33(1), 139–62.

Hume, D. 1983 [1778]. *The History of England From the Invasion of Julius Caesar to The Revolution in 1688 in Six Volumes*. Indianapolis, IN: Liberty Classics.

Hume, D. 1985a [1777]. Of refinement in the arts, in *Essays Moral, Political and Literary*, edited by E.F. Miller. Indianapolis, IN: Liberty Classics, 268–80.

Hume, D. 1985b [1777]. Of the balance of power, in *Essays Moral, Political and Literary*, edited by E.F. Miller. Indianapolis, IN: Liberty Classics, 332–41.

Hume, D. 1985c [1777]. Of the populousness of ancient nations, in *Essays Moral, Political and Literary*, edited by E.F. Miller. Indianapolis, IN: Liberty Classics, 377–464.

Hutcheson, F. 1747. *A Short Introduction to Moral Philosophy in Three Books: In Three Parts. Containing the Elements of Ethicks and the Law of Nature*. Glasgow: printed by Robert Foulis.

Kant, I. 1970a [1784]. An answer to the question: what is enlightenment? in *Kant's Political Writings*, edited by H. Reiss. Translated from German by H.B. Nisbet. Cambridge: Cambridge University Press, 54–60.

Kant, I. 1970b [1784]. Idea for a universal history with a cosmopolitan purpose, in *Kant's Political Writings*, edited by H. Reiss, translated by H.B. Nisbet. Cambridge: Cambridge University Press, 41–53.

Kant, I. 1970c [1792]. On the common saying: 'This may be true in theory, but it does not apply in practice, in *Kant's Political Writings*, edited by H. Reiss. Translated from German by H.B. Nisbet. Cambridge: Cambridge University Press, 61–92.

Kant, I. 1970d [1795]. Perpetual peace: a philosophical sketch, in *Kant's Political Writings*, edited by H. Reiss. Translated from German by H.B. Nisbet. Cambridge: Cambridge University Press, 93–130.

Kant, I. 1996. *Anthropology from a Pragmatic Point of View*. Translated from German by V.L. Dowdell. Carbondale: Southern Illinois University Press.

Keal, P. 2003. *European Conquest and the Rights of Indigenous People: The Moral Backwardness of International Society*. Cambridge: Cambridge University Press.

Lahontan, Baron de. 1970 [1703]. *New Voyages to North America*, vol. 2. New York: Burt Franklin.

Lawrence, P.K. 1999. Enlightenment, modernity and war. *History of the Human Sciences*, 12(3), 3–25.

Marriott, J. 1765. *Letter to John Pownall, 15 February*. LAC, R216–193–4–E. Ottawa: Canadian National Archives.

Montesquieu 1985 [1748]. *Spirit of the Laws*. Translated from French by A.M. Cohler, B.C. Miller and H.S. Stone. Cambridge: Cambridge University Press.

Pagden, A. 2003. Human rights, natural rights, and Europe's imperial legacy. *Political Theory*, 31(2), 171–99.

Pocock, J.G.A. 1999. *Barbarism and Religion,* vol. 2. *Narratives of Civil Government*. Cambridge: Cambridge University Press.

Pufendorf, S. 2003 [1691]. *The Whole Duty of Man According to the Law of Nature*. Translated by A. Tooke, edited by I. Hunter and D. Saunders. Indianapolis, IN: Liberty Fund.

Rink, M. 2010. The partisan's metamorphosis: from freelance military entrepreneur to German freedom fighter, 1740 to 1815. *War in History*, 17(1), 16–36.

Robertson, W. 1827 [1769]. History of the reign of Charles V, in *The Works of William Robertson, D.D.*: to which is prefixed, an account of the life and writings of the author, vols. 3–5. London: Printed for T. Cadell et al.

Salter, J. 2001. Hugo Grotius: property and consent. *Political Theory*, 29(4), 537–55.

Schmitt, C. 2007. *Theory of the Partisan.* Translated from German by G.L. Ulmen. New York: Telos Press.

Smith, A. 1976 [1759]. *The Theory of the Moral Sentiments*, edited by D.D. Raphael and A.L. Macfie. Oxford: Oxford University Press.

Voltaire 1756. *The History of the War of 1741.* London: s.n.

Voltaire 1859. Fontenoy: a poem, in *The Select Works of Voltaire*, vol. 2, edited by O.W. Wight. New York: Derby and Jackson, 251–74.

Weigley, R. 1993. *The Age of Battles: The Quest for Decisive Battle From Breitenfeld to Waterloo.* London: Pimlico.

Chapter 8
Indigenous Inspiration and Herder's Peace Woman

Vicki A. Spencer

In the tenth collection of his *Letters for the Advancement of Humanity* (*Briefe zu Beförderung der Humanität*, 1797), the late eighteenth-century German philosopher, Johann Gottfried Herder (1744–1803), offers his views on the formation of peace that he personifies in his 'great *peace woman*' ('große *Friedensfrau*') (Herder 2002: 403; 1991: 717). Herder is well known as a champion of indigenous rights and spent much of his intellectual life urging Europeans to recognize that other cultures possessed many merits that they could learn from. It is perhaps unsurprising then that he draws inspiration for his emblematic figure from the alliance between the Iroquois and Delaware nations in North America whereby the Delaware took on the role of peacemaker by donning female clothes and becoming the peace woman. The immediate intellectual context for him setting out his views was, however, the intense flourish of interest in eternal peace plans generated in Germany with the publication of Immanuel Kant's essay *Toward Perpetual Peace: A Philosophical Sketch* (*Zum ewigen Frieden. Ein philosophischer Entwurf*, 1795).

Herder, like Kant, can be classified as a moral cosmopolitan who insists 'that there are universal commitments to respect the moral worth of individuals everywhere' and that they 'should be equally applied' (Brown and Held 2010: 2). Both thinkers are highly critical of the atrocities committed against indigenous peoples by the European colonial powers and abhor the institution of slavery. In common, they challenge the realist perspective towards international relations by applying normative principles to the conduct of states. They also reject the viability of a world government and combine a significant degree of pragmatism with their desire to counter war. Yet such similarities should not obscure the important differences between them.

In this chapter I argue that Herder provides an embedded cosmopolitan alternative to Kant's legal state-based cosmopolitanism. The central component of Kant's peace plan is the establishment of a pacific federation of republican states through their voluntary agreement to give up their lawless freedom and to submit to international and cosmopolitan law. Perpetual peace is realized, as Howard Williams (1983: 258) indicates, 'by gradual reform from the top downward'. By contrast, Herder's inclusion of the story of the indigenous peace alliance is a direct challenge to Kant's privileging of the state as a prerequisite for peace and his euro-centric, Hobbesian claim that war is endemic in 'primitive' societies. Although Herder concedes that the Delaware–Iroquois alliance was ultimately as unsuccessful as attempts to stop war-thirsty nations in Europe and Asia, his attention to the history of warfare means he has little, if any, faith in the attainment of peace through a reliance on European state cabinets. Rejecting visions of one ideal political constitution and formalistic plans for eternal peace as unworkable, Herder provides us in many respects with an 'anti-plan' for peace by instead promoting seven dispositions we each need to cultivate if humanity is to work towards the gradual diminishing of war and the cultivation of peace. In contrast to Kant's top-down, legalistic approach to political reform, Herder offers us a grassroots bottom-up approach that still holds considerable resonance today for activists frustrated with the political machinations of states' interests evident in the United Nations.

Moral Cosmopolitanism, Colonialism and Slavery

Herder begins his discussion of peace in Letter 114 with a series of rhetorical questions challenging the value of colonial ambitions as displayed by the Huns and Mongols in Asia; the Phoenicians, Greeks and Romans in ancient times; the Germans; and most recently, the Spaniards, Portuguese, English and Dutch. Whatever art the imperial powers may have spread, he argues, it does not compensate for the misery they have produced by their oppression of foreign peoples. 'And what good did the *crusades* do for the Orient?' he asks. 'What happiness have they brought to the coasts of the Baltic Sea? The old *Prussians* are destroyed; *Livonians*, *Estonians*, and *Latvians* in the poorest condition still now curse in their hearts their subjugators, the Germans' (Herder 2002: 381; 1991: 672). The peoples in Africa, the East and West Indies, and the islands in the southern world similarly 'cry for revenge'. Far from viewing Europeans as having advanced humanity through their interactions with peoples in the rest of the world, Herder writes,

> Let the land be named to which Europeans have come without having sinned against defenseless, trusting humanity, perhaps for all aeons to come, through injurious acts, through unjust wars, greed, deceit, oppression, through diseases and harmful gifts! Our part of the world must be called, not the wise, but the *presumptuous, pushing, tricking* part of the earth; it has not cultivated but has destroyed the shoots of peoples' own cultures wherever and however it could. (Herder 2002: 381–2; 1991: 672)

As early as the sixteenth century humanist thinkers in Europe – such as the French philosopher Michel de Montaigne and the Spanish historian and theologian Bartolomé de las Casas – were equally appalled at the atrocities Europeans committed against indigenous peoples in the Americas. Herder places his peace proposal within this rich intellectual tradition by acknowledging the efforts of a wide range of European thinkers in promoting peace and justice. He agrees with the general consensus among his contemporaries that the Abbé Saint Pierre's 1713 peace plan to create a European federal power sufficiently powerful to suppress wars between states is naïvely optimistic. But just as the Abbé's plan nonetheless inspired both the Swiss-French philosopher Jean-Jacques Rousseau and Kant in the development of their peace plans (Williams 1983: 256), Herder follows his general method in establishing 'firm first principles' that he sees as a 'quietly effective means if not for an eternal peace then certainly at least for a gradual diminution of wars' (Herder 2002: 404; 1991: 720). Central to this objective is the elimination of both slavery and colonialism.

Kant similarly recognizes the necessity to overcome Europeans' exploitation and abuse of people on a global scale for the attainment of peace. More reminiscent of the formality of the Abbé's plan than Herder's first principles, however, Kant's peace proposal takes the form of a treaty in which he outlines the normative rights due to others within a cosmopolitan and international legal framework. His critique of European colonialism appears in his third definitive article where he outlines a cosmopolitan right to universal hospitality that entails 'the right of a stranger not to be treated with hostility when he arrives on someone else's territory' (Kant 1991: 105), while equally assuming the corresponding hospitable behaviour of the visitor. Kant thereby invalidates the inhospitable practices of the European commercial states in Africa, in the Spice and Cape Islands, and in East India where 'foreign troops were brought in under the pretext of merely setting up trading posts. This led', he writes, 'to oppression of the natives, incitement of the various Indian states to widespread wars, famine, insurrection, treachery and the whole litany of evils which can afflict the human race' (Kant 1991: 106). Kant's disdain for the behaviour of many Europeans abroad is further apparent in his commendation of 'the cruellest and most calculated slavery' in the Sugar Islands (Kant 1991: 107). Kant did not adhere to a universal principle of justice based on any substantive conception of equality; he denies women and the working class full citizenship rights and he attributes different capacities for moral virtues to people on the basis of race and gender (Kant 1991: 139, Nussbaum 2010: 34, Sikka 2006: 151–3, Reiss 1991: 27). Commentators (Williams 1983: 260, Wood 1998: 62, Ellis 2005: 76, Brown 2009: 8) nonetheless agree that at least Kant's basic respect for others entails universal application irrespective of race, nationality or political status. Both slavery and the worst excesses of colonialism clearly violate this basic universal respect and Kant's cosmopolitan law.

Though Herder is often attributed with the development of cultural relativism (Goldie and Wokler 2006: 742, Sikka 2011), he is no less than Kant a moral cosmopolitan who promotes a universal respect for all persons. He commends the promotion of 'Universal reason and justice, virtue and beneficence' in the Abbé Saint Pierre's peace plan and he calls his own great peace woman '*universal justice, humaneness, active reason*' (Herder 2002: 389, 404; 1991: 692, 719). Throughout his works he consistently rejects the right of any people to conquer another. And while he is also commonly depicted as the father of nationalism (Goldie and

Wokler 2006: 742, Adams and Dyson 2003: 93), Herder's praise for the universal, humane sentiment in the statement he endorses by the seventeenth-century Catholic archbishop and theologian, Francois Fénelon – '"I love my family", says the noble man, "more than myself; more than my family my fatherland; more than my fatherland humanity"'(Herder 2002: 389; 1991: 692) – is a far more accurate summation of his position. Love of humanity means that the right of all peoples to determine their own fate and local ties must be respected. For Herder, a foreign culture that is foisted on another so that an indigenous culture cannot develop out of a people's own needs and dispositions can only deform and oppress. No progress can arise from the cultural oppression of others (Herder 2002: 383; 1991: 674).

Thus, while Herder was a Lutheran minister who ends his discussion of peace with two letters praising Christianity for its '*sovereign law of freedom*' (Herder 2002: 421; 1991: 747), he is deeply ambivalent about the role of Christian missionaries with respect to European colonialism (Löchte 2005: 70–71, Dreitzel 1987: 279–80). In a strategic move designed to encourage sympathy for the plight of African slaves among Europeans, he empathetically compares their perspective towards Christian missionaries with the Latvians' attitude towards their German oppressors:

> The negro depicts the devil as white, and the Latvian does not want to enter into heaven as soon as there are Germans there. 'Why are you pouring water on my head?' said that dying slave to the missionary. 'So that you enter into heaven'. 'I do not want to enter into any heaven where there are whites' he spoke, turned away his face, and died. Sad history of humanity! (Herder 2002: 383; 1991: 674)

Following this statement is a series of five poems ironically entitled the 'Negro–Idylls'. Each relates a poignant story of extreme suffering experienced by an individual slave with the traditional equation of black with evil, and white with good, reversed and the moral superiority of the oppressed emphasized (Solbrig 1990: 43).

Scholars (Solbrig 1990: 44, Logan 1980: 391, Shelley 1938: 55, Forster in Herder 2002: 383 n. 9) disagree over the precise sources Herder employed for his poems with the stories they are based on having appeared previously in various other works. Importantly, too, he liberally adjusts the original stories when it suits his rhetorical purpose. In his first poem, *The Fruit on the Tree (Die Frucht am Baume)*, he relates the horrific punishment of a slave caged and hanging from a tree for days so that the birds had gouged out his eye. His crime, according to Herder, was having defended his fiancé from the advances of a white man. Herder neglects to mention that the slave had reportedly killed the man, although it hardly diminishes the horrendously inhumane nature of his punishment (Herder 1991: 674–5, Logan 1980: 396).

Herder equally exonerates the protagonist Zimeo in his fourth poem by presenting him as untainted by blood and playing a moderating and just role in the slave revolt that had taken place in Jamaica against the white owners. By contrast, in Johann Ernst Kolb's account of Zimeo published in 1789, he was a black leader who participated in a bloody rampage against his former oppressors (Logan 1980: 391–3). Yet it is inaccurate to claim, as Susanne Zantop (1997: 149) does, that in cleansing Zimeo of violence Herder 'depoliticizes' him. In Herder's Idyll, Zimeo is no less the leader – someone 'born to rule' – of a hill-dwelling community of escaped slaves who formed an independent republic in Jamaica (Herder 1991: 680 line 11, my translation, also see 680 n. 224).

All of Herder's depictions of slaves in his 'Negro–Idylls' evoke the image of the 'noble savage' and 'the Black as victim' (Musgrave 1977: 90, 94). His purified depictions also accord with the general tendency of humanitarian anti-slavers to refuse to condemn or even to mention black violence and vengeance. Some critics (Musgrave 1977: 93–4, Zantop 1997: 149) suggest that such a view perpetuates a paternalistic and colonial message by portraying Africans as excessively obedient and subservient. But while these poems might appear condescending in hindsight to modern sensibilities, it is nevertheless important to recognize that Herder's poetic aim is to evoke readers' emotions and provoke a sympathetic identification on behalf of his protagonists, not to provide rational justifications and reasoned argumentation. Justified or not, he clearly did not want the actions of the slaves in avenging themselves to detract from his objective of drawing attention to the appalling cruelties and injustices done to them.

It is noteworthy too that Herder situates his 'Negro–Idylls' in the same letter that empathetically acknowledges Africans' 'cry for revenge'. His poems clearly need to be read in this context. In the following letter, Herder directly confronts those who regard people as 'savages' because they 'defend themselves against foreign visitors with cunning or with violence' to protect their land and loved ones. 'It is', he insists, 'a poor manner of thought that holds this against them' (Herder 2002: 385; 1991: 687). Self-defence against a direct attack is Herder's one exception to his prohibition on war (Herder 2002: 404; 1991: 720). Significantly, he extends this principle not only to states, but also to peoples (*Völker*) or nations[1] residing within multi-national states and in a stateless condition.

Kant and Stateless Peoples

Based on Kant's anti-colonial statements, the conclusion that Herder and Kant provide similar protection to indigenous peoples and their autonomy might be

1 Herder uses the term *das Volk* (the people) in the plural (*die Völker*) interchangeably with nations. However, he also applies it to tribes and it therefore has a far wider meaning than the modern concept of nation in nationalist studies where it is linked to the formation of the modern state. Elsewhere (Spencer 2012: 144) I have defined a *Volk* 'as *a socially cohesive community with shared historic memories, a common culture, and a sense of solidarity and belonging that unites its members*'. It needs to be emphasized that Herder's use of the term culture to denote a community's way of life also includes a community's political institutions (both formal and informal). See Spencer 2012: 70–71, 81–4, 128–44.

arrived at. Sankar Muthu (2003: 147) and Williams both emphasize that Kant's belief in the innate right of individuals to be free of coercion means his thought 'undermines any justification a nation or race might have for placing another under its tutelage' (Williams 1983: 260). For example, due to the misbehaviour of European states, Kant supports the restrictions both Japan and China placed on foreign access to their territories (Kant 1991: 106–7, Waligore 2009: 38–9). The members of his pacific '*federation of peoples*'[2] also have clear duties based on cosmopolitan law towards those who do not belong to the federation (Kant 1991: 102, Brown 2009: 103, Ellis 2005: 95). None of the peoples in Africa, the Americas or the Cape and Spice Islands would, for example, have met his criterion for entry into the federation by having a republican state. Yet he is critical of those Europeans who treated them 'as ownerless territories' so that 'the natives were counted as nothing' (Kant 1991: 106). It is indisputable that Kant had an aversion as deep as Herder's towards the worst atrocities Europeans committed in the name of progress and culture.

When Kant's views on the state are considered, however, the rights of stateless indigenous peoples to autonomous coexistence begin to look far more precarious within his theoretical framework. For Kant, reason prescribes that people ought to leave the state of nature and enter into a civil state by submitting to the coercion of public law (Kant 1991: 73, 90). Echoing the political realism of the English philosopher Thomas Hobbes, he declares that 'the state of nature ... is rather a state of war' (Kant 1991: 98). And just as he follows Hobbes in describing existing international relations as a state of nature, Kant is not merely referring to a hypothetical state when he relates his disdain for the stateless condition in which certain indigenous peoples live:

> We look with profound contempt upon the way in which savages cling to their lawless freedom. They would rather engage in incessant strife than submit to a legal constraint which they might impose upon themselves, for they prefer the freedom of folly to the freedom of reason. We regard this as barbarism, coarseness, and brutish debasement of humanity. (Kant 1991: 102–3)

For Kant (1991: 118), belonging to a state with a legal constitution, even a despotic one, is better than existing in a stateless condition. Kant's cosmopolitan law is designed, not to protect the rights of peoples or nations to coexistence, but to protect the rights of individuals, while his international law outlines the rights of states. Thus article five of his peace plan – one that he considers requires immediate implementation – stipulates that '"No state shall forcibly interfere in the constitution and government of another state"' (Kant 1991: 96). Despite

2 Kant (1965: 208–10), like Herder, employs the term *Volk* to mean nation. However, his federation of peoples (*Völkerbund*) is a union of nation–states (*Völkerstaat*). In this context, he is not therefore referring to nations/*Völker* in Herder's broad sense also to refer to tribes and his usage is more akin to that in current nationalist studies.

its despotic nature according to Kant's classificatory scheme of governmental forms (1991: 101), the right of the Chinese state in international relations to non-interference is thereby ensured.

By contrast, stateless peoples have no such guarantee within the terms of his legal framework. According to Kant (1991: 98), only states possess legitimacy to form peaceful alliances so that 'unless one neighbour gives a guarantee to the other at his request (which can happen only in a *lawful* state), the latter may treat him as an enemy'. It follows that all those living within a stateless condition constitute the enemy. Those who refuse to enter into a lawful state threaten the very foundations of peace so that Kant (1991: 98) justifies pre-emptive action against them:

> It is usually assumed that one cannot take hostile action against anyone unless one has already been actively *injured* by them. This is perfectly correct if both parties are living in a *legal civil state*. For the fact that the one has entered such a state gives the required guarantee to the other, since both are subject to the same authority. But man (or an individual people) in a mere state of nature robs me of any such security and injures me by virtue of this very state in which he coexists with me. He may not have injured me actively (*facto*), but he does injure me by the very lawlessness of his state (*statu iniusto*), for he is a permanent threat to me, and I can require him either to enter into a common lawful state along with me or to move away from my vicinity.

Thus, while Kant prohibits the brutality associated with the worst excesses of colonialism and the slave trade, he nevertheless opens the door for either the removal of stateless peoples from their territory or their assimilation into a neighbouring state.[3]

Indigenous Peace

Herder responds directly to Kant's peace plan and his views on the barbarous, warlike condition of stateless peoples in Letter 118 (van der Laan 2009: 341, Schultz 1989: 416) by pointedly providing in the place of all the recent 'talk of plans *for eternal peace* … a real attempt made with this purpose' among the Delaware (also known as the Lenape) and Iroquois in North America (Herder 2002: 400; 1991: 713). His source from which he quotes extensively was the German,

---

3 Later, in *The Metaphysics of Morals* (*Die Metaphysik der Sitten* 1797), Kant (1991: 172) stipulates that his cosmopolitan right to hospitality does not entail 'a right to *settle*' and insists that settlements cannot be established legitimately by violence where pastoral and hunting peoples exist as in the case of American Indians. Kant's position is deeply ambiguous and requires far more detailed analysis, but since it is his comments in *Toward a Perpetual Peace* that Herder addresses in his *Letters for the Advancement of Humanity* they are my focus here.

Christian missionary George Henry Loskiel whose *History of the Mission of the United Brethren among the Indians in North America* was published originally in German in 1789 (*Geschichte der Mission der evangelischen Brüder unter den Indianern*). Although the Delaware and Iroquois both acknowledged the formation of this alliance in the distant past and the Delaware's feminized role as the peace mediator, Loskiel (1796: 124–6) relates disagreement between them over the origin of the alliance and its meaning for the status of the Delaware. It is the Delaware account, which situates them as the constant victors in their wars with the Iroquois that Herder reproduces. On this account the Iroquois came to the realization that if they were to avoid eventual destruction they needed to establish peaceful relations. With this objective they sent representatives to the Delaware and suggested that the Delaware become the woman whose role it would be to preserve the peace. They proposed that the five (later six) nation members of the Iroquois confederacy would live around the woman. The Iroquois were to remain the men with the ability to wage war on others but none of them would touch or harm the woman. In place of taking up arms, the Delaware would play a mediating role and remind those within the alliance who came to blows 'that your wives and children are bound to die if you do not stop. Do you, then, want to be responsible for your own annihilation from the face of the earth?' It was determined that the men would then listen to 'the *woman* and obey her' (Herder 2002: 401; 1991: 714).

The Delaware accordingly accepted the position of tribal matron and a ceremonial celebration was conducted in which the Iroquois stated three propositions. In the first, the Iroquois symbolically dressed the Delaware in women's clothes with a long dress and earrings. In the second, the Iroquois gave them a bottle of oil and medicine to wear. The purpose of the oil was for the Delaware to '"clean the ears of the remaining nations so that they pay heed to good and not to evil"'. The medicine was meant for those nations already engaged in warlike activities so that they would be cured and returned to peaceful ways. In the third and final proposition, the Delaware were assigned agriculture as their future occupation in keeping with the traditional economic role performed by women in both Iroquois and Delaware society. As was typical in such treaty negotiations (Schutt 2007: 11), each of these three speech acts was accompanied by the giving of a belt of wampum (beads), which together became known as the belt of peace (Herder 2002: 401–2; 1991: 714–15).

Neither the existence of this peace alliance nor the Delaware's feminized role as the peacemaker has been disputed in subsequent scholarship. Nevertheless, still at issue are the original reason for the alliance and the status attached to the feminization of the Delaware. Interestingly, Herder ignores the imputation of inferiority to the Delaware's feminization that is evident both in Loskiel's claim that the Delaware considered themselves to have been duped by the Iroquois and in the Iroquois account that Loskiel reports in which the Iroquois were placed as the conquerors of the Delaware whom they had forced into a subservient female role (Loskiel 1794: 125–6). The probable falsehoods that the Delaware were humiliated by being deprived of the masculine prerogative to wage war and that the Delaware were reduced to a dishonourable female role as a penalty for having been defeated in battle have persisted ever since (Weslager 1972: 180–82; 1944; 1947, also see Speck 1946). Much of the evidence for the Iroquois account stems from a speech made by the Onondaga[4] spokesperson, Canasatego, during negotiations with the Pennsylvanian authorities in 1742 when he claimed that the Iroquois had conquered the Delaware and had made them into women. Subsequent colonial records further show that by the mid-eighteenth century gendered language designating men as women was understood as an insult and became commonplace in Delaware–Iroquois–English interactions from that time (Fur 2009: 162–8).

Yet no direct evidence exists of any conquest and many scholars consider Canasatego's suggestion that the Delaware were subordinate to the Iroquois due to their feminization was an invocation of Euro-American perceptions of female subservience designed to give them the upper-hand at a time when they were struggling for their survival. Unlike Euro-American society, Iroquois society was strongly matrilineal with each of the senior women possessing the power to appoint and dismiss their tribe's representative (or sachem) at the confederacy's main deliberative body, the Great Council. The women's role as agricultural producers was, moreover, not a lesser one to any role held by the men but formed the mainstay of their economy (Schutt 2007: 89–91, Snow 1994: 62–5, Camerino 1978: 7–9, Miller 1974, Wallace 1947: 9–10). As Vicki Camerino writes (1978: 8): 'Women were the most honored, most respected and most powerful people in [Iroquois] society'. It is therefore highly implausible that at the time of the alliance (most likely in the seventeenth century) that the Iroquois would have employed the term woman in reference to the Delaware to denote inferiority.

With a similar matrilineal structure there was also no reason why the Delaware would have considered their designation as women as anything other than honourable. And while the Iroquois came in their political machinations to adopt Euro-American perceptions of female inferiority that the Delaware would have certainly found insulting, evidence from the 1940s suggests that the Delaware continued to interpret their role as matron as a dignified one of the highest authority (Speck 1946: 385, Schutt 2007: 21–2, 90, Camerino 1978: 7–10, Wallace 1947: 13–14). Herder's use of Loskiel's account does not therefore mean his depiction is inaccurate as some commentators (van der Laan 2009: 340) suggest. Instead, his own refusal to accept a Euro-gendered, hierarchical evaluation of masculinity and femininity where the former is associated with war, strength and superiority and the latter is equated with peace, weakness and inferiority means his depiction accords with an important perspective within current scholarship concerning traditional gender relations in both Iroquois and Delaware societies.

Herder further pre-empts the gendered devaluation of the Delaware's role as peacemaker in subservient terms and undermines the potential strangeness of this

4 The Onondaga were one of the five founding nations of the Iroquois confederacy.

story to Europeans by drawing an analogy with the Catholic hierarchy that 'too wore the long dress; oil and medicine were in her hand'. He notes that the Catholic Church had nevertheless failed to fulfil its intended role as peacemaker and was even blamed by many for 'having stirred up and fanned wars between the men' (Herder 2002: 402; 1991: 716). There is also no possibility, according to Herder, of any nation in the middle of Europe ever successfully taking up a mediating role equivalent to that of the Delaware. Reminding his readers of the history of wars conducted in Europe since the crusades, he concludes: 'In a world where dark cabinets initiate and continue wars, all the efforts of the *peace woman* would be lost' (Herder 2002: 402; 1991: 716). Herder therefore does not suggest that we ought to adopt the Delaware–Iroquois alliance as a model for future peaceful relations. By contrasting it with the willingness of European nations to go to war, it serves instead to challenge Kant's assumption that those living outside the state system are a greater threat to peaceful relations than states.

Herder recognizes that the Delaware–Iroquois alliance was ultimately unsuccessful. When the Europeans pressed closer, the Iroquois wanted the Delaware to take up the war axe again and shorten the long skirt that they originally and symbolically had dressed her in. But failure to maintain peace is by no means unique to indigenous peoples; Herder insists that 'A foreign, unforeseen dominant force' will always be able to disturb such alliances 'as long as the tree of peace does not bloom for the nations with firm, inextirpable roots *from within to outside*' (Herder 2002: 403; 1991: 716). History is replete with examples of failed attempts by peoples in Europe, Africa and Asia to set limits on the ability of war-thirsty nations to inflict destruction and to fashion unsuccessful peace alliances and leagues (Herder 2002: 403; 1991: 716–17). As John Pizer (2007: 359) indicates, 'in arguing against Kant, Herder uses the "peace woman" as a metonym for the futility of creating confederative institutions designed to establish perpetual peace'.

Formal Peace Proposals

We cannot deduce, however, from these past failures that all future attempts at establishing peace will fail. Herder does not draw from them a static and essentialist conception of human nature that elevates specific personality traits to a universal status; he is not a realist in a Hobbesian sense. In his early work, he rejects Hobbes's one-sided focus on the selfish and competitive side of humanity that leads Hobbes to confer an inevitable status on the necessity of the coercive apparatus of the state to maintain just and peaceful relations (Herder 2002: 151; 1985: 796). In his *Letters for the Advancement of Humanity*, he also repudiates Kant's 'hypothesis of a *radical wicked basic force in the human mind and will'* posed in his *Religion within the Bounds of Reason Alone* (*Die Religion innerhalb der Grenzen der bloßen Vernunft*, 1793) (Herder 2002: 420; 1991: 746). 'Where there is evil', Herder (2002: 421; 1991: 747) responds,

> the cause of the evil is the *corrupted character* of our species, not its nature and character. Sloth, impudence, pride, error, callousness, carelessness, prejudices, bad education, bad habit – through and through evils that are avoidable or curable if new life, diligence for good, reason, modesty, justice, truth, a better education, better habits from youth on, arrive individually and universally.

For Herder (1989: 316, my translation), 'peace is the natural state of humankind when at liberty'. It is oppression that deforms us; but even if we become malformed, human beings are born with a capacity for the good. Furthermore, it is the purpose of humanity to overcome the corrupted character of our species that leads people to wage war against each other. Herder therefore sees little value in the success of '*Machiavelli's Prince*' measured solely in terms of the maintenance of power. As morality and politics are, for him, inextricably linked, the truly successful prince is a morally worthy one who cares for the well-being of his people through the simultaneous advancement of humanity's welfare (Herder 2002: 411; 1997: 103; 1991: 732–3, 130).

Herder's rejection of political realism does not mean that he is a utopian. His strong sense of human fallibility leads him to believe that 'an eternal peace will only be *formally* made at the day of judgment' (Herder 2002: 409; 1991: 726). Due to people's ability to learn from their mistakes, Herder remains optimistic that the frequency of wars can at least be diminished. The human species can understand 'why we fell, fall, and will fall' (Herder 2002: 422; 1991: 748). Understanding is nevertheless insufficient; it needs to be 'accompanied by active goodness' (Herder 2002: 422; 1991: 749). 'The work is great', Herder (2002: 422; 1991: 748) writes, 'but it should also be continued for as long as humanity lasts'. It does not follow from the obstacles entailed in obtaining greater peace that we ought not strive to achieve it. Even if perpetual peace is never realized on earth, 'no first principle, no drop of oil, is in vain that prepares for it even if only at the remotest of distances' (Herder 2002: 409; 1991: 726). It is instead the construction of formalistic plans for perpetual peace that he associates with a self-defeating utopianism.

Urging us not to be misled by their seductive allure, Herder raises four main objections to formalistic plans for peace. First, when the focus is on the beauty of a future vision, people often commit themselves 'too early and too exactly to the definition of the formalities of the outcome' and they thereby neglect the essential 'means for helping to promote this outcome' (Herder 2002: 409; 1991: 726). Second, people become deceived, believing that they will soon arrive at their desired outcome only to see it move further and further away. There is then the danger that 'the deluded person gives up all hope' (Herder 2002: 410; 1991: 727). Third, people become too attached to the letter of formally defining and fulfilling such plans with the repercussion that they progressively deviate from the original vision. Finally, unlike general first principles, precise, formalistic plans militate against the flexibility required to suit different times and places, and to adapt to new and unpredictable circumstances (Herder 2002: 410–11; 1991: 726–7).

This final objection forms the basis of Herder's critique of Kant's proposal for a federation of republican states. Kant's teleological conception of history in his earlier *Idea for a Universal History with a Cosmopolitan Purpose* (*Idee zu einer allgemeinen Geschichte in weltbürgerlicher Absicht*, 1784) is summarily dismissed. For Herder (2002: 412–13; 1991: 734), Kant's '*calculation of undertakings towards a future better republic; towards the best form of the state, indeed of all states*' is a 'dazzling phantom'. It is important to acknowledge that Kant, like Herder, is no utopian. As Martha Nussbaum (2010: 37, 28) argues, despite his view that there is an inherent human wickedness, Kant offers a 'truly optimistic' political project. It is, however, people's rational self-interest rather than any propensity for the good that he appeals to in his argument for the establishment of a formal cosmopolitan peace (Williams 1983: 17, 259). Nor does he envisage an immediate adoption of his programme. He is, as Williams (1983: 5, 251) indicates, cautious about its short-term prospects. Although he thinks nature will ultimately propel us towards this end, his model is an ideal system gradually achieved in a manner similar to Herder's first principles.

Since the defining feature of a republican state is, for Kant (1991: 101), the separation of the executive and legislative functions of government, it is sufficiently broad to encompass more than one form of government, including monarchical rule and the American representative system. Yet it is undeniably limited and, by definition, excludes the Westminster system of representative democracy where the executive resides within the legislature. Though Herder rejects monarchical rule and supports a democratic, republican system in the context of Europe in the late eighteenth century, his anarchist tendencies mean that, unlike Kant, his acceptance of the state is purely pragmatic (Spencer 2012: ch. 6). Further pivotal to the differences between his position and Kant's is that Herder does not believe any particular form of government or sovereignty is universally suitable for all peoples in all times and places:

> The roses for the wreath of *freedom* must be picked by a people's own hands and grow up happily out of its own needs, out of its own desire and love. The so-called *best form of government*, which has unfortunately not yet been discovered, certainly does not suit all peoples, at once, in the same way; with the yoke of badly imported freedom from abroad a foreign people would be incommoded in the worst possible way. (Herder 2002: 413; 1991: 734)

Though Kant never suggests that violence ought to be employed to force states to become republican, Herder recognizes that a 'badly imported freedom' need not be imposed by direct force. Whether blind imitation of foreign ways is by choice or imposition, he considers it detrimental to the authenticity necessary for self-determination. Herder also recognizes that power is effectively exerted by any ideological pronouncement of progress that 'blinds with the names of "freedom", "enlightenment", "highest happiness of the peoples"' (2002: 413; 1991: 734). While he encourages people to learn from other ways of life, adaptation to one's own circumstances is essential. Even the best ideas and models introduced into the wrong place and time can become deformed. Thus, unlike Kant, he nowhere suggests that indigenous peoples ought to forsake their own forms of governance by adopting a state, republican or otherwise.

It is, moreover, impossible to determine what could possibly be the best form of government for a people in the future. To dictate in advance what political system would be right for future peoples amounts to placing them in a straightjacket that violates their capacity for self-determination. For Herder, progress towards the realization of the minimal normative principles contained in his concept of *Humanität*[5] and that he personifies in his great peace woman is possible. We can improve our avoidance of radical harm to others by advancing peace, justice and people's general welfare through the advancement of individual and collective self-determination (Spencer 2012: 115–18, Adler 2010: 105–11). Particular individuals and peoples must, however, interpret the precise form in which these general principles are best realized to suit their particular time and circumstances. In contrast to Kant, Herder possesses an open teleology in which the particular ends people strive for to achieve their *Humanität* are forever emerging and evolving (Spencer 2012: ch. 4).

The best we can therefore do to advance peaceful relations is to 'Secure good first principles; they will take effect through their own force – but not otherwise than with modifications which only time and place can give them and will give them' (Herder 2002: 410; 1991: 727). It is the role of Herder's great peace woman to secure these first principles by cultivating seven dispositions of peace. He admits that her path will be a slow one, but he considers the establishment of a strong foundation will more surely lead to a long-lasting peace than any formal, legal proposals for an international federation of republican states. Rather than a top-down process where the motive force for change lies in the hands of state leaders, Herder advocates a bottom-up process that relies first and foremost on the moral education and mobilization of the people. The key to the eventual achievement of a more enduring peace is to alter people's fundamental attitudes towards war and other peoples.

Herder's Great Peace Woman

First, we need to cultivate a horror of war. For Herder (2002: 404; 1991: 720), 'a mad attack on a peaceful, neighboring nation, is an inhuman, worse-than-animal

5 *Humanität* can be translated into English as humanity but Herder deliberately chose to adopt the English term to distinguish his concept from the German, *Menschheit*, which can be substituted in English with humankind or humanity. Unlike the English term, Herder's concept of *Humanität* is both descriptive in that it designates specific features characteristic of the human species and normative in that it outlines a number of basic principles that human beings need to follow in order to live well. To acknowledge this difference I will therefore use Herder's term. See Spencer 2012: 112–18, Adler 2010, 1994.

thing'. It not only threatens an innocent nation, but also inflicts terrible harm on the nation that conducts it. No state's authority to declare war legitimizes 'the horrible sight' of 'two standing armies standing in opposition to each other which without having suffered abuse murder each other' (Herder 2002: 405; 1991: 720). Wearing a soldier's uniform does not therefore transform murder into legitimate killing when it is conducted against an innocent people.

The empowering feature of Herder's proposal is that we do not need to wait for state leaders to decide that war should cease to take action. He (2002: 405; 1991: 720) insists that all human beings – and especially parents to their children – can and should inculcate revulsion towards war and its after effects, emphasizing that the 'diseases, military hospitals, starvation, plague, robbery, violence, desolation of lands, degeneration of minds into savagery, [and the] destruction of families' that come in its wake are often more terrible than the war itself. Rather than sanitizing the subject, its atrocities need to be imparted to people so they become fully aware of the extent of its devastating impact on people's lives. The objective should be 'that the terrible word "war" which people articulate with such ease not only becomes hateful to human beings but people, with the same horror as in the case of St. Vitus's Dance, plague, famine, earthquake, the black death, hardly dare to name it or to write it' (Herder 2002: 405; 1991: 720).

Second, we need to develop a reduced respect for the heroic glory that is perpetuated by 'the land-conquering heroic spirit' we have inherited from the Greeks, Romans and 'barbarians'. We need to encourage instead the idea that rulers can develop a far nobler spirit and character in their ongoing efforts to rule in the interests and welfare of their people. Herder fundamentally rejects the proposition that their interests are ever advanced by a state leader sending them to fight against others unless they are forced to defend themselves due to a direct attack. The ruler who embodies the principles of universal justice, *Humanität* and reason as personified in Herder's great peace woman, is the noblest hero. People of understanding therefore need to work together to dispel the false shimmer that surrounds historical military figures. The songs written for them should make it evident that their form of 'heroism' is equivalent to that possessed by the ringleader of a criminal gang (Herder 2002: 405; 1991: 721).

The third disposition we need to promote is revulsion of dishonest statecraft. 'More and more', Herder (2002: 405; 1991: 721) writes, 'there must be an unmasking of the *false statecraft* that places a regent's glory and his government's fortune in expansion of borders, in capturing or seizing foreign provinces, in increased income, sly negotiations, in arbitrary power, cunning, and deception'. Employing the examples of a number of French politicians during the reign of Louis XIV's absolutism, Herder (2002: 406; 1991: 722) argues that it is necessary for the people to perceive them, in their dishonesty, as the 'weaklings' that they are 'so that it becomes as clear as one-times-one that every deception of a false statecraft in the end *deceives itself*'.

Fourth, patriotism needs to be reformed and purified so that respect for the self-determination of all peoples or nations, and not only states, is upheld. Earlier in the first collection of his *Letters for the Advancement of Humanity* (1793), Herder (1991: 66) urges sovereigns to respect and honour the languages and cultures of all peoples under their jurisdiction. Here he focuses on our need to cultivate a critical perspective towards our state so that we view its interference in foreign quarrels and every invasion of foreign lands with contempt for disturbing our peace and welfare. For Herder (2002: 406; 1991: 722–3),

> It must become ridiculous and contemptible when native inhabitants quarrel with each other, hate each other, persecute each other, vilify each other, and slander each other over foreign affairs which they neither know nor understand, in which they can change nothing, and which are none of their business at all. They must appear as foreign bandits and assassins who from mad passion for or against foreign people undermine the peace of their fellow brothers.

It might be objected that the danger with such a strong principle of non-interference is that it can legitimize the international community standing idly by as it watches a sovereign brutally attack its own people. In the context of eighteenth-century imperialism, however, Herder's immediate concern was to prevent the kind of egoistic patriotism and narrow nationalism that gives rise to an arrogant sense of superiority towards others without taking the time to understand them empathetically in their own terms (Herder 1991: 104, 700). It does not mean that Herder invalidates all criticism of practices in other cultures. He rejects, for example, the legitimacy of hereditary systems of government and he is highly critical of oppressive cultural practices that radically harm others (Herder 1989: 363–4, 455–7). But, unlike many liberal thinkers, he understands the harm inflicted on individuals through the oppression of their culture and community and he therefore sees collective autonomy as a necessary prerequisite for individual self-determination. He considers it impossible to impose values successfully through the use of external forces and he warns that attempts to do so can simply cause greater harm by causing the breakdown of an existing community. Herder is acutely aware of the attachments that people develop to their way of life even when it might not, in the eyes of others, provide them with a good and just life. Thus, the best we can do is plant the seeds of justice and freedom in others through peaceful and respectful means where we avoid impudently insulting other peoples due to our prejudice and ignorance. Otherwise, rather than having strong roots embedded in people's dispositions, such values are bound to become perverted through our interference (Herder 2002: 394, 413; 1991: 698, 734; 1989: 34, 367–9, 635).

Fifth, we simultaneously need to inculcate a feeling of justice and universal empathy[6] so that all nations 'gradually come to feel it as unpleasant when another

---

6 The English Romantic poet, Samuel Taylor Coleridge, coined the English word empathy from Herder's term (*Sichhineinfühlen*) for the historical and cross-cultural research method he developed where the objective is to transport oneself into the culture under study and to attempt to see events from the perspective of one's subjects (Morton 1989: 147,

nation gets disparaged and abused; there must gradually awaken a *common feeling* so that every nation feels itself into the position of every other one' (Herder 2002: 406–7; 1991: 723). Again Herder's immediate concern is with the colonialism of his time:

> People will hate the impudent transgressor of foreign rights, the destroyer of foreign welfare, the brazen abuser of foreign ethics and opinions, the boastful imposer of his own advantages on peoples who do not want them. Under whatever pretext someone steps over the border in order to cut off the hair of his neighbor as a slave, in order to force his own gods upon him, and in order in return to steal from him his national sacred objects in religion, art, manner of representation, and mode of life – he will find in the heart of *every nation* an enemy who looks into his own breast and says: 'What if that happened to me?' (Herder 2002: 407; 1991: 723)

Based on this transnational empathy, Herder (1991: 723, my translation) envisages an informal '*alliance of all educated*[7] *nations* against every individual presumptuous power'. As this alliance is among peoples and nations, and not merely states, it opens the possibility for mutual aid against a state authority that wantonly attacks an innocent people within its jurisdiction in cases of genocide and ethnic cleansing. It therefore mitigates the potential danger noted above with his principle of non-interference.

Realists would undoubtedly dismiss the idea of transnational empathy as a utopian vision, but it is important to recognize that Herder grounds its development in rational self-interest and not on self-sacrifice. To feel the pain inflicted on other peoples who are abused, we only need to think about how we would feel in the same situation. Just as love of others, according to Herder's analysis of the human psyche, is only possible if we first love ourselves, sympathetic identification for others is derived from seeing ourselves in their place (Herder 2002: 214; 1994: 360–61). To be sure, we need to be encouraged to take this step and Herder could be seen to underestimate the difficulty those in powerful positions have in moving beyond their own perspective to imagine what it would feel like to be abused. Yet

---

also see Spencer 2012: 103–5). Herder (2002: 393–7; 1991: 698–702) provides a summary of his method, which he developed most notably in his early *Yet Another Philosophy of History* (*Auch eine Philosophie der Geschichte*, 1774), in Letter 116 of his *Letters for the Advancement of Humanity*.

7 Michael Forster (Herder 2002: 407) translates the original *gebildeten* as 'civilized'. Herder's idea needs, however, to be distinguished from notions of civilization in European terms. Instead he is referring to nations that embody the basic moral principles contained in his concept of *Humanität*, which he sees as having been evident in different cultures and in the actions of various individuals throughout history (Herder 1991: 689–95). On his use of the term culture with reference to all peoples and his rejection of the Eurocentric idea of a cultivated people see Herder 1989: 11–12; 2002: 419; 1991: 741.

he recognizes that the imaginative ability to place oneself in another's situation needs to be cultivated and, most importantly, he does not assume a benevolent disposition. It is 'In the degree of the depth of our self-feeling', he indicates, that 'lies also the degree of our other-feeling for others, for it is only ourselves that we can, so to speak, feel into others' (Herder 2002: 214; 1994: 361). Our sense of justice for others that can motivate mutual co-operation at an international level arises from the desire of justice for ourselves and for effective defence against potential transgressors of our own autonomy.

The great peace woman's sixth disposition entails the overcoming of 'impudent presumptions in trade' (Herder 2002: 407; 1991: 724). Like many of his contemporaries, Herder sees trade as having the potential to unite people. Even if it is often conducted from less than noble motives, he maintains that it can nevertheless teach us to know both our individual and common interests. It is important to remember that Germany at this point was still emerging from feudal oppression and in this context capitalism was a progressive force. But unlike Kant, whom commentators (Cheah 1998: 291, Williams 1983: 252) find overly optimistic regarding the progressive and benign nature of the '*spirit of commerce*' (Kant 1991: 114), Herder acknowledges that greed can equally undermine trade's potential to unify humankind so that instead it creates greater division. Although he believes, like Kant, that the trading powers would prosper most from a long-lasting peace, he does not assume that they will act from rational self-interest over their immediate gain. He is also far more attuned to the exploitative nature of the trading powers. For trade to serve the interests of humanity, then, Herder (2002: 407; 1991: 724) thinks that we need actively to cultivate and awaken indignation among all nations against those who use trade to subjugate others as 'the presumptuous possessor of *all* the treasures and fruits of the earth'.

The seventh and final disposition is activity. Here Herder returns for direct inspiration to the Delaware peace woman with the Iroquois having assigned the Delaware agriculture as their future occupation. According to Herder (2002: 408; 1991: 725), the more people are rewarded with the 'fruits of a useful activity and learn to realize that by the war ax nothing is won but much devastated', the more the glory of war will diminish. These seven dispositions, he concludes, are 'the *oil* and the *medicine* of the great peace goddess *Reason*' (Herder 2002: 408; 1991: 725).

Conclusion

It is often said that Kant's peace plan prefigured the United Nations (Wood 1998: 62), although contrary to his vision of a federation of republican states the United Nations is inclusive of all states. Kant also cannot be held responsible for the undemocratic nature of the United Nations' Security Council with the veto power of its five permanent members and the inertia that often ensues in its decisions when dealing with state violence. However, Herder's critique of formalistic peace plans astutely anticipates the straightjacket in which the United Nations has placed future generations with its continued resistance to structural reform and its institutionalization of the state over peoples or nations as the legitimate entity in the global arena. Reliance on states to initiate reform through a top-down legal process has also failed to prevent the proliferation of war. Even if it can be said that republican states do not go to war with each other, they have far from shown themselves to be committed to peace.

In rejecting state-based legal cosmopolitanism, Herder offers in its place an embedded cosmopolitan alternative that emphasizes local ties and loyalties while it supports informal mechanisms for mutual co-operation at the international level based on the cultivation of a transnational empathy. It may be objected that in his attempt to invalidate colonialism he over-emphasizes the right of communities to non-interference. Yet Herder also promotes peace among peoples and nations within states and provides for their mutual aid against violent attack that would include an unwarranted attack by a state against a people within its jurisdiction. The main insight of Herder's great peace woman over Kant's top-down approach to political reform lies, however, in her reminder that long-term peace depends first and foremost on us working to change people's fundamental attitudes towards war and other peoples. For those frustrated with the pursuit of states' interests and power politics evident in the United Nations, it is an empowering message that means we do not need to wait passively for state leaders to act. Though power politics continues to override grassroots movements for peace just as it too often corrupts the ideals of liberal institutionalism, ultimately those at the top are dependent for their power on support from below.[8]

Bibliography

Adams, I. and Dyson, R.W. 2003. *Fifty Major Political Thinkers*. London and New York: Routledge.

Adler, H. 1994. Johann Gottfried Herder's concept of humanity. *Studies in Eighteenth-Century Culture*, 23, 55–74.

Adler, H. 2009. Herder's concept of *Humanität*, in *A Companion to the Works of Johann Gottfried Herder*, edited by H. Adler and W. Koepke. Rochester, NY: Camden House, 93–116.

Brown, G.W. 2009. *Grounding Cosmopolitanism: From Kant to the Idea of a Cosmopolitan Constitution*. Edinburgh: Edinburgh University Press.

---

8 I would like to thank Paul Corcoran for his very helpful comments on my chapter and the University of Toronto Press for its permission to reproduce some of my ideas originally published in my book *Herder's Political Thought: A Study of Language, Culture, and Community*, © University of Toronto Press 2012. Material used with permission of the publisher.

Brown, G.W. and Held, D. 2010. Editor's introduction, in *The Cosmopolitanism Reader*, edited by G.W. Brown and D. Held. Cambridge: Polity, 1–14.

Camerino, V. 1978. The Delaware Indians as women: an alternative approach. *American Indian Journal*, 4(4), 2–11.

Cheah, P. 1998. Rethinking cosmopolitical freedom in transnationalism, in *Cosmopolitics: Thinking and Feeling beyond the Nation*, edited by P. Cheah and B. Robbins. Minneapolis, MN and London: University of Minnesota Press, 290–328.

Dreitzel, H. 1987. Herders politische Konzepte, in *Johann Gottfried Herder, 1744–1803*, edited by G. Sauder. Hamburg: Meiner, 267–98.

Ellis, E. 2005. *Kant's Politics: Provisional Theory for an Uncertain World*. New Haven, CT and London: Yale University Press.

Fur, G. 2009. *A Nation of Women: Gender and Colonial Encounters among the Delaware Indians*. Philadelphia, PA: University of Pennsylvania Press.

Goldie, M. and Wokler, R. 2006. Biographies, in *The Cambridge History of Eighteenth-Century Political Thought*, edited by M. Goldie and R. Wokler. Cambridge: Cambridge University Press, 711–86.

Heinz, M. 1996. Kulturtheorien der Aufklärung: Herder und Kant, in *Nationen und Kulturen: Zum 250. Geburtstag Johann Gottfried Herder*, edited by R. Otto. Würzburg: Königshausen and Neumann, 139–52.

Herder, J.G. 1985. Abhandlung über den Ursprung der Sprache, in *Frühe Schriften 1764–1772*, edited by Ulrich Gaier, vol. 1 of *Werke in zehn Bänden*, edited by Günter Arnold et al. Frankfurt am Main: Deutscher Klassiker Verlag, 695–810.

Herder, J.G. 1989. *Ideen zur Philosophie der Geschichte der Menschheit*, edited by Martin Bollacher, vol. 6 of *Werke in zehn Bänden*, edited by Günter Arnold et al. Frankfurt am Main: Deutscher Klassiker Verlag.

Herder, J.G. 1991. *Briefe zu Beförderung der Humanität*, edited by H.D. Irmscher, vol. 7 of *Werke in zehn Bänden*, edited by Günter Arnold et al. Frankfurt am Main: Deutscher Klassiker Verlag.

Herder, J.G. 1994. Vom Erkennen und Empfinden der menschlichen Seele, in *Schriften zu Philosophie, Literatur, Kunst und Altertum 1774–1787*, vol. 4 of *Werke in zehn Bänden*, edited by Günter Arnold et al. Frankfurt am Main: Deutscher Klassiker Verlag, 327–93.

Herder, J.G. 1997. *On World History: An Anthology*, edited by H. Adler and E.A. Menze. Translated from German by E.A. Menze with M. Palma. Armonk, NY and London: M.E. Sharpe.

Herder, J.G. 2002. *Philosophical Writings*, edited and translated from German by M.N. Forster. Cambridge: Cambridge University Press.

Kant, I. 1965. Zum ewigen Frieden. Ein philosophischer Entwuf, in I. Kant, *Werke*, vol. 6, edited by E. Weischedel. Frankfurt: Insel Verlag, 191–251.

Kant, I. 1991. *Kant's Political Writings*. 2nd Edition, edited by H. Reiss. Translated from German by H.S. Nisbet. Cambridge: Cambridge University Press.

Löchte, A. 2005. *Johann Gottfried Herder: Kulturtheorie und Humanitätsidee der* Ideen, Humanitätsbriefe *und* Adrastea. Würzburg: Königshausen and Neumann.

Logan, P.E. 1980. Images of the black: J.E. Kolb's *Erzählungen von den Sitten und Schicksalen der Negersklaven. Monatshefte*, 72(4), 389–400.

Loskiel, G.H. 1794. *History of the Mission of the United Brethren among the Indians in North America*, 3 parts. Translated from German by C.I. La Trobe. London: Printed for the Brethen's Society for the furtherance of the Gospel.

Miller, J. 1974. The Delaware as women: a symbolic solution. *American Ethnologist*, 1(3), 507–14.

Morton, M. 1989. *Herder and the Poetics of Thought: Unity and Diversity in* On Diligence in Several Learned Languages. University Park, PA and London: Penn State University Press.

Musgrave, M.E. 1977. Herder, blacks, and the 'Negeridyllen': a study in ambivalent humanitarianism. *Studien Africana*, 1, 89–99.

Muthu, S. 2003. *Enlightenment against Empire*. Princeton, NJ: Princeton University Press.

Nussbaum, M.C. 2010. Kant and cosmopolitanism, in *The Cosmopolitanism Reader*, edited by G.W. Brown and D. Held. Cambridge: Polity, 27–44.

Pizer, J. 2008. The German response to Kant's essay on perpetual peace: Herder contra the Romantics. *The Germanic Review*, 82(4), 353–68.

Reiss, H. 1991. Introduction, in I. Kant, *Kant's Political Writings*. 2nd Edition, edited by H. Reiss. Translated from German by H.S. Nisbet. Cambridge: Cambridge University Press, 1–40.

Schultz, K.L. 1989. Herders indianische Friedensfrau. *Monatshefte,* 81(4), 413–24.

Schutt, A.C. 2007. *Peoples of the River Valley: The Odyssey of the Delaware Indians.* Philadelphia, PA: University of Pennsylvania Press.

Shelley, P. 1938. Crèvecoeur's contribution to Herder's 'Neger–Idyllen'. *The Journal of English and Germanic Philology*, 37(1), 48–68.

Sikka, S. 2006. Herder and the concept of race, in *Herder Jahrbuch/Herder Yearbook*, vol. 8, edited by W. Koepke and K. Menges. Heidelberg: Synchron, 133–57.

Sikka, S. 2011. *Herder on Humanity and Cultural Difference: Enlightened Relativism.* Cambridge: Cambridge University Press.

Snow, D.R. 1994. *The Iroquois*. Oxford and Cambridge, MA: Blackwell.

Speck, F.G. 1946. The Delaware Indians as women: were the original Pennsylvanians politically emasculated? *The Pennsylvania Magazine of History and Biography*, 70(4), 377–89.

Spencer, V.A. 2012. *Herder's Political Thought: A Study of Language, Culture, and Community*. Toronto: University of Toronto Press.

Solbrig, I.H. 1990. American slavery in eighteenth-century German literature: the case of Herder's 'Neger–Idyllen'. *Monatshefte*, 82(1), 38–49.

van der Laan, J.M. 2009. Johann Gottfried Herder on war and peace. *Monatshefte*, 101(3), 335–46.

Waligore, T. 2009. Cosmopolitan right, indigenous peoples, and the risks of cultural interaction. *Public Reason*, 1(1), 27–56.

Wallace, A.F.C. 1947. Women, land and society: three aspects of aboriginal Delaware life. *Pennsylvania Archaeologist*, 17(1), 1–35.

Weslager, C.A. 1944. The Delaware Indians as women. *Journal of the Washington Academy of Sciences*, 34(12), 381–8.

Weslager, C.A. 1947. Further light on the Delaware Indians as women. *Journal of the Washington Academy of Sciences*, 37(9), 298–304.

Weslager, C.A. 1972. *The Delaware Indians: A History*. New Brunswick, NJ: Rutgers University Press.

Williams, H. 1983. *Kant's Political Philosophy*. Oxford: Basil Blackwell.

Wood, A.W. 1998. Kant's project for perpetual peace, in *Cosmopolitics: Thinking and Feeling beyond the Nation*, edited by P. Cheah and B. Robbins. Minneapolis, MN and London: University of Minnesota Press, 59–76.

Zantop, S. 1997. *Colonial Fantasies: Conquest, Family, and Nation in Precolonial German, 1770–1870*. Durham, NC and London: Duke University Press.

Chapter 9
Liberal Peace Plans and Cultural Difference: Jeremy Bentham and the Limits of Enlightenment Universalism

Katherine Smits

One of the central and most controversial issues in contemporary western liberal thinking about peace and war concerns the correlation between states organized along liberal democratic lines and peace at the international level. Michael Doyle made an influential case for the 'democratic peace' in 1983, arguing that the historical record shows that democracies do not go to war against each other – although they are not less likely to be belligerent towards non-liberal democratic states (Doyle 1983a, 1983b). Although scholars since have debated whether or not the claim holds and whether liberal democratic organization and principles or the *Pax Americana* is responsible for the correlation (Sigelman 2005: iv), it has passed into popular political opinion and been reiterated by public leaders. Doyle (1983a: 205, n.1) cites Ronald Reagan in 1982, asserting that a 'crusade for freedom' and the spread of liberal principles would strengthen the prospects for world peace. Since then, the same argument has been made by Presidents Clinton and Bush, and was used by the Bush Administration to justify the invasion of Iraq in 2003 (Owen 2005, Devetak 2007).

Doyle locates the theoretical origins of this argument in German philosopher Immanuel Kant's 1795 essay *Perpetual Peace*, in which Kant argues that republican reform within states, along with the adoption of international law and cosmopolitan principles between states and peoples will bring about lasting international peace. Kant did not himself advocate democracy in any modern sense, but his structure and principles of republican government underpin modern liberal democracies. Liberal republics would not, Kant argued, fight each other because they recognized the moral rights of each other's citizens, and they understood that it would be contrary to their interests to do so. Universal peace was thus possible, but only between states in which political culture and institutions are organized according to particular normative principles.

As the political uses to which it has been put suggest, the democratic peace argument is vulnerable to the charge that it justifies imposing Western liberal values and principles upon other states in order to ensure international peace. In this chapter, I explore an alternative and less well-known source for contemporary ideas about the democratic peace in the work of the British utilitarian philosopher

Jeremy Bentham (1748–1832). There are several similarities between Kant's and Bentham's recommendations, despite their quite different philosophical justifications, and both may be described as cosmopolitan (Brown 1992). However, Bentham's peace plan is, I argue, more amenable to including diverse non-Western cultures and states based on different ethical principles in a pacific network of nations. In order to explore this claim, we must examine not only the audience for the plan explicitly addressed and imagined by the author, but also whether or not the principles that underlie it are consistent with admitting cultural diversity. I suggest here that Bentham's peace plan allows for the inclusion of non-Western and non-liberal states which are accountable to their citizens.

My focus here is not to determine whether Kant or Bentham takes the most defensible approach to peaceful relations with non-European states but rather to trace the origin of an alternative liberal approach to the problem of universal peace, which is less concerned with the moral principles underlying individual autonomy and government within states. This is of more than historical interest; the proper relationship between Western liberal states and non-liberal nations remains a key question in normative philosophy about international relations today. As we have seen, moreover, the 'democratic peace' argument has been used to justify military intervention to liberalize states. While realists in international relations argue that state interests trump concerns about liberal principle when it comes to foreign policy, there are few liberal arguments made for recognizing the potential to cooperate pacifically with non-liberal states. One notable exception is liberal philosopher John Rawls, who argues in his 1999 *The Law of Peoples* that international law based on respect for sovereignty and human rights extends not only to liberal states, but also to 'well-ordered states' – those organized according to a principle of justice, known and approved by their members (Rawls 1999). This encompasses non-liberal states, although ones where there is a measure of accountability. Rawls thus embraces a degree of 'normative pluralism' when it comes to the legitimacy of the internal structure and values of states (Garcia 2001: 666).

Peace Plans in Western Political Thought

Proposals for lasting peace in Western thinking date back at least to the fourteenth century, appearing in early form as exhortations to Christians to renounce violence against each other – as in, for example, Erasmus's 1521 *The Complaint of Peace (peace speaks in her own person)* (Aksu 2008, Hinsley 1963). From around the seventeenth century and the emergence of the early modern state system, peace plans were recognizably political in nature, based as Sissela Bok (1990) argues not on Christian pacifism, but rather on the assumption that nations could break away from the destructive behaviour patterns of the past, and that war was not an inevitable aspect of the human condition. The Enlightenment's commitment to rational argument and political reform meant that these plans and proposals flourished during the eighteenth century. Early Enlightenment peace plans proposed federations of states, while those written later tended to rely less on the machinery of government and more upon shared human interests in peace. In both cases, a key question is whether provision is made for coercive force to be used against delinquent member or signatory states. In his critical essay on the Abbé de Saint-Pierre's 1713 peace plan, written in 1761, Swiss-French philosopher Jean-Jacques Rousseau reflects the tension between government and individual-based perspectives, arguing that Saint-Pierre's was a noble, beautiful but utopian scheme, dependent upon human goodwill. He also recommended a federation, but one which encompassed all significant states and which had provision for coercive force against delinquent members.

The authors of these peace plans addressed the European world they knew, but differed on the degree to which their plans were restricted to European or Christian states, or to those with political constitutions organized according to Enlightenment principles. Early plans focused more specifically upon the need for European political unity, while later schemes combined universalist language concerning human interests with specific policy proposals addressed to European citizens and monarchs (Aksu 2008: 15–16). Several authors addressed specifically the question of whether non-Christian – Muslim, in the political context of the period – states should be included in peaceful relations. In his 1693 *Essay Towards the Present and Future Peace of Europe,* William Penn's description of 'man' was universalist, and as Aksu (2008: 16) argues, he does not emphasize the importance of Europeanness and Christianity. While his plan focuses on Europe, Penn envisages it as extending to cover the Turks, as an imperial power with interests affecting Europe. In 1713[1], Saint-Pierre published his *Project for Settling an Everlasting Peace in Europe*, in which he argued that a federation of the states of Europe would prevent war between them. Saint-Pierre's federation was explicitly between Christian states, although he also argued that European states could make lasting peace treaties with Muslim sovereigns. John Beller's peace plan of 1710, *Some Reasons for an European State* (Bellers 1987) included Turks and Russians (then regarded as beyond the European pale), and appealed in universalist terms to the happiness and welfare of all mankind and the damage done by religious persecution (van den Dungen 2000). Bellers (1987: 152) wrote:

> The Muscovites are Christians and the Mahometans Men, and have the same faculties, and reason as other men … to beat their Brains out … is a great Mistake, and would leave Europe, too much in a state of War, whereas, the farther this Civil Union is possible to be Extended, the Greater will be the Peace on Earth and Goodwill among Men.

1 The Abbé de Saint-Pierre published an original sketch for his peace plan in 1712, but expanded this to a two volume essay the following year. This longer version was translated into English in 1714.

Kant's *Perpetual Peace*

Kant's *Perpetual Peace,* the best-known of Enlightenment peace plans, reflects his deontological ethical perspective and couches its argument in universalist and cosmopolitan terms. He rejects the imposition of world government on moral grounds – states are the necessary context in which individuals achieve moral freedom and autonomy, and any peace plan must be based upon their cooperation. Kant advocates instead the liberal reform of states and their cooperation in a pacific federation. His plan is not addressed to the specific interests of European states: he argued that the universal right of all people expressed itself not only in terms of domestic government, which was to be republican – what we would now describe as liberal – but also in the right to a peaceful union of states, which protected the cosmopolitan rights of individuals. As Williams (1983: 253) points out, the founding of a just and peaceful international order is similar to the foundation of civil society. States give up their arbitrary natural freedom in exchange for a self-regulated lawful freedom. But they will only be sufficiently mature to do this when their internal constitutions are based upon rightful freedom. In these properly constituted republican states, citizens are educated in their rights and duties, the rule of law is established and representative government is instituted with separate legislative and executive arms. These states, Kant argues, would agree to form a peaceful federation respecting the law of nations and would also recognize the cosmopolitan rights of citizens of other republics (Kant 1991). As Doyle (1996) summarizes, peace between nations would be guaranteed by a three level structure: the republican constitution of states, international laws and cosmopolitan principles.

At the basis of this structure – and most relevant for our comparison with Bentham – is the moral status of domestic political organization and principle. It is important to note that for Kant, majoritarian democratic governments alone are not enough to guarantee peace between states. Kant divides such governments into two categories: those that are republican and those that are despotic. Republican governments separate the executive power from the sovereign body – the people. Individual liberties and the legal equality of citizens are protected, while the state maintains a commitment to human rights and individual freedoms, and the protection of private property. These are characteristic of the moral maturity of individuals and states for Kant, and are linked with the spread of what he believed to be rational religion: universal Christianity (Williams 1983: 260–68). Republican political societies have, as Doyle (1983a: 225) puts it, 'solved the problem of combining moral autonomy, individualism and social order'. Morally autonomous individuals make laws to which they themselves are subject. There are thus quite stringent requirements for international peace. Not only must political systems be accountable and separate legislative from executive power, but they must also embody particular values concerning individual liberty, autonomy, morality and private property.

We should note here that in the first supplement to his peace plan, Kant does explicitly acknowledge cultural and religious differences among peoples as one of the causes of warfare. But he assumes that progress within and contact between them will lead to great moral and political homogeneity:

> [Nature] uses two means to separate the nations, and prevent them from intermingling – linguistic and religious differences. These may certainly occasion mutual hatred and provide pretexts for wars, but as culture grows and men gradually move towards greater agreement over their principles, they lead to mutual understanding and peace. And unlike that universal despotism which saps all man's energies and ends in the graveyard of freedom, this peace is created and guaranteed by an equilibrium of forces and a most vigorous rivalry. (Kant 1991: 113–14)

Bentham on Peace, War and Colonialism

Kant's contemporary Bentham shared his scepticism about the machinery of international government, although Bentham was not concerned with the ethical value of the state as the necessary context for individual autonomy. He viewed with suspicion the extension of government power within states and thus opposed the creation of new governing institutions between them (Hinsley 1963: 82). Central to his peace proposal is the assumption that people in all states wish to avoid war and it is only their governments which propel them into it. His peace proposals appear in a collection of his essays written in the period 1786–89, in the context of Britain's manoeuvres against Russia (Britain had entered into a Triple Alliance with the Dutch and Prussians, and was using it to place pressure on Russia). These were not published until 1843, when Bentham's friend and posthumous editor John Bowring collected them together as *Principles of International Law.* Bentham was a prolific writer and commentator over a long career, and there are many references to peace and war across his scholarly work, pamphlets and letters – which do not always display consistent attitudes. While for the most part he was a trenchant critic of war, describing it as 'mischief upon the largest scale' (Bentham 1843 vol. 2: 544), he was not a pacifist in all cases (Conway 1989). The ultimate test for whether war could or could not be justified was, for Bentham, that of utility: whether it was more or less likely to promote human happiness and welfare. In most cases, he concluded, it would not, but there were exceptions. Defensive wars might be justified as the lesser of evils: his editor records him as claiming that 'Defence is a fair ground for war. The Quaker's objection cannot stand. What a fine thing it would have been for Buonoparte to have to do with Quaker nations!' (Bentham 1843 vol. 10: 581). Nevertheless, Bentham was convinced that in most cases, wars occurred because governments acted against the interests of their citizens.

It is important to note the many similarities between Bentham's and Kant's peace plans. Both argued against colonialism, for the development of international law and international institutions, for disarmament and for transparency in foreign policy. Both see peace as obligatory and rational. Where ethical commitment will not persuade populations to peace, then self-interest will. Both agree that free trade and commerce is likely to produce peaceful relations between states. Both argued for the importance of publicity to peaceful relations – blaming secret treaties and machinations by statesmen for leading to war. In Kant's theory, individuals must be able to judge the political actions of leaders by the moral standards that they are themselves striving to recognize (Ellis 2005: 97). In Bentham's argument, simple self-interest guarantees that citizens are likely to oppose the bellicose plans of their leaders. As we shall see, these peace plans reflect the quite different deontological and consequentialist philosophical positions of Kant and Bentham respectively, and this has implications for their inclusiveness.

Bentham's peace plan is set out in his essay *A Plan for an Universal and Perpetual Peace*, written in 1789. It is the fourth of four essays; the others address the objects of international law, the subjects to whom it applies and the causes and consequences of war. Bentham describes his peace plan as universal: he announces at the beginning that his object is 'to submit to the world a plan for an universal and perpetual peace; the globe is the field of dominion to which the author aspires' (Bentham 1843 vol. 2: 546) – but he addresses his argument specifically to Great Britain and France, as the possessors of colonial territories and the great powers most likely to recognize that war was inimical to the true interests of their citizens. The peace plan would take Europe as its nucleus – its primary goal was 'the reduction and fixation of the force of the several nations that comprise the European system'. But Bentham expects that it will be extended to other 'civilized nations'.

Bentham does not propose a formal federation, or any form of global government, but rather agreement between countries reflecting the shared interests of their citizens. As F.H. Hinsley (1963: 82–3) has pointed out, Bentham, like other later eighteenth century radicals, was not interested in world government; it was in fact protection from the machinations of government that was required in order for states to best get along together in the interests of individual citizens. International peace was to rest upon international law, which Bentham argued should be rationalized and codified in the same way as domestic law. He saw his life's work as the rational improvement and codification of law, at both domestic and international levels, and underpinning all his proposals for legislative reform is his empiricist view that legislation and morals should be guided not by transcendental moral principles or by universal human rights, but rather by the principle of utility – by the degree of happiness or welfare that they produce in people affected by them. Bentham argues that human beings are governed by 'two sovereign masters' – pain and pleasure. Thus:

> By the principle of utility is meant that principle which approves or disapproves of every action whatsoever, according to the tendency which it appears to have to augment or diminish the happiness of the party whose interest is in question.

> … I say of every action whatsoever; and therefore not only of every action of a private individual, but of every measure of government. (Bentham 1988: 2)

Bentham's views on the form of domestic constitution most likely to adopt utility as a principle developed over the course of his life, but he gradually became convinced of the superiority of democracy over benevolent monarchical rule, his final views on the subject being clearly expressed in his *Constitutional Code* of 1830. Here Bentham (1843 vol. 9) advocates universal suffrage, annual parliaments and a public opinion tribunal. Government was to be based upon the express wish of the people; an argument distinct from that of Kant, who was suspicious as we have seen of majority rule and saw good government as reflecting and enabling individual moral development.

As Baum (2008: 442) comments, Bentham's peace plan may be regarded as a translation into the international context of his utilitarian framework. War is an evil to be prevented in most situations because of the cost and suffering that it produces. Apart from the loss in terms of human life, it is financially ruinous. Bentham begins his peace plan by tackling what he sees as the two main causes of war. The fundamental propositions of the plan are, first, military troops should be reduced among European nations and, second, colonies should be relinquished. These increase the likelihood of war by providing subjects for dispute and because people care less about war when it is fought at a distance (Bentham 1843 vol. 2). Colonies, he argues, are of no financial benefit to mother countries – an argument he also made forcefully in *Emancipate Your Colonies* addressed to France in 1793. Bentham's opposition to colonization reflected, typically, not a deontological ethical position against it, but rather a consequentialist assessment of the value of colonial possessions and the impact of colonial rule. Like moral philosopher and early theorist of capitalism Adam Smith and later opponents of imperial expansion, Bentham believed that colonies drained funds and resources and distorted trade. Colonization led to undesirable growth in the size and influence of the military and increased opportunities for corruption in government. In terms of the interests of the colonized themselves, Bentham argued that colonial government was based on ignorance of local needs and conditions, and subsumed the interests of the subject people to their rulers. In addition to abandoning standing armies and colonies, Bentham (1843 vol. 4) argued that states – he addresses Britain and France – should enter into no treaties or alliances, including trade agreements, as these were likely to lead to wars.

Bentham rejected the criticism that his plan was visionary, arguing that it was in the clear and already recognized interests of parties to maintain it. The most important consideration here was the relief in the burden of supporting a military, which the peace plan would afford to ordinary citizens. Once people had been freed from the prejudices that subvert their interests, Bentham assumed in true Enlightenment fashion that they would realize that peace would best ensure their personal and economic security and prosperity. Rulers referred to concepts like honour, glory and the national interest to persuade people to go to war against their own interests. Bentham (1843 vol. 2: 553) exhorted: 'Oh my countrymen! Purge your eyes from the film of prejudice – extirpate from your hearts the black specks of jealousy, false ambition, selfishness and insolence. The operations may be painful, but the rewards are glorious indeed!' Bentham believed that once the populace could no longer be manipulated by leaders who had selfish economic interests in going to war, then wars would end among democratic states. Progress depended upon peace and the free trade that would ensure peace and be maintained by it – here he prefigures the later free trade internationalist radicalism of British politicians Richard Cobden and John Bright in the nineteenth century (Conway 1989).

In practical terms, Bentham proposed a confederation of nations, which would develop and harmonize international law, and be guided by it. A congress or diet to consider matters of common interest would proceed entirely in public. Ensuring freedom of the press in all signatory states would mean that renegade states would be forced by their populations to fall into line. Publicity is key here and Bentham emphasized that foreign policy must not be conducted in secret. Secret treaties and diplomacy must be abandoned, as must treaties that restrict trade. Peace should be maintained by a 'common court of judicature' to resolve disputes between nations. However neither the court nor congress should have any coercive powers; rather its decisions should be enforced by the weight of international public opinion (Bentham 1843 vol. 2). In an international system where states were accountable to their citizens, Bentham assumed that popular opinion would promote the rational and pacific interests of people.

With no coercive power, it would be inevitable that some 'rogue states' would not heed the deliberations of the congress or decisions of the courts. Bentham recommends his tribunal for solving disputes between states in good faith. In those cases of bad faith, where there is a legitimate grievance, circumstances must be considered in determining whether or not recourse to warfare is justified. In cases where one state injures another and seems bent on continuing to do so, and war seems the only way of preventing this – and is likely to be successful – then it may be the prudent course. Bentham supported broadly-based citizen's militias ready to wage defensive wars and advocated applying humanitarian principles to the conduct of war (Conway 1989).

As we have seen, Bentham addressed his proposals to Great Britain and France, but envisaged his peace plan as applying more widely – first to Europe. It is consistent with his utilitarian moral argument that the happiness and welfare of all people count when assessing policy proposals, including those for international peace. In order for governments to commit themselves to peaceful relations, it was necessary that they be dedicated to the welfare of their citizens and that those citizens should be able to hold them accountable. Ideally for Bentham, this required representative government with political institutions modelled on those in Britain. However he was prepared to accept that other cultures might allow different ways of pursuing a common good and different conceptions of accountability. Religious toleration and accounting for the cultural impact of religion upon law were particularly important: in the third essay in *Principles of International Law,* on the causes of war, he listed religious difference as a prime cause and recommended toleration as a solution (Bentham 1843 vol. 2: 545). Bentham was similarly an advocate of toleration within states – arguing that political institutions should accommodate and negotiate a range of religious perspectives, by reinforcing the importance of social cooperation and citizenly duty (Canuel 2002: 38–40). He opposed the compulsory use in Britain of religious oaths and other measures designed to ensure religious conformity.

Non-Western Peoples and Bentham's Peace Plan

As Bentham wrote comparatively little explicitly on the question of cultural and political difference between states in his peace plan, we must turn to his views on the moral and political legitimacy of non-Western societies in other contexts. This issue has been the focus of considerable attention recently, as scholars working on the historical interpretation of Enlightenment thinkers have examined attitudes towards the legitimacy of the imperial project (Mehta 1999, Muthu 2003, Pitts 2006). Bentham's views on empire have been the subject of much debate – he famously influenced a generation of British utilitarian governors and officials in British India, who were trained in Britain but, frustrated with the pace of legal reform at home, implemented in India utilitarian approaches to the codification of law and rationalization of administration (Stokes 1959). However Bentham was also a vocal critic of colonialism as is clear in his peace proposal and in earlier pamphlets exhorting European nations to give up their colonies.

Unlike later Victorian liberals, including James and John Stuart Mill, Bentham did not categorize races and cultures in hierarchies based on purported historical progress, and he displayed a greater toleration for cultural differences than was shown by either Mill. He did not share the belief that the more historically 'advanced' peoples were bound to intervene to hasten the progress of the supposedly 'backward'. Bentham writes in *Emancipate Your Colonies*: 'Is it then for their advantage to be governed by a people who never know, nor ever can know, either their inclinations or their wants? What is it you ever can know about them?' (Bentham 1843 vol. 4: 409). For J.S. Mill, utilitarianism was modified by concepts of national character and historical progress (Pitts 2006). 'Uncivilized peoples' were not capable of knowing their own interests, as they were not sufficiently historically developed. It followed, as Mill argued, that peaceful relations should apply between 'civilized' nations, but not in their relations with 'uncivilized' peoples (Mill 1984).

Bentham, however, assumed along stricter utilitarian lines that people in any cultural context were in the best position to judge their interests and to assess the impact of government upon their welfare. He did not distinguish between 'civilized' and 'uncivilized' peoples in this respect (Pitts 2006: 205). Colonial rule was thus in most cases wrong because subordinated peoples knew their own interests better than did colonial rulers. Even in the case of India – Bentham's only concession to continuing colonial rule – colonialism was justified not by any 'backwardness' of the people, but rather by pragmatic concerns: Bentham argued that given the existing facts of colonial rule, a power vacuum would be created by withdrawal. In any event, he insisted that Indians should participate in their own government, which should be adapted to their specific cultural values and practices. The interests of subordinated people should not be identified despotically for them (Pitts 2006: 205).

A similar acknowledgement of the importance of local and particular culture can be seen in Bentham's approach to legal codes. Critics have argued that he advocates in his influential *Introduction to Morals and Legislation* a universalist understanding of law (den Otter 2007). He did in fact regard the science of utility and principles of human nature as universal and drafted several proposed legal codes for other nations. However, as den Otter (2007: 97) points out, on many occasions he demonstrated a sensitive appreciation of the ways in which universal and immutable principles should be adapted for particular circumstances. His essay 'On the Influence of Time and Place on Legislation' examines English law making in Bengal and demonstrates that he recognizes the importance of cultural difference in modifying principles of law – because such difference affects what produces happiness and welfare in a people. Bentham writes: 'The same individual event, which would produce pain or pleasure in one country, would not produce an effect of the same sort, or if of the same sort, not in equal degree, in another' (Bentham 1843 vol. 1: 172). Legislators adapting codes of law to Bengal must take account of 'the circumstances influencing sensibility … the moral, religious, sympathetic and antipathetic biases of the people' (Bentham 1843 vol. 1: 173). Because legislation must be suited to local circumstances, the people of Bengal retained the right to withhold their consent from new laws.

We see the tension between Bentham's belief in the universal applicability of utility and his concern for the specific national factors that impact upon it in the constitutional codes that he drafted for various societies – sometimes by request and sometimes on his own initiative. The systems of government he devised for Greece and Tripoli are based upon the fundamental principle that government should advance the utility of citizens and must thus be subject to public scrutiny and accountability. Constitutions must therefore take into account local cultural, social and political practices and institutions. We might note that in his commentary upon the Spanish constitution, Bentham recommends limiting the right to representation for 'Mahometans', that is, Muslims. However, the ultimate objective is gradually to admit them to the status of citizen (Bentham 1990: 254–5). He writes:

> Strange it were, if by such treatment, the Mahometans were not rendered good Citizens. By the faculty of voting, even supposing no Mahometans were allowed to sit as Representatives, they would be raised to a situation high in dignity, as well as security, in comparison of the highest which any of them can occupy at present. To no Christian could in that case any Mahometan be, as such, an object of contempt. (Bentham 1990: 255)

In the same essay, he rejects polygamy for Muslims on the grounds of their own religious precepts (Bentham 1990: 255).

In the constitutional code for Greece, he temporarily excludes Muslims from full political participation. However he does so expressly on the grounds of self-preservation because they are long-standing enemies of the Greek state, rather than on the grounds of cultural difference:

> In their case so long as the danger from admission continues, so long must the exclusion be continued. So long it must be, but not a moment longer ought to be. No sooner has the danger ceased than self-regarding prudence joins with effective benevolence in dictating the removal of the antisocial bar. (Bentham 1990: 263)

In the meantime, laws around marriage and inheritance should be structured so that they were consistent with Muslim law (Bentham 1990: 255–6). Bentham also refers to local custom in Greece on the question of suffrage for women:

> As to persons of the female sex, if the only proper mode of receiving the declaration of a person's will, namely that of *secret suffrage openly delivered*, be employed, no reason consistent with the principle of general utility as above can be assigned why they or any of them, being of relatively mature age, should stand [excluded]. But no prepossession, howsoever adverse to the principle of general utility, can on the sudden be eradicated: and it would be idle to propose to all that to which acceptance it is certain would not be given by any one. (Bentham 1990: 260)

The case of Tripoli clearly exemplifies some of the ambiguities around Bentham's views on relations with non-Western states. Tripoli was then a kingdom governed by Pashas semi-independent under the Ottoman Empire and Bentham was asked by a Tripolitan friend to draft constitutional proposals to stabilize government in the kingdom. His investigation of local practices and cultures appears in his *Account on Tripoli,* written in 1822; as he had recommended legislators in Bengal to do, he collected information about the territory, population, language, religion and procedures of government in the kingdom (Bentham 1990: 3–23). His chief concerns were the arbitrary nature of the Pasha's power and the problem of succession, and he proposed constitutional principles which could be agreed to by a representative assembly. Bentham maintained that the best chance for achieving constitutional reform in Tripoli would come from the education of people, particularly in principles of government. Books on legislation should be translated into Arabic, and local customs and practices absorbed into new political structures.

At the same time, Bentham's private correspondence suggests that he flirted on occasion with a much more interventionist approach to relations with non-Western societies. As it became clear that the Pasha in Tripoli would not introduce a representative assembly, some people including Tripolitan friends corresponding with Bentham developed plans for an armed intervention. Bentham even drafted a letter to US President John Quincy Adams asking for American support for an armed uprising (Bentham 1990: 145–80). On the strength of this, Peter Niesen (2007) characterizes Bentham (in contrast to Kant) as a liberal universalist who justified intervention to institute liberal regimes. This private adventurism must be weighed, however, against Bentham's published work from the 1780s until his death in 1832, in which he argues consistently that people must be able to choose their own systems of government in line with their own beliefs and customs.

Bentham's acknowledgement of cultural difference with respect to colonial government and law-making is not inconsistent with his realistic recognition of the role of power in international relations. As is clear from his address to Britain and France in the peace plan, Bentham accepted the dominant role of great powers in international relations. His approach to international relations combines, as Gunhild Hoogensen (2005) argues, aspects of realist and liberal international ideology. Niesen draws a comparison between Bentham's acknowledgement of great power hegemony and Kant's view of international peace as depending upon each state being sovereign and equal. While Kant counselled 'egalitarian restraint' in dealing with non-liberal states – whether weak, tyrannical or chaotic – at the margins of international relations, Bentham defended intervention in such cases (Niesen 2007: 96).

This does suggest a more realist acceptance of power relations, which is characteristic of Bentham. But it also reflects a less prescriptive approach to the political and cultural conditions that had to precede peace and explains his confident claim that his peace plan was aimed at the entire world. He focuses on great power hegemony because he understands it to be a crucial empirical fact, without the acknowledgement of which, progress to peace cannot take place. As long as it is compatible with the preservation of accountability within states, there is no reason that it cannot provide a basis for international peace. Similarly, cultural difference did not preclude peaceful relations between states – as long as in all states, citizens could identify and impose their opposition to warfare as being contrary to their interests. There were of course some cases where warfare might be consistent with the interests of people: Bentham's sole modern example is 'New Zealanders', by which he meant Maori who were regarded by the British at the time as notoriously cannibalistic: 'Conquests made by New Zealanders have some sense in them. While the conquered fry, the conquerors fatten' (Bentham 1843 vol. 2: 557). But for most peoples, war was contrary to the public good, and governments required to conduct foreign policy in the open, subject to the scrutiny and consent of citizens, would be unable to prosecute it.

Bentham's belief in the possibility of extending peaceful relations to non-European and non-Christian nations strengthened later in his life. In the late 1820s, he addressed international law again, and formulated a draft of guiding articles for international relations. This draft code is still unpublished, although it is, as Hoogensen (2005: 98) points out, uncharacteristically succinct. It is, moreover, the clearest and most explicitly inclusive proposal for international peace. Bentham proposed a 'Confederacy' in which nations recognize each other's equality, and the following three articles dealt with questions of national heterogeneity. Article Three reads 'Each has its own form of government – each respects the form of government of every other'. Articles Four and Five provide that each state has 'its own opinions and enactments on the subject of religion' and its own 'manners, customs and opinions', and in each case respects those of all other states (Hoogensen 2005: 98–9). The unqualified nature of these recommendations suggests that while Bentham believed that states should be encouraged to adopt constitutional codes based upon the principle of utility, this was not essential to the maintenance of peaceful relations between them.

Conclusion

Any assessment of Bentham's views on the legitimacy of non-Western and non-liberal political systems runs into two interpretive problems: first, as we have seen, Bentham sometimes expressed quite contradictory views, particularly as between his private and public writings. It is hard to reconcile his plea to the US to intervene in Tripoli with his insistence that states respect each other's forms of government. Second, Bentham's views changed over time. His later writings – from the turn of the nineteenth century – are much more definite in their support for democracy as the legitimate system of government. Nevertheless, the principles formulated in his draft code for an international confederation shortly before his death suggest that his final conclusion was that international war posed the most fundamental threat to utility, and that recognizing the distinct culture and religion of each state was most essential for preserving the utility of its citizens. This outweighed any increase that might be gained from imposing democratic regimes around the world. There is no reason to think that in his final writings on the subject Bentham abandoned his belief that only governments accountable to their citizens were likely to be able to maintain peace, but it is clear that accountability does not require that same reflection and embodiment of moral principles that Kant advocated for the domestic constitutions of states in his pacific confederation.

We might note here that both Kant and Bentham evinced some ambivalence when it came to the question of intervention in the affairs of other states. As we saw at the beginning of this chapter, Kant's arguments in *Perpetual Peace* have been invoked to justify 'democratizing' interventions into non-democratic states. Jeremy Moses (2006) argues that this is an illegitimate interpretation of Kant's peace plan, which defends a strict position of non-intervention. However Kant also suggests some circumstances in which intervention might be justified (Devetak 2007).

On the related but distinct question of inclusiveness, however, there is a clearer distinction between Kant and Bentham, and we might see the latter as an alternative liberal source for peace plans – one which distinguishes between accountability on the one hand, and a liberal structure aimed at realizing individual moral freedom on the other. Like Kant, Bentham offers a cosmopolitan view of international society. Bentham's view, however, is based upon the universal principle of maximizing the utility of all people, and recognizing the validity of cultural difference as a factor which contributes to that utility. Following this approach, Chris Brown (1992: 71) concludes that 'the only reason for taking Kant rather than Bentham as the archetypal cosmopolitan is because Kant offers a more elaborate series of texts on the subject than his consequentialist opponent'.

Bentham's pragmatic acceptance of differently ordered states as 'partners for peace' recalls the non-Ideal theory of Rawls's law of peoples – which establishes, as he puts it, a 'Realistic Utopia' (Rawls 1999: 11–23). As we saw at the beginning of this chapter, Rawls advocates principles of international law based on respect for sovereignty and human rights, which are acceptable to both liberal societies and 'well-ordered' but non-liberal societies. These include hierarchical societies which have a 'decent consultation hierarchy' allowing for the expression of different voices and which satisfy two criteria: first, they must not have aggressive aims and second, they must respect the social and political order of other societies. The second criterion consists of three parts: such states must respect basic human rights, they must impose duties and obligations on members consistent with the common good idea of justice and finally, the legal system in well-ordered societies must be guided by a common good idea of justice (Rawls 1999: 64–6).

Rawls's example is of an Islamic nation in which there is no separation of church and state and allows only Muslims into positions of political leadership (Rawls 1999: 75–8). Such a society must allow, Rawls argues, for the representation of minority groups in consultation procedures, so that their interests are taken into account, although minorities do not themselves make final political decisions. These conditions recall Bentham's opposition to the Pasha's arbitrary rule in Tripoli and his recommendations for temporarily limiting Muslims' political rights in Spain and Greece. In their emphasis on consultation and government according to an accepted conception of the common good, they provide for the inclusion of non-liberal states in peace pacts.

Despite the fact that Bentham's peace plan has not been as widely read and cited as Kant's, it merits renewed attention on the part of contemporary students of international peace. His consequentialist argument is not one that can be relied upon to oppose war in all circumstances, but in this respect it reflects post-1945 international law concerning resort to the use of force. Bentham's approach combines a universalist recognition of the moral value of individuals and their preferences, with the recognition that specific cultural circumstances are likely to produce differences in what constitutes legitimate government. Disputes will continue over what constitutes internal legitimacy, but in a culturally and politically heterogeneous global context no single political and economic model may in practice be considered essential to international peace.

Bibliography

Aksu, E. 2008. Introduction, in *Early Notions of Global Governance: Selected Eighteenth-Century Proposals for 'Perpetual Peace'*, edited by E. Aksu. Cardiff: University of Wales Press, 1–2.

Baum, T. 2008. A quest for inspiration in the liberal peace paradigm: back to Bentham? *European Journal of International Relations* 14(3), 431–53.

Bellers, J. 1987. Some reasons for an European state, in *John Bellers,* edited by George Clarke. London: Routledge and Kegan Paul, 132–53.

Bentham, J. 1843. *The Collected Works of Jeremy Bentham,* 11 vols. edited by John Bowring. Edinburgh: Tate.

Bentham, J. 1988. *The Principles of Morals and Legislation.* Amherst, NY: Prometheus.

Bentham, J. 1990. *Securities Against Misrule and other Constitutional Writings for Tripoli and Greece: The Collected Works of Jeremy Bentham*, edited by P. Schofield. Oxford: Clarendon Press.

Bok, S. 1990. Early advocates of lasting world peace: utopians or realists? *Ethics and International Affairs*, 4, 145–62.

Brown, C. 1992. *International Relations Theory: New Normative Approaches.* Hemel Hempstead: Harvester Wheatsheaf.

Canuel, M. 2002. *Religion, Toleration, and British Writing 1790–1830.* Cambridge: Cambridge University Press.

Conway, S. 1989. Bentham on peace and war. *Utilitas*, 1(1), 82–101.

Den Otter, S. 2007. 'A legislating empire': Victorian political theorists, codes of law and empire, in *Victorian Visions of Global Order,* edited by Duncan Bell. Cambridge: Cambridge University Press, 89–112.

Devetak, R. 2007. Between Kant and Pufendorf: humanitarian intervention, statist anti-cosmopolitanism and critical international theory. *Review of International Studies*, 33, 151–74.

Doyle, M.W. 1983a. Kant, liberal legacies and foreign affairs, Part I. *Philosophy and Public Affairs*, 12(3), 205–35.

Doyle, M.W. 1983b. Kant, liberal legacies and foreign affairs, Part II. *Philosophy and Public Affairs*, 12(4), 323–53.

Doyle, M.W. 1996. Three pillars of the liberal peace. *American Political Science Review*, 99(3), 463–6.

Ellis, E. 2005. *Kant's Politics: Provisional Theory for an Uncertain World.* New Haven: Yale University Press.

Garcia, F.J. 2001. Review of *The Law of Peoples* by John Rawls. *Houston Journal of International Law*, 23(3), 659–73.

Hinsley, F.H. 1963. *Power and the Pursuit of Peace: Theory and Practice in the History of Relations between States.* Cambridge: Cambridge University Press.

Hoogensen, G. 2005. *International Relations, Security and Jeremy Bentham.* London: Routledge.

Kant, I. 1991. Perpetual peace, in *Kant's Political Writings*. 2nd Edition, edited by Hans Reiss. Translated from German by H.B. Nisbet. Cambridge: Cambridge University Press, 93–130.

Mehta, U. 1999. *Liberalism and Empire: Nineteenth Century British Liberal Thought.* Chicago: University of Chicago Press.

Mill, J.S. 1984. A few words on non-intervention, in *The Collected Works of John Stuart Mill,* vol. 21, edited by John M. Robson. Toronto: University of Toronto Press, 109–24.

Moses, J. 2006. Challenging just war and democratic peace: a critical perspective on Kant and humanitarian intervention, in *Ethics of War in a Time of Terror*, edited by Christian Enemark. Canberra Papers on Strategy and Defence no. 163. Canberra, 71–84.

Muthu, S. 2003. *Enlightenment against Empire.* Princeton: Princeton University Press.

Niesen, P. 2007. The 'Divided West'? Bentham and Kant on law and ethics in foreign policy, in *Rethinking Ethical Foreign Policy: Pitfalls, Possibilities and Paradoxes,* edited by David Chandler and Volker Heins. New York: Routledge, 97–115.

Owen, J.M. 2005. Iraq and the democratic peace: who says democracies don't fight? *Foreign Affairs*, 84(6), 122–7.

Pitts, J. 2006. *A Turn to Empire: The Rise of Imperial Liberalism in Britain and France.* Princeton: Princeton University Press.

Rawls, J. 1999. *The Law of Peoples*. Cambridge, MA: Harvard University Press.

Sigelman, L. 2005. Notes from the editor. *American Political Science Review*, 99 (3), iii–iv.

Stokes, E. 1959. *The English Utilitarians and India.* Oxford: Oxford University Press.

Van den Dungen, P. 2000. The Abbe de Saint-Pierre and the English 'Irenists' of the eighteenth century (Penn, Bellers and Bentham), *International Journal on World Peace*, 17(2), 5–31.

Williams, H. 1983. *Kant's Political Philosophy*. Oxford: Basil Blackwell.

Index

For Product Safety Concerns and Information please contact our EU representative GPSR@taylorandfrancis.com
Taylor & Francis Verlag GmbH, Kaufingerstraße 24, 80331 München, Germany

www.ingramcontent.com/pod-product-compliance
Lightning Source LLC
Chambersburg PA
CBHW050710280326
41926CB00088B/2909

* 9 7 8 1 1 3 8 2 6 9 9 6 5 *